BADGER CLAN

My Badgers and Other Family

Caroline Greville

To my God who held me through this obsession;
I think I know you better now.
And to my family, found in these pages –
now older and wiser, but adorable still.

CONTENTS

SUMMER

1: Badger contact

We're in a field at dusk, the day stilling around us as we look into a small patch of woodland, hoping we'll see the badgers come out. *We* is Maddy, my twelve-year-old, and me. Much of nature is packing up for the night: the wood sorrel are folding their shamrock-like leaves into protective little shelters, and the birds have stopped singing, except for a lone blackbird. His alarm call tells me he'd like to reclaim his territory, and asks if we would mind taking ourselves home so he can settle for the night. It's turning cold, and although it's May now we're glad of our winter coats. Maddy has chosen an old one of her sister's, and is rustling in the pocket for peanuts that might tempt the badgers out. It's too late for that, we should have scattered them hours ago so our scent could wear off a little.

'Let's try further along,' I say to her.

Although they are born in February, it is usually April or May by the time the badger cubs first come out of their setts. We've been watching these new ones for about a month. I wonder if their boldness is already starting to waver. Till now they've shown none of the reticence of their parents, often coming close to us to get a better look. We take the path into a sheltered area of woodland and sit down on a log, side by side. It feels a more intimate space in here than it did just three weeks ago. Red campion has grown tall, and most of the lords-and-ladies are lost among waist-high glossy greens and pinks. The smell of wild garlic is strong tonight. Badgers are known to take it down into their holes to keep fleas at bay.

This is becoming something of a habit of ours, and is our favourite place to wait for them. We have tried sitting near the badger holes in a graveyard just a quarter of a mile from home. I like to think modern day fears about the perils of such places are overblown, the real danger being to stay within our own four walls and process the world through a screen. Yet a small part of me objects to loitering in a graveyard after dark. It's not a fear – just a feeling that it is in some ways inappropriate. What if someone walks past? We'd freak them for sure. There is a slight anxiety that we may be seen, wherever we wait. I understand Robert Frost's embarrassment when he writes of his night wanderings, "I have passed by the watchman on his beat /And dropped my eyes, unwilling to explain."[1] At least in the woods the badgers are often

---

[1] Robert Frost's poem 'Acquainted with the Night' was first published in his poetry collection *West-Running Brook* in 1928.

out before nightfall this time of year. There are fewer noises for them to fear – back in the village a road passes within metres of their graveyard holes.

We started coming here as soon as I discovered the badger sett. I was out in the woods on a February day when I spotted some scorched tree stumps, and as I crouched down to look saw a hole at the base of each one. There was graffiti on a tree and cans and broken glass scattered around the place, in amongst a deep layer of beech leaves. 'The teenage wood,' I labelled it in my mind. I searched the internet when I was home – I needed to see pictures to clarify everything – But was this a badger sett? Weren't they protected? What should I do? My internet searches told me that I was most probably right – the holes were at least ten inches wide, a group of them close together, which were more than likely connected. I came across the East Kent Badger Group and made contact. I collected the rubbish the next day, and started to watch the sett.

Nothing is happening tonight and I give Maddy a nudge. As we step over the fallen tree and out of the wood we realize how dark it is. Then there is a noise. Screeching interspersed with keckering. We climb over a fence, and at that moment find two badger cubs skidding to a halt at our feet, like kids who find their bike brakes aren't all they'd hoped. I grab Maddy's hand and push her in front of me, out of their way as much as she possibly can be, but they've already turned and have run into the woods. I don't tell her of my brief feeling of panic and wonder how she's feeling. We pause to absorb the shock when they're back again, running at us just as fast as the first time. They look like small remote control toys stuck on fast-forward, something has gone wrong with the wiring and they really can't stop. That static-hair look doesn't help matters, but they are still endearing and we're not scared, I decide, just overwhelmed.

'I counted at least four of them,' Maddy tells me on the way home.

I'm not so sure, but it did feel like a small mob. 'Don't you think it was the same ones, coming back to check on us?'

Maddy doesn't answer, she's looking over her shoulder and back across the field. 'I didn't expect that to happen,' she says after a minute or two. 'Wait till I tell the others, they're going to be so jealous.' She pauses. 'But perhaps they won't. It sounds a bit freaky.'

I remind her that they are harmless creatures, that they really wouldn't attack us. It's as much for my benefit as hers, I'm repeating the textbook mantra that's easy enough to take when you're sitting on a sofa at home. I'm determined that she won't feel frightened in the woods. She's such a shy girl, but out here there's an edge to her that's slightly different. It's where she forgets herself and her eyes shine brightest.

'It could happen though, couldn't it?'

'You know, it would need to feel cornered by a very real threat. These ones had plenty of space to turn and run, though it took them a moment to realize.'

I want to get to know these badgers better – or any badgers that I can. I feel as if I've rediscovered a piece of my past that had been lying dormant for a while. I saw a dead badger on the side of the road last winter and complained to a friend that's the only way I see them these days. That as a child I had watched them from a holiday cottage window and been captivated, that the fascination continued for years, but there seemed no way of recapturing the experience. She challenged me to track them down, said that if there was a dead one in the village the rest of the clan couldn't be far away. Then I found the sett in the woods. And so a childhood obsession was hooked up like a dropped knitting stitch, and life feels the better for it.

I have got myself involved in this badger group, too. A member came out and confirmed for me that it was a sett, and showed me evidence that the badgers were nesting, with bedding material drying out in the sunshine. I was quickly trained to identify setts myself, and though I know I'm all too inexperienced, it feels like an exciting time, that anything could happen as I make space for badgers in the routine of life. I'm told this corner of east Kent is a badger-rich area, that they like our chalky soil that's so easy to dig. This wasn't a consideration of ours when we moved here, but it's fortuitous all the same.

*

'Mum, there's some post for you here,' says Annie, my fifteen-year-old, who has her own ideas about what should interest me. 'It's probably another *badger* book.'

It is, it's my copy of Ernest Neal's *The Badger*, a classic on understanding badgers, with all the important information a newcomer needs. Neal himself became interested in badgers as a young school teacher in the 1930s, and made use of his sixth form students to help him conduct a scientific study. I am aware that my own knowledge of badgers is very patchy, and am reading all that I can now before the badger group require anything much of me. I have discovered that the regional badger groups provide a vital role around the country, visiting members of the public who need advice, instructing councils when a badger sett is on a proposed development site, rehoming orphans and sometimes providing badgers with medical attention. The police and RSPCA refer cases on to these groups, and they are not simply clubs for enthusiasts, but there to deal with all the badger related problems in their communities. They are run by volunteers, though the level of knowledge and experience is exceptional. I am told that the local contact for the Dover area wants to retire, and my phone might just start to ring with badger problems. I've heard of the sludge-filled latrines marking badger territory on once pristine lawns and of badger-triggered road closures. I think I'm in for some fun.

The Eurasian badger (Meles meles) is perhaps the best loved species of British wildlife, distinctive for its white facial stripes and small bear-like appearance, with short legs and a stout carriage. It is a true native, and Neal writes in his preface of how the badger lived here even when Britain was a peninsula. The average badger weighs between 9 and 12 kg (more in the autumn) and is around 70cm long, with some males measuring up to one metre. They are omnivorous, though they are not 'hunters' in the way we think of foxes and wolves; they sometimes eat rabbits, but their staple is the earthworm, and they can each consume several hundred in a night. They will eat whatever is seasonal: windfall apples, berries, roots, beech-mast, nuts, and have a particular liking for red-skin peanuts. These, I was told, will significantly increase my chances of seeing a badger, and can be put out during the day in anticipation of their nightly forage. Badgers are sure to seek them out if they are placed on their usual hunting ground – although their vision is poor, their sense of smell is possibly 750 times better than our own. Perhaps this is why they do not bring food into their setts or defecate there.

The presence of badgers has been linked to the spread of TB in cattle in the UK, and culls have taken place in various counties in the south-west as a misguided endeavour to control its spread. The £50 million trial in 2005 judged that culling 'can make no meaningful contribution to cattle TB control in Britain',[2] and the Independent Expert Panel, who concluded the 2013 cull a failure on humaneness grounds, has been removed, so that the process can continue without scientific interference.[3]

---

[2] The Randomized Badger Culling (Krebs) Trial, 1998 – 2005. This can be read online. Follow a link at: www.wildlifetrusts.org/bBTscience

[3] In 2017 the cull continues, having been extended into South Herefordshire, West Dorset, North Cornwall and North and South Devon. The Badger Trust suggest 'Over £100 M could be spent by 2020 on killing badgers.' The science is shaky at best, and experts agree attention should instead focus on compromised cattle and farming practices, with funding re-directed towards assisting farmers and a vaccination programme.

There's a part of me that questions the wisdom of focusing so intently on a creature that is doomed. And yet it intrigues me, and perhaps I'm responding to that feeling that lurks in all of us, to protect those that cannot protect themselves. Besides, there is no TB in Kent, and any badgers I may get to know are not going to be done away with. So I can dare to draw close and not fear the consequences.

*

My mornings usually start like this, just me alone in my little square kitchen, putting things in order before the four children get ready for school. Plates from the dishwasher onto the old cream plate rack above. Dry clothes to be taken from the airer on the ceiling. Today five grimy chicken eggs of varying sizes have been left by the children on my clean ceramic draining board. And the wooden floor is unusually muddy and needs to be swept and washed. We went for a walk yesterday afternoon and now the wellies are encrusted and ready to be cleaned outside. Tyndale, our Border terrier, is waiting to be let in, adding to the muddy patch on the glass door with his front paws. I open it, then spray the window and wipe off the mud he's shaken onto the cream cupboards. Exactly whose idea were those? Mine I think.

I clean the eggs and set about making myself some tea and toast. If I can just get on top of all this now I'll be able to settle down to some writing once they're at school. I find a pencil and write the date on each egg before putting them in the egg house. There's noise on the stairs and the family start to appear.

'Shut the door,' I say. 'The toaster's smoking again.'

It's Annie, and she pulls the door behind her, then reaches inside a high cupboard. 'Mum, my contact lens box is empty,' she says, shaking it over the oak counter.

'I'll sort it today.'

The door opens and now my husband Rupert comes through, catching the tail end of the conversation. He fills the kettle that's open on the side before wandering through to the boot room. 'If you're shopping, I need a new foil for my razor, it'll cut my chin to pieces otherwise,' he says, his head now inside the fridge.

A tapping on the kitchen door and Annie opens it for Jem, our six-year-old and youngest of the brood. 'My knickers are all too small this morning,' she says. 'The ones I can find anyway.'

'Can you get me some too,' says Annie, stuffing her sandwich into a bag. 'They all say seven to eight.'

'And the dog needs his flea treatment, if you're going that way.'

A shopping trip, that wasn't what I'd planned, though it needn't take long. We love our rural location, but being seven miles from anywhere is at times a little inconvenient. We chose this village for its close proximity to woods and countryside, and I'd still rather be here than in a town. I take a tea-towel and wipe up the spilt water from the kettle. I feel an arm across my shoulder and a gentle dig in the ribs. 'You're so OCD, you know that don't you,' says Rupert. 'There's still not a ring mark on them.'

'And you're so messy. They only look good because I clean up after you.'

'But I love you.' He smiles at me and gives me a hug. 'See you tonight, once I've helped Terry move house.'

'Bye, Dad,' says Eliott. 'Don't let anyone escape.'

'Yeah, yeah.'

He works in the education department of the local Immigration Removal Centre.

'Girls, where are you?' he shouts up the stairs. 'Time to go.'

'I don't know why they need to learn English when they're going home,' continues Eliott.

'Not now.'

'But what's the point?'

'It might help impress the judge if they've bothered to try.' He smiles with a provocative tilt of the head. 'You know, things might just go their way if they listen to me.'

'Yeah, Dad. We should always listen to you. You're so wise,' says Eliott.

'And I pay your pocket money.'

'Katie's allowance has gone up by £5,' says Annie, picking up her school bag.

'Good for Katie, maybe you should go live with her then. They've got plenty of space.'

Soon I hear the car leave the driveway. Just Eliott and Jemima left, and I go up to the bathroom and lock the door while they chatter away downstairs. These two are still at primary, though Eliott won't be for much longer.

'Mum! *Mum!*' calls Jem.

'What?'

'It's all red.'

'What's all red?'

'The strawberry. I found one in the window-box, it's ready.'

'Have it then,' I say.

'Mum, *phone*,' says Eliott from outside the door.

I make my way back down and pick it up –

'Is that Caroline? I've got a badger problem, it's on my land. I live in Eythorne. I hear Ken's retired.'

I push shut the door and sit down on the top kitchen step. 'Of course I'll come, I'm glad to help. Where are you? And what time's good?' Three-thirty, I repeat, smiling to myself. 'I'll see you then.'

'What are you looking so happy about?' says Eliott when I put the phone down.

'Oh, nothing. Just my first badger visit on my own.'

'Can we come?' says Jem, entering the room.

'We're *coming*,' says Eliott.

'You're going to have to. I've arranged the visit for when you're home from school.'

Jem gives me a giant hug and climbs onto my lap. 'You won't see any badgers,' I tell her. 'We're just helping an old lady out.'

'We might,' she says, her brown eyes wide and unblinking. 'You never know.'

We find the track that joins our road, a once made-up lane that's now crumbling. It narrows to a footpath and we take the turning for the last house on the right. Eliott and Jemima are proud to be out on badger group business, though disappointed I have no lanyards or business cards for them. Jemima takes my hand as three geese come over and confront her at eye-level, squawking. Her "fally-down" ponytail is in her eyes but she can still see more than she wants to.

'They're just being friendly,' I tell her, but she's convinced they're out to get her, like the black geese in the Russian folk tale who steal the little boy Sergei away.

This has to be the house; the geese are Mrs Stephens' reason for calling me. They are still stalking us. We can't find a front door, but a dog barks as I tap on a side window. There is no doorbell, or letterbox that I can see. The dog trots through, followed by a much slower elderly lady who walks with a stiff limp. She looks surprised to see me – mine is a familiar face to her – and I'm reminded of that saying about a prophet not being accepted in his home town. Well, I'm not exactly a prophet, but I have been well-briefed by a wiser being. 'Martin's given me some advice,' I say, referring to the chairman of our badger group who's devoted some time to training me up. I hand her the information sheets I've spent the morning preparing. She needn't know this is my first visit unaccompanied, or that, in his words, I'm 'a little green'.

'It's over here, the problem. Come and have a look.'

We follow her through her garden, more of an over-grown meadow in truth, but her fixed, apologetic smile shows exactly how much she loves it. 'My friend says he's coming with his tractor to cut it, but it won't be before the end of the month. The nettles have never been so long,' she says. 'It just hasn't stopped raining, has it?'

Jemima is in her red-gingham school dress, her legs bare except for her pink wellies. 'Go carefully, Jem,' I say. She heads off to collect large white feathers while we walk over to the goose house. Mrs Stephens shows me a gap where animals have begun to tunnel underneath. I place my hand inside – I can rotate it easily, a sure sign it's a badger hole, and it's not a likely haunt for a rabbit anyway.

'It has a concrete floor,' I say as I examine the goose house more closely. I catch Eliott smiling to himself. 'You haven't any worries there, they'll never get in.'

She is not convinced, and I'm persuaded to lower a concrete slab across the top of the hole. She clearly loves these three remaining geese, and has lost dozens of birds to foxes over the years. I don't block off access completely, and if anything were down there it could breathe, and with a bit more digging make its way out. *There are no badgers living under there*, I tell myself, *I'm merely cutting off a bolt-hole*, but I can't help feeling guilty. Under the Protection of Badgers Act 1992 it's considered an offence to 'Intentionally or recklessly damage or destroy a badger sett, or obstruct access to it.' This isn't a sett, it's a one-off hole, that's my defence. It seems to be an 'outlier', or a blind-end tunnel, isolated and not within sight of any other holes. More of a purpose built stopping point between wooded areas. And it's a disused one at that, I don't think a badger has been here in a very long while. There's no evidence of fresh hairs, and I'd had to pull out a bundle of leaves before placing my hand inside. With a hole that's in use you would expect to find loose soil, the occasional footprint, perhaps evidence of a little digging or stray bits of 'bedding' – that is, dry stems of grass or other vegetation. I'm still not sure I should have covered it but nothing else seemed as if it would appease her.

Jemima comes over, the 'little Staffy' at her heels. She tugs on my coat, '*Mum!*' Eliott is looking flustered, with that '*Do something, Mum*' expression.

'Oh, Ruby wants a feather,' says Mrs Stephens. 'She likes to play with them.' Ruby is baring her teeth.

'Give her one,' I tell Jemima. 'You've got loads there.'

'Is there any chance Martin can come?' asks Mrs Stephens. 'He did come once before, a long time ago.'

'I'll mention it to him, but he's really busy at the moment,' I say. Is it just that she knows me? Will I be able to convince a stranger that I know what I'm talking about? I honestly thought it'd be easier than this. 'You really don't have a sett here and your geese aren't in any danger.'

I offer to come back when the children are at school. Then I can brave the nettles and walk the perimeters to see where the badgers are getting in. Mrs Stephens is adamant she doesn't want me to. 'It's not a problem,' I say. 'Perhaps we can block off their entrances.' She isn't budging and seems a little defensive. Well, it would be a hard task, anyway. Perhaps she's embarrassed by the long grass but she shouldn't be. She has a complete wildlife haven here, an open invitation to birds, butterflies and bees. Just not badgers. Over 97% of wildflower meadows have been lost in the UK since the 1950s and most of us would be amazed by what we could bring to our gardens with a small amount of neglect.

'Thanks for coming,' she says to us as she and the geese accompany us to the path.

'I'm glad to help,' I reply. She smiles her fixed smile back at me, her eyes have glazed over.

'That dog was chavvy,' says Eliott on the way home. 'It's not the badgers I'd be worried about if I were her.'

'Ruby's harmless,' I tell him. 'She's just a frail old lady with a few over-protective pets. There's nothing unusual about that.'

'You do know she wants to build houses on her land?' Rupert says to me later.

I glance out of the back door to make sure our own chickens have been put away for the night. 'But you can see how much she loves it, it doesn't make sense.'

'It's all a bit run down though,' says Rupert, turning off the family room light as we head through to the sitting room together. 'She probably needs the money.'

'That could be it. She wouldn't let me take a proper look, I guess she's worried I'll find a hole and tell the planning office. If they find badgers to relocate it could stall things for months.'

My throat is hurting, and a tickle starts to build till it reaches a spasm and I have to cough – Maddy looks at me with a disapproving stare she must have picked up in school. A badger appears at the hole and watches, her attention directed at me alone. Satisfied that I'm a harmless nuisance, she turns and walks away.

'It's because you coughed,' Maddy whispers. 'It came because you coughed! Do it again, Mum.'

'No!'

I rustle a cough sweet out of its wrapping – it's sticky and I place it in my mouth with half the plastic still intact. More disapproval: 'They'll smell it,' she says, stuffing her hands in her pockets and turning from me. I can't seem to win.

The badger is back – a small female, or perhaps one of last year's cubs. Maddy turns to see it just in time. Then it's gone, and a young cub takes its turn just minutes later, far smaller than the last and content to stop and stare. We feel compelled to do the same. This cub – we'll call it he – does not look like he could have possibly emerged from the earth. His coat is of the cleanest white and smartest grey. It is fluffy and long, as if untamed after a blow-dry. I think that if I could touch it I would spoil it – it is the stuff of dandelion clocks and makes him look just as fragile. And vulnerable he is, for this first year will be the most dangerous of his life. Though he is wayward, his mother needn't worry too much for now – it will be a few weeks before he ventures far from home.

There is not a speck of dirt in this badger's eyes, bright in the light they are not yet accustomed to. Everything about him shouts newness. There is a pink patch in the white strip just above his nose, perhaps where the fur is still to grow. His slim head looks too big for his body and his feet oversized, like a puppy's. The claws are not touching the ground, as if the padding on his feet has not been sufficiently worn in. Now he shakes his head as if woken from a daydream and runs into the enclosure. Maddy and I have seen more than we could have hoped for, and turn for home.

A perfect oak platter is in the centre of the table the next morning. It's a present from Rupert, the reason he wasn't much help last night. Shaped from a three inch block of wood, it's been rounded, smoothed and waxed so not a flaw remains. I hold it and rotate it in my hands, watching as the pale wood absorbs the light.

Rupert will have to be in charge tonight, I'm going to my first badger group committee meeting. The current secretary thinks she may need to retire, and I've offered to be the replacement. So at six thirty I'm driving through abandoned countryside like a tourist, glad no one's behind me as I slow to watch a lone sheep, then a farmhouse with acres of land. This high road gives an unbroken panoramic view of the scenery below, an 'Area of Outstanding Natural Beauty' that is rich in chalk and dominated by pasture. The valley was formed by the River Nailbourne that is absent most of the time, reappearing only in late winter after a year or two of heavy rain. Then I spot a pub, The Doll's House, which Jem would love. We could bring the kids out here and walk into the hills and beyond. There must be accidents along this stretch as drivers look sideways for just a moment too long. I wonder if I've missed the Elham turning. The road seems to go on for miles without a single signpost; perhaps they are thought to spoil the view.

The village hall is equally hard to find, tucked behind a high hedge and only accessible with a u-turn in the road. The short driveway opens into a large car park with a purpose-built modern hall. Two elderly couples are playing tennis together and I watch from the car for a minute, being the first of the group to have arrived. The serves and ball retrievals seem to be carried out in slow-motion, but I think their game is as much about getting some fresh air and taking in the scenery as competing.

The committee members start to arrive and assemble tables in the small meeting room. I meet Marion the planning officer, who tells me from under her heavy, precision-cut greying fringe of the hundreds of planning applications she deals with each year. Ben and Jan, the married couple on the committee, unpack a box containing tea, coffee and biscuit provisions. Mugs with rural scenes are placed on the table, including one or two with a predictable badger. It all seems pretty normal so far. The group appears to be run by a small group of faithful folk, mostly with grey hair (though Jan's has purple streaks) and I'm not feeling this is going to be especially challenging. But as the meeting unfolds I imagine myself responding to a 1am call to see to an injured badger. Navigation skills: zero. Strength to deal with jaws and claws: minus one… I'm even useless with hamsters and banned them long ago. It was a combination of factors: the sharp nip that would draw blood – Tabitha the Savage we nicknamed the first – the dying-then-reviving act that brought swings of grief to ecstasy and back, and our cold house that made their average lifespan shrink to little more than six weeks. And they are so small and easy to drop – maybe I'll be better with a badger.

I say to the group that I should probably have Rupert involved. They agree, but tell me I need to sign him up as a member. It's decided that if anything happens near me, we'll get there and cover the badger with a cage or a blanket, then wait for Martin or Ed to arrive. All okay so far. It's easy to trust Martin, with his hand-lens permanently slung round his neck on its green cord, and his kind face. He clearly knows what he's doing, and so does Ed, the other ecologist in the group.

So how much do I tell Rupert about Martin's past injuries? He's running through them now, for my benefit, as he sits at the head of the table. He's had a serious bite on his thumb – it's lost some mobility, but 'it's not terrible.' Is my tetanus up to date, he asks. 'You have to tell them at the hospital, "It's *not* a dog bite," that you need an antibiotic injection. Tell them. Don't ask them. Caroline, I think you're able to do this.' He is quiet and serious for a moment, and no one says a word. I'm beginning to wonder if this is some initiation lecture to weed out the faint-hearted and I'm half-expecting a pain test at any moment. 'Badger bites are messy,' he says. 'They do bleed – not like a dog bite, they're clean. An old male can have teeth here' – he's pointing to his canines – 'like rusty old razor blades, full of bacteria.'

On one occasion he encountered a badger at head height in the course of his work. 'Neither of us could stay where we were. I thought it's going to hurt him and it's going to hurt me. Like the pictures you see of those old baiter boys holding the badger at arm's length by the tail. You can't do that for long. They couldn't.' Martin's humour conceals a deep compassion for these creatures, and I get the impression he needs plenty of both – badgers can be challenging, but so can the members of the general public that encounter them.

Ben and Jan tell me together that a badger's jaws will lock on you. 'It's happened to us,' says Ben. He speaks in a soft, Welsh voice, but his tolerance for pain is seen in the fading tattoos along his arms. And 'their skin is loose and they can twist round on you,' continues Jan, her silver cat earrings swinging in time as she demonstrates. 'It really did happen to us once, almost went inside out.' I can tell from their sincerity they are not simply trying to frighten the new recruit. They could be telling me about the post they've received today and I sense they are just as calm when these things happen.

I tell Rupert when I'm home that I've signed him up as a member so he can come out on mercy missions. I don't tell him about potential injuries, there's time for all that later.

'What, you mean we've got to go and rescue badgers? I didn't say I'd be up for that.'

'It's not a big deal. It won't happen very often I'm sure.'

He raises a smile at me, then hesitates before saying something. 'Don't you think you're getting a bit carried away with all this?'

'Look, you weren't there. Most of them are older than us and they manage.'

'Yeah, well, I'm going to bed. You coming?'

'In a minute, I just want to read some of this document that Martin's given me.'

An exasperated look from Rupert – 'What?' I say. 'You know I won't sleep without unwinding first anyway.'

I take the pamphlet from my bag as I hear his steps on the stairs and flick to the page that I've cornered. 'For the national survey we used the term "sett" to describe either a single, isolated hole, or a series of a few or many holes that seemed to be connected underground.' What have I got myself into? With the best of intentions I have unwittingly broken the law. Helping old ladies isn't as straightforward as it seems.

Saturday morning, and Madeline's awake early and calls out when she hears me. 'How did it go last night?'

'Good,' I say, coming to sit on her bed. I tell her about the possible rescues I'll be involved in.

'Can I come?' she says, up on one elbow and then sitting upright. 'I never get to do anything useful at my age.'

'Probably better not. We'll have to stop the car in dodgy places and deal with injured animals. They may be bleeding and frightened.'

'Oh. Won't Martin be there?'

'Not always. But what's the rush? You've a lifetime of badger adventures ahead of you.'

She's met Martin before and was charmed by his suggestion that left-handed people change the world, as she gave him hers to shake. She feels she knows him better than she does, but her picture of him is pretty accurate. Whenever we're out walking I pass on his knowledge, teaching her to find evidence of badgers. She's getting pretty good, as it happens.

'Mum, I saved you a jelly baby.' She hands it to me. 'Who does this remind you of?'

It's a green one. 'Martin,' I say. 'You need to stretch it out like this,' and I give it a tug.

Jemima must have overheard from her neighbouring bed but makes no comment for now. Perhaps she realizes that for her these adventures are so far off they're not even worth contemplating. But by supper time she has to air her thoughts.

'Mum, I want to be a member of the East Kent Badger Group,' she says.

The family are all seated round the big pine table and I sense she's been holding onto this request, wanting the full attention of everyone. I continue to pass out the remaining plates of veggie lasagne before looking straight at her.

'You are a member, I forgot to tell you. I signed you all up last night – family membership for an extra quid.'

'Is there any meat in this?' says Eliott, inspecting his meal with a fork.

'What do you think?' says Maddy. 'You don't need any dead animal in that anyway.'

'I didn't have time, it's the same for everyone.'

Jem bangs on the table with her fork. 'No, I'm ready to be a *proper* member, looking for badgers, rescuing them and all that stuff.' She's using that knowing, disgruntled voice saved for when grown-ups are unreasonable, and continues to press peas into her potato waffle. 'Martin did rescues when he was seven.'

When did she hear this? The expressive hands and strength of her argument are admirable, she'd be great in Maddy's school debating society. But the fact that she's sitting in her swimming costume with party beads slung round her neck convinces me that, after all, Mummy knows best. Besides, she's not yet seven.

Annie stops gazing at the chicken that's pecking the sweet peas outside the patio window. 'Am I a member too?'

'You are.'

'Why?' She rolls her eyes. 'I didn't ask to be. Don't I get a say in it?'

'What's not to like?'

She chooses not to answer this one, but her vexation comes out when we're watching Springwatch. This programme provides the nation's fix of British wildlife coverage whatever the weather, with live filming from five locations around the UK. 'They're not even talking about badgers, why's this even on?'

'So you admit they're cool,' says Eliott.

'Well, better than birds, but that's all.'

'So you are interested,' I say.

'No, I want them to get it over so you stop watching it. It's like it's your child on TV or something. I bet you weren't so interested when I was on that advert.'

Annie's moment of fame, the *Today* yoghurt drink ad when we lived in Nepal. She was filmed by chance when we visited the Ajima grocery stores, a carton in hand as she reclined in her pushchair. Her usually wide eyes were even wider for all the attention. It was shown in Nepalese homes every night just before the news. 'Putali justai' ('she's like a doll') they said wherever she went, and she and baby Maddy became objects of fascination, to be held, photographed, taken behind counters and into neighbours' houses. Given sweets, flowers, shoes that squeak, they –

'It's on!' says Eliott.

We stare at the screen as at last they play the footage we've been promised. A badger swims to a scrape and eats all but two of the avocet chicks it finds there, and all the eggs. Maddy is out of the room but she's going to hear about it. I wonder if her loyalty will start to wane.

'Mmm, these avocet chicks are delicious,' says Rupert. 'I think I'll have another one. Or another nineteen. Ha ha ha.'

A phone call soon reminds me of my much-needed allegiance, not that it was ever in any doubt. 'Is that Caroline from the badger group? We need a bit of advice here, something's not right,' says a quiet, worried voice. The lady introduces herself as Sandra, and she thinks I'll be able to help. 'We've had a large number of badgers on our land for years, but this summer all is quiet. We haven't seen one in months. They used to come close to our dining room window and watch from the top step while we all sat around the table,' she says.

They are exactly the sort of people who should have badgers, even allowing them to dig up their lawn.

As the story unfolds I know this one is beyond me. A few days ago, they found a skinned mole – perfectly intact – in the field that borders their property. They mentioned it to a neighbour, who told them of a skinned badger beside the stable on his own land. It has left them all feeling very anxious. There have been 'other suspicious goings on', but she won't elaborate on the phone. 'Could you come and see if you can find any evidence of badgers still being around here, or explain how to encourage them back? And help us to stop this persecution.' If only it were that simple, but I know I have to try.

The day of my visit arrives and I set out early, convinced as always that I'm going to get lost. It's the perfect mid-summer morning, and house martins fly up off the road as they're disturbed by the car. Bind-weed bells are bright and open, and the wheat is ripe already here, just five miles from home. I'm looking for the Ham/Sandwich signpost that I'm told has been replaced now – taken as a holiday souvenir, perhaps – and soon find it. The old

Been a farm worker all his life I'd say.'

'Spot on,' she says.

'You probably have a name.'

'Oh, we know who it is.'

I squint in the bright sunshine as I look out across the garden. I'm imagining some old farmworker dragging a dead badger into place and stepping back to admire his work. And is he responsible for the skinnings? Martin seems to think so. We all stand silent in the frustration of there not being enough evidence to prosecute, so cross he's got away with it. Apparently with the dead animals gone there's not a lot that can be done. I'm studying the nettle rash across my knuckles, I'd rather not look at that area of grass again.

'You know what to do if he leaves you another offering?' asks Martin.

'Oh we'll be right on it,' says David. 'Contact you or the police while the evidence is fresh.'

'If we're still here,' comes a quiet voice from beside me.

'You still have one or two,' says Martin. 'I think your most recent decrease is down to the sett having been flooded by the nearby well. Give it time, you never know.'

Talk of dead badgers always drives me out to watch living ones. We witness many badger antics now summer is well underway, and we're not seen as a threat very often. Are they familiar with us now? Do they know our scent and choose to ignore us? It's hard to tell. It worries me that someone with less-than-kind intentions could trick them into acceptance.

One evening I am out in the field with Rupert and Maddy, leaving Annie at home to babysit. We see a small face under the nettles and then a bottom with candyfloss tail as a cub goes down the hole. I turn on my phone to use the camera and it rings. I turn it off – we won't be long, it's probably my neighbour – it usually is. Rupert takes it from me and walks back along the field. 'I'll talk quietly,' he says.

Maddy is in an unusually annoying mood. She breaks wind and smiles at me, defiant and proud. She has the giggles now, and starts to fidget with the zip on her body-warmer.

The phone sounds again and we can hear Rupert muttering – little hope of seeing any more badgers tonight. He's back. 'It was Annie. She wanted to know about the Double Decker by the phone – was it for her?'

'Unbelievable.'

'I don't get it,' she says when we're home, the empty chocolate wrapper on the arm of the sofa beside her. 'Why do you have to see them again when you've seen them once?'

'Look Annie–' says Rupert in a voice that's too loud for the room. He stops himself and after a long pause starts again. 'Save your emergency calls for when the house is burning down.'

She looks at us with her piercing blue eyes. They make her confrontational without even trying, as one glance from a jackdaw can send predators flying from its nest. 'It was a chocolate crisis. You really don't get it, do you?'

A few evenings later, and we return home from a dentist check-up to a recorded message from Martin. Something about a big problem in our village, and he's told those concerned that I live elsewhere: 'Thought I'd better protect you a bit.' I can't understand what he means and I phone back straight away. He's out. I grab the dog lead and Maddy asks what's wrong. 'I need to check on the sett in case there's a problem with our badgers. Tell you on the way.'

I set a fast pace and Maddy and Tyn are almost running to keep up. A bruised sunset is spreading across the sky, all purples and pinks with a strange yellow hue, while swollen clouds build in the distance where the colour is yet to seep. The trees are wind-whipped and turning to silhouettes from the top down. Surely it can't be our badger sett, and how does Martin know what's going on here before me? I should have been keeping a closer eye. It seems we're in the field already, and a rabbit runs across our path – silent, except for its landing as it tumbles and rights itself at speed. It would be time to settle up here now, on a good night, but it's too windy, there'd be no chance of walking undetected. Grasses are blowing every which way and obscuring the paths. 'Could it have been the teenagers again?' says Maddy, breaking into my thoughts. 'Setting fire to their entrances?'

'I don't know, let's hope not.'

We check the holes – everything seems okay, and there's no evidence of tampering all the way along. We walk the loop and back into the teenage wood, but nothing.

'It's okay, Mum,' says Maddy, looking at me for a moment and then away. She's not one for holding eye contact, even with the family, but I check myself. I'm looking a little wild and have frightened her with my mad chase out here, barely stopping to engage with her.

'He must've got it wrong,' she says.

'Perhaps I did.' I sling an arm around her shoulders as we turn to walk home.

Martin phones again later when I'm tucked up in bed and reading my book. He tells me about a lady in my village who'd woken to find soil dug out from beneath her bungalow. 'She'd blocked all but one hole up. I read the riot act, gently,' says Martin. 'Digging right under her house. We're going to have to get a licence.'

Apparently we could get into trouble if we intervene immediately ourselves, which would slow down the process no end. Things always have to be done by the book. It seems ridiculous when a house is in danger and an elderly resident is frightened, but Martin does know what he's doing. But is this really the 'big problem' he said it was? The old lady's life isn't in danger, though at worst she might have to move out of her house, at least while it is fixed. His greatest fear has to be that one of us does more than we are legally allowed to, which could result in a fine, or even a short prison stay. Would the law really be this harsh towards an old lady who feels vulnerable in her own home or people who are trying to help her?

The following morning I take an early call from Mrs Joss. 'They've opened them up again,' she says. There's mess everywhere.'

'I'll be along as soon as I can,' I say. I've never seen a house with badger damage, this is actually quite exciting. As I take the short walk up the road I quicken my pace and start to run. This could be dramatic, and right here in our village. Some journalists love anything like this, particularly if their paper supports the cull and wants to sully the badger's reputation. We're going to have to try to keep this whole thing quiet. I ring the bell and a tall elderly lady in pink lipstick opens the door a fraction as two white dogs cause a blur around her feet. 'I'll just put my boots on,' she says, opening the door wider and stepping out of her pink fluffy slippers. 'You two, go in there, behave!'

She takes a stick from behind the door. 'It's round the side there, Caroline. I'll come and open the gate. You know, I thought there'd been a top-soil delivery to the wrong house.' Well she's managed to tidy most of it away. It's a magazine-perfect garden, small but immaculate – except for the badger holes. She's filled them in again as best she can, though soil is smeared over her neat paths. Do I tell Martin? How? I'd asked her not to touch them, but she's desperately worried about her two West Highland Terriers getting out through the holes. And I am somewhat confused – didn't Martin say they'd been digging *under* her house? They've come close, but there's a paving slab between their entry point and her bungalow.

'I think it'll all be okay,' I tell her. 'You really mustn't worry.'

'But what about the dogs?' She smooths her Princess Diana side-fringe though it was in place anyway.

'Just let me know if anything happens,' I say. 'I'm not far away.'

'Look at this, they've moved these bits of slate. I've had to put some logs in beside the fence here, but I really shouldn't lift things with my back.'

The next morning she calls me when I'm sitting down to check my emails. 'They're back. They've broken a concrete bar. The dogs are going to escape. It's awful, just awful, Caroline.'

'I'm sure I can temporarily block your holes,' I say. She has Martin coming today. *Today*? How did she manage that? I search the garden and then the garage, and find some old logs propped up in a corner. I gather up a bucket of rubble and drive round to plug the gaps.

I'm back again at 7 p.m., and invited inside to wait for Martin and Ed. I leave my wellies at the door and seat myself on the sitting room floor, allowing the dogs to clamber on me. The puppy climbs onto the sofa I'm leaning against and licks the back of my neck. So this is what it's like to be retired. No longer the pockets of muddle round the house, or stray objects that the children have dropped and left. Polished wooden surfaces that gleam and cut flowers from the garden in crystal vases. Soon the *Coronation Street* theme tune starts and I settle in for a different kind of

'You used those? I've been seasoning those for months. My seasoned cedar.'

He's in one of his rare but nightmarish sulks. Is it really so important? It's a lump of wood; well, a few, but there's some perspective missing here. It's an uneasy silence and I feel the need to fill it: 'I was dealing with a stressed-out old lady who was beside herself with worry this morning. How many people do we ever get to help in our community? You can hope the badgers dig them out tonight and then you can go and get your bits of wood back!'

'They won't be much good then, they'll be all wet.'

'Your lathe isn't even working at the moment.'

'You didn't ask me.'

'You were at work, what was I supposed to do?'

Our first badger argument. We rarely argue, just sink into a bit of sarcasm from time to time, so this has surprised me. He'll see the funny side of this one before too long. He needs things broken to him gently.

Two days later and another call from Martin. 'Gilli and I have rescued a badger that was tangled in netting under someone's shed,' he says. 'We thought you might like to come out tonight and help release it. It's a strong-willed boar, mind you.'

'Sounds great,' I say. 'I'd love to.'

'So what's the story?' whispers Rupert as Martin carries on

talking in my ear.

'He has a badger to release,' I say, covering the mouthpiece. 'It won't be easy. A difficult male. Do you want to come? We'll have to leave the kids at home.'

'I'm up for it,' he says, with no hesitation in his voice.

A golden sunset is reflected in the puddles as we take Rupert's winding back-lane route, the day's glory captured and held like clear honey dripped into a jar. It's just all so perfect. I glance across at him. His blond hair is shining in the light and his arms are tanned a colour I can never hope to reach. Is he over the wood-thing yet?

'You know, I am sorry about your cedar,' I tell him. 'It didn't look that special,' I say, going for some eye contact but his eyes are on the road.

'Oh well, it's done now.'

Soon we're in a part of Kent I don't know and driving through dark leafy lanes. Most of the place names are ending with 'ington'. Rupert slows the car and turns into a driveway concealed by overhanging shrubs and trees. I would never have found it on my own. We take the steps down to the house – it's lost in a wash of green, with limited sky visible through a dense canopy. I feel I have stepped into the setting of Hardy's *The Woodlanders,* where 'Except at midday the sun was not seen complete by the Hintock people, but rather in the form of numerous little stars staring through the leaves'. I didn't think anyone should own woodland until I met Martin – after all, you can't own a sunset, or the birds that fly through the trees – but I can't imagine anyone more trustworthy. He's a keeper of native species that thrive under his care. He greets us and we gather up a cage that we put in the wheelbarrow, a heavy-duty torch and some thick gloves. Something squeaks just off the path. 'Gilli, that's that baby weasel again,' he calls to his wife as we leave. Gilli is back in the house already, badger releases are normality for her living here and she lets Martin get on with it.

Rupert goes up to the road to wait for Karen, another new member, and Martin takes me to the holding pen, where we stand outside and chat. It's an old Pfizer cage for beagles, the size of a small garage, and is where injured badgers are kept until ready for release. Timing is crucial, and if they're away for more than ten days they won't be accepted back on their home turf.

Eventually Rupert gets fed up with waiting and comes to find us. Martin takes us both inside the cage; I can just about stand up straight in it, though my hair is catching as I move. There in the corner is a large dog carrier with a cover. Martin instructs us to place the small cage we've brought in front, in the hope the badger will run straight in when he lifts the lid.

'He'll probably go for one of our legs. I won't mind if you swear. He is pretty lively.'

Martin has been bitten by this one already, and underneath his thick gloves has plasters on his finger and thumb. He places both hands on the lid and slowly begins to lift it. I can feel my stomach tensing up, and I'm telling myself that I mustn't behave like a stupid girl and do anything I'll later regret.

'Ow. I can't believe it,' says Martin. 'Of all the –. Well. He only had to wait a few hours.'

Is he dead? What possibly could've happened to him? Perhaps he injured himself as he struggled in the net.

Martin stands back so we can see. The small carrier is *empty*. Martin looks closer, and Rupert and I step over to check, too. It really is empty. A few large strides and Martin is on the other side of the holding pen. 'Come and look at this,' he says and there at the back is a hole – the badger has bitten through weld mesh and steel rods. It will need fixing with cement before it's useable again. Then we notice that the food bowl has been broken – it's as if this badger worked himself into a frenzy and released himself.

'Well, it looks like I've got myself another badger. That really wasn't the plan. And you've come all this way.'

'Don't worry,' I say. 'Hopefully there'll be a next time.'

'You must at least come up to the house and have a coffee. It'll be time for the bats to come out soon. Would you like to watch them instead?'

'Of course,' we say together. But first we're given a tour around his wood in the fading light. Apparently he has a four-foot adder here – affectionately known as Ada the adder to begin with, until he discovered it was a male. He's still apologetic for the lack of badger, doesn't seem to get that it's simply fascinating to see him in his home environment and we don't really mind how we spend our time with him. Martin is such a natural with wildlife I always learn something without him even trying.

'How's Mrs Joss getting on?' says Martin.

'Okay I think.' I glance at Rupert. 'I got into trouble at home though,' I say smiling. 'Apparently that was seasoned cedar, prized it was.'

'Oh, it doesn't matter,' says Rupert.

'I've got lots of wood you can take away and use, there's no shortage. You must take something tonight.'

There is talking beyond the trees and Gilli arrives with Karen. The men talk woodland management while the rest of us get to know each other. Karen is in bare legs and flip-flops. What was she expecting? 'I'm new to the group, too,' she tells me. That kind of shows. It's nice to feel I'm perhaps no longer the greenest member of the group.

Martin takes us back up to the house and seats us outside on garden chairs to watch his bat spectacle. 'There are thousands in that little roof,' he says. 'We'll hear them before we see them. Get yourselves comfy.'

We are dotted down the slope as in the tiers of a theatre, and he passes around his sonic equipment so we can hear the echolocation. I'm confused as I seem to be hearing it in stereo; I'm clearly picking up some of this without the technology. I won't say anything – I'm not sure if it's possible or if I'm just imagining it, and I don't want to feel foolish. But some of their chatter was audible before he even switched it on. 'I'm going to help you pick out the sound of the serotine bat. Can you hear the noise of lips being smacked together? That's the serotine.'

Soon they start to emerge in ones and twos, making their way over our heads and into the trees. They favour this particular gable end we're looking at. Martin tells us of the infant bats he's witnessed in his attic, doing press-ups in preparation for flight. And now bats are spilling out of the roof, dissolving into the darkening sky like ink in water. I have never stopped to watch them before, and now that I've seen them I'm fascinated. Their flight paths are outlandish and you want them to slow down so you can form a picture of them in your mind.

I'm ashamed of my lack of bat knowledge. Like most people I've lived with a slight feeling of repulsion about them, perhaps compounded by their depiction in fiction and film. I confess that I know very little about their real-life existence. Bram Stocker has of course coloured our perception: 'Good God, Professor!', says Dr. Seward, 'Do you mean to tell me that Lucy was bitten by such a bat; and that such a thing is here in London in the nineteenth century?'. But that other-worldly appearance, like a malformed mouse crawling inside a wet sheet, can't help either, nor their ability to negotiate complete darkness. Francis Bacon wrote, 'Suspicions amongst thoughts are like bats among birds, they ever fly by twilight.' In our human narrative we often fill in gaps of knowledge with explanations that seem plausible, but that are based solely on fear. What are they fleeing, we wonder? What's the hurry? During the Celtic New Year festival of Samhain bats would have feasted on insects lured by the communal bonfires.

These autumnal fires have continued under various names for centuries, with the bat association firmly established in the collective imagination. Most varieties of bat fly out at dusk anyway, so the literal and figurative link with darkness is impossible to shift. And then there's their attachment to caves, giving rise to the belief that they are messengers between worlds. We may conclude that they are evil – or a little sinister anyway – and best kept out of sight. There's an old saying that has been attributed to many authors, 'A lie will go round the world while truth is pulling its boots on.' Meanwhile every species of Britain's bat is endangered, and we are its greatest threat. They've done nothing to deserve their lack of popularity, and for many simply fall short in the lottery of cuteness.

The next morning the youngest three want to hear about the badger we helped to release.

'I'm glad I didn't miss out on anything', says Maddy as she clicks shut the lid on her lunch-box. 'Bats? Bats. No substitute at all.'

'Well I think they're cute,' says Jemima, running her finger along her marmalade-covered knife, then putting it in her mouth.

'About as cute as you,' says Eliott, pulling his best boss-eyed face at her.

Annie comes down last of all, carrying a spider that she's caught in the bathroom. She opens the back door and puts him outside.

2: Shared spaces

The Crown has been filling the village with sound this Saturday. Earlier it was a charity fundraiser – Eliott played his cornet there, together with the rest of the silver band. An ex-mining community, the village was paid off with a stockpile of instruments that keep teenagers off the street (well, the good ones), and fill the community with a sense of pride. The pub has been dressed and waiting all week, with two-tier hanging baskets trailing flowers, and bunting strung from the roof in red, blue and green.

Now dusk is approaching and Rupert, Maddy and I are in the woods, half a mile away; we can hear them blasting out the Britain's Got Talent final from here. Much of the nation will be watching this tonight, with dancing granny Paddy Jones battling with singers, impressionists and other dance acts. It's on at home too. I had thought of inviting Eliott to come for the first time, but he looked so chilled out in front of the TV, the excitement of his 'gig' having worn him out. He and Annie will enjoy watching it together without Rupert's cynical comments. Annie will strut around the sitting room before raiding the fridge and kitchen cupboards. Maddy felt she'd rather come with us to watch badgers. 'I won't remember who won when I grow up, but I will remember this,' she says.

This kind of noise pollution doesn't often happen here and I don't resent the party atmosphere. We hear a high-pitched squeak from a cub as we come to our watching place, but that's it for a while. They'll have to get on with it at some point if they want to eat tonight.

It's the warmest night so far and I try to undo my jacket, pressing my thumb against the zip to muffle the sound; I'm sure they're listening from underground and any noises close by will be picked up all the same. I have a chest infection – 'You need to look after yourself' my mum said recently, equating my ongoing illness with my late-night wanderings – so I'm trying to dress for when the temperature drops. I place my hand in a pocket and find fragments of sweet wrapper from last time.

Something's happening and we all look into the oak tree overhead – the leafy coverage is dense and we can't see what's going on. 'It sounds like a badger up there,' says Maddy. She can't be serious, but it does sound like a heavy creature attacking something. They have been known to climb trees after all.

'Could it be?'

'No,' I whisper. 'But it does sound like it. It's probably just squirrels.'

It *is* squirrels – we see them bound off across the branches in different directions, leaping from one tree to the next, free runners of the woods with no fear of falling.

'He's coming,' whispers Rupert, already focused again on the woodland floor. The thrashing of nettles and a cub makes its way to the hole, three metres away. It's still early but this cub could be feeling hungry and out for an early supper; sows wean their cubs from the end of May. He sniffs the entrance before putting his head inside the tunnel and disappearing from sight.

We wait a while, but the badgers aren't out in force tonight. They need plenty of time to forage, and I'm starting to feel we could be in the way. We put on the torch and walk back across the fields and then down the fenced footpath towards the street.

'I thought we'd see more than that,' says Maddy.

'I know. We should be glad they're cautious though,' says Rupert. 'Self-preservation skills and all that.'

The litter on the ground increases as we near the pub and a covering of sycamore 'helicopters' rests on top, like a child's attempt at hiding veg with a knife and fork. The music is getting louder: 'Shout, shout, let it all out, these are the things we can do without...' Perhaps some nights are best left to noise and revelry.

Soon it's Monday morning again and Maddy thinks she's lost her keys at school – that is, her house key, locker key and memory stick. She won't leave anything in her locker and is carting a bag to and fro that's half her body weight, as if fearful of a Dover

Girls' crime ring. She's stressed with the thought of her Year 8 exams this week and I've assured her we won't go badger watching without her. Last night she couldn't sleep and I gave her an espresso cup of lager that knocked her out, but now she's tearful and is trying to reconcile Mum's counselling with her fears. *What's the worst that can happen? A resit? A detention? The tests are as much for the teachers as for you, to make sure they've been getting across what you need to know. If you all bomb on the same questions, they've got some explaining to do. There's always bottom set – no shame there, just an easier ride.*

I bump into Mrs Stephens and her little staffy whilst out walking Tyn. He tugs towards them, then backs off to wait behind my legs. 'Now, what have you done or not done?' she asks. I'm not sure what else there was to do. I'd shown Martin the pictures on my phone and he agreed the badgers weren't going to get in. He had suggested chicken wire tacked onto the lower part of her goose house, but she wasn't having it, so we'd agreed to watch and wait. I explain this to her.

'I can come and check for any more digging if you like,' I offer.

Now she seems to think I've done quite enough and feels sure all is well.

I can only imagine there must be evidence of badgers in her lower field and she's worried about the planning application. Badgers needn't halt her building plans anyway, though it's true they will slow things down considerably. I'd love an excuse to take a look. I would do practically anything to have badgers in my back garden, but they always seem to choose the places where they're not wanted. Perhaps we could redirect them towards our house – it's very close as the crow flies, we could even be on their radar, come to think of it. After all, what's a few hedges and back gardens to a badger?

I get the feeling she remains unsettled by what happened to the goose house, though she is at least happier than before my visit. Still, I'm relieved to know Martin thinks I've done enough on this one, even if she remains unconvinced.

Later I bring Eliott and Jemima home and they race down to the chicken house to look for eggs. I'm still pulling on the hand-break. 'Mum, *Mum!*' calls Jemima.

'What's the emergency?' I say, following them down the garden. The chickens are all fine, pecking round the garden as usual.

'In there,' says Eliott. 'It's a trapped squirrel. D'you want me to go in and get it? I can you know.'

I prop open the door with the usual log, but the squirrel is distressed and dives at speed over every surface of the run and into the chicken house, before launching out the door and into the trees behind.

We have a new resident in our garden, too: we keep spotting a lone kit rabbit on the back lawn. It's probably an orphan and the children are concerned.

'Can we take him in?' asks Madeline early one Saturday. 'We've got so many empty hutches and things.'

'I don't think it'd be right,' I say. 'He's a wild rabbit.'

'Yeah,' joins in Eliott. 'Imagine taking him to the vets and having to explain.'

'Is he a boy or girl?' asks Jemima.

'I wouldn't know without looking,' I say, 'and even then I wouldn't be sure.'

'I think it's a boy,' says Maddy. 'He's got darker ears.'

'Oh really.'

'Don't laugh, I heard it somewhere. Look, he's hopping around with a blackbird, he thinks it's a friend.'

Jem is now 'playing' a recorder and is trying a little too hard. 'Did you like my music?'

'Mmm.'

'Did you wonder what the noise was?'

'Yes but stop, you'll disturb the bunny. Come away from the window. Just this once I'll let you sit on the table.'

A hop and a flick of the tail. He's looking in our direction and seems unsure what to do.

'Mummy, can I go out and get him? *Please.*'

*

The phone is ringing and I step between the sleeping bag rolls and rucksacks that are covering half the kitchen floor. Annie and Maddy are camping this weekend with friends and pitching their tents is our next job.

'Caroline, there's an injured badger for you to deal with,' says Martin. 'It's in the next village to you.'

I flick on the kitchen light and settle on the top step. 'Go on.'

'It has a gash and I just need you to take a photo. We think it's living under the neighbour's shed.'

I'm put in touch with Beryl and Alan who run the Dover animal rescue and live closer to me than Martin. Beryl tells me she hopes the badger can be treated on site, 'but if it's really bad you'll need to look at trapping it.'

They make it sound so easy. It probably would be for them. So I have actually to get a sighting, and if it's really bad make plans to move it. Perhaps I can do it tonight, as long as we can put the tent up quickly enough. I worry that Martin and Beryl are putting too much trust in me but perhaps this is the only way I'll learn. I suppose I just need to get on with it, see what happens. I call the number that's been passed on to me and speak to Glenn. 'It's now starting to dig up my drive, which is quite annoying really,' he says.

'I can come tonight if you like. It sounds like your badger needs help as soon as possible.'

'I think we all do.'

I meet no other cars as I take the quiet lanes between fields and around the wood yard. The sun is low in the sky but there's time to settle before the badger ventures out. Insects and seed pollen are suspended mid-air and grass cuttings pad the verges. Scabious heads nod at the field edge. This plant was once used to treat skin conditions such as scabies, eczema and weeping sores, its name coming from 'scabere', the Latin term for scratch. I wonder if badgers instinctively know which plants to chew on, as pregnant women crave foods containing the nutrients they lack.

At 8.30 p.m. I pull into the parking bay a short walk from the end-of-terrace house. As I walk up the driveway I look for signs of badger digging and sure enough there's a nice little pit hollowed out over to one side. I rap on the door and Glenn comes to meet me. He leads me through the sitting room and I spot school photos propped up on a bookcase – I recognize the faces from school and realize whose house I'm in.

'I've got kids at the school, too,' I say, pointing at the picture. 'My Jemima knows your daughter, Chloe. They're friends at Brownies too.'

'Do you know my wife, Sally?' he asks, scratching his scalp through his mop of curls.

I nod. 'Sorry, she's out tonight,' he says. That's probably just as well, there's no way we'd be quiet enough for a badger. He shows me into the kitchen and seems slightly embarrassed by my being here – that makes two of us then. 'Do you want a drink? Please, sit down.'

The table is placed right up against the window, creating the perfect domestic wildlife hide. I pull out a chair for myself. 'We have squirrels on that windowsill, most days,' he says. 'The girls love it at breakfast time. They've seen a pair of squirrels raise their young and can hand feed them from here –.' He opens the window in front of me and sticks out his hand. 'You see the bird-table? That's where the badger comes up and feeds most nights.

I've made a platform for him at the bottom, but he's been known to climb right up.'

It's no more than two metres away from where I'm sitting. I'm trying not to feel jealous, but in this small patch they see more wildlife in one day than we see in a year.

Why don't we just move house? I'd like to, but the girls have already resisted the idea. I remind myself that I'm here for a reason, and Glenn passes me a mug of tea. 'I'm often out there watching the badger,' he tells me. 'Though sudden movements will send him flying for cover.' I sympathise with him while I sip slowly and wait.

'Perhaps I should wait outside,' I say. 'It's what I had imagined.'

'There's nowhere for you to hide really. I tend to go out once he's settled. No, you're all right.'

Glenn leaves me to it, which is something of a relief and I check my camera is working okay. It makes a loud noise and I put it on the table in front of me.

I finish my tea, the mug grows cold. Nothing. I sit for an hour and a half but the badger doesn't show. Glenn comes back into the kitchen and looks at the clock. I think the noise from the washing machine isn't helping, it's as close to the window as the bird-table. Glenn's on his feet now and drumming his fingers on the counter. 'I don't think he's coming tonight,' I say. 'I can wait longer if you like.'

'No, it's okay.'

'I was really hoping to get a photo, then we can work out how to help him.'

'I know. Why don't you come on through, I've got some pictures of him on the computer.'

He presses a button and the screen comes to life. 'Hang on a minute, they're on here somewhere.' He runs a short film and then finds the still shots. 'I can see an obvious line around the badger's neck,' I tell him. 'It looks like he's been caught in a snare.' He thinks the badger has been slower since the injury. That's worrying.

'So the badger is coming from next door?' I ask.

'He's living under their shed, but it's being pulled down within the month – perhaps even a couple of weeks.'

'That's no good. Your badger looks like one of last year's male cubs – that fits with what you say. They're forced to relocate once a new litter is born.'

'Well where's he gonna go? I expect he'll start digging under our house, it happens doesn't it?'

'It's unlikely,' I say.

'We're built on mud with no foundations here.'

I can see his point; if the badger is fond of this spot – and who can blame it – there's really nowhere else to dig; it's a small enclosed garden, semi-wild, edged with a railway line to the rear.

'So you're going to catch him? Move him on?'

'I need to get some more advice,' I say. 'But I think we can treat him here.'

'You sure? He is looking poorly. He's had an injured ear for a couple of months, too.'

'Let's give it a few days, anyway.'

Glenn agrees to keep a look out for the badger and will monitor any changes. I ask if anything else eats the food they put out – he thinks there are no foxes around and tells me they keep their dog inside after eight o'clock. This means we should be able to put medicine in his food and be pretty certain he'll take it.

I begin investigating snares when I'm home. I think Glenn's badger's been injured by a light rabbit snare, they are very common. 'If you learn to observe the ground and know what game trails to look for, snares will provide more food than you can handle,' says one site. And unseen damage to wildlife of course. But the thought of that shed coming down is starting to bother me more. I'll have to talk to Martin.

The next morning there are texts from Maddy, full of badger concern. I tell her I think he's escaped from a snare and I'll need to get him some antibiotics.

'Aww is the badger ok? Maddyxxx.'

'I think he's on the mend, but needs medicine to be on the safe side. Xx.'

'Ok hope he gets better soon love Maddyxxx

Ps i had beans on toast for breakfast!'

'Could've been worse,' says Rupert as I read out the texts to him.

'Yes,' I say. 'I think it could've been a lot worse.'

'I mean the beans on toast. You've got badgers on the brain.'

The girls come home on Sunday, their eyes watering with tiredness, their long blonde hair somehow still immaculate, though Annie's hair-straighteners had to stay at home. We unload the car and dump bags on the kitchen floor. They make their way through to collapse into comfy chairs, but Eliott stays to rifle through the luggage.

'Where's my tent?' he asks.

'It'll turn up,' says Rupert. 'It's probably come home in someone else's car.'

'I don't think so,' says Maddy. She's sounding tearful. 'I had it all ready but it'd gone from the rest of my stuff when it was time to go.'

'It'll probably still turn up,' says Rupert. 'If it doesn't we'll just have to find you another one.'

I speak to Sally, Glenn's wife, a few days later. 'We saw the badger the night after you came. It had a wound on its shoulder,' she says. 'It was definitely an open wound, not just a scrape.'

I ask for their neighbour's details and Sally says she'll pass mine on to them. Within minutes I take a call from Samantha who informs me that she is Sally's neighbour, and they won't move the shed now. She seems genuine, which is something of a relief. I still tell her what Martin has asked me to say – 'We could organize a licence for you, but we have to be there when it happens.' I quote 'It's "a resting place for badgers and therefore protected by the 1992 act."'

'We love that badger,' she says. 'Every night we leave food for it under the trampoline. It won't come to any harm, I can assure you.'

I can't believe how easy that was. I can only hope she's telling the truth. Beryl had prepared me too, and I had been ready to say more – 'We need a week to ten days to sort it out,' she'd instructed me to say. 'We respectfully ask that you let us know before doing anything.' *We will win*, she had said to me. I was really expecting a fight.

I speak to Beryl again for advice on the injury – she's just back from her day job at the funeral directors that she runs with her husband, and now she's on animal duty through the night. She thinks the badger will need trapping, but will speak to Martin first.

I land myself on the sofa next to Rupert. 'You know, Beryl is talking about bringing a cage.'

'It would be quite exciting,' he says.

'Yeah, but not for the badger.'

'But if it needs doing…'

Then the plan progresses further. I'm to pick up antibiotics at a local vets, and we'll give these time to work before we do anything else. It all sounds good, but the vets won't oblige unless I bring the badger in. I tell them that this is what we're trying to avoid. Back to Martin. Children's vitamin drops are decided on; a child's dose must be soaked into bread. These are easier to obtain, and I take them round with instructions in the bag, and a request that they keep us posted.

Sally is home and tells me they saw the badger on Friday night: 'He fled when I put the outside light on – he's getting more fearful of us. He'd been sitting on our knee-high bird table and got down rather clumsily.'

'That's a good sign,' I say. 'He doesn't sound like he's deteriorating if he's able to climb. We're all so jealous. Jemima keeps talking about Chloe's badger.'

'You know, she hasn't seen the badger yet – she's usually in bed by the time he's out. She'd rather not see him, anyway. The other night we got home late and she was afraid to get out of the car in the dark, worried he'd be down the hole.'

The next morning I take Tyn on an early morning walk to check on the sett. It's June and the badgers are very active in our village now – I worry their presence may have become obvious to others, too. The footpath to the woods is dry and cracked, like some old worn leather relic, long since forgotten. Holly leaves have fallen and crunch underfoot. It is sunny and warm already though it's not yet eight o'clock. I reach the teenage wood and want to make sure there are no more signs of disturbance – and if I'm quiet I may see something. The ground is covered in beech mast husks though, so there's not a chance. I check on the enclosure too and drop peanuts for later. Has that hole been filled in? I think it's just underused. Even the main hole has plant growth concealing it now, heavy dock leaves drape over the top like swagged curtains; everything about this sett is well-hidden. I step closer to look at the balled cobwebs on the bushes – they resemble dropped wet cloths and remind me of tales of housewives spreading washing over shrubs to dry, a habit recorded in the sixteenth century.

I hear the movement of a heavy animal inside the thicket. Badgers occasionally wander above ground in the mornings, though I'm yet to see one. I stand quietly for a time but I've been detected and should just go home.

The dog and I take our usual circuit and enter the teenage wood from the other side. Here I find plenty of rubbish, and an empty Argos carrier bag – I fill it with broken bottles and cans, and a piece of broken yellow sign that reads 'Danger of death'. The bag is soon full and I hope it will hold until I reach the village. Conkers lie strewn over the ground here; they have fallen too early and are still in their shells – a reason to come back later with the children. Beech leaves from autumn still glow from the floor, and foxgloves are spreading along the path. Jemima will like the old names: Fairy Thimbles, Fairybells and Goblin Gloves. They grow where foxes tread – and badgers.

Days later I run into Sally near the school. Her badger is bleeding behind his ear – 'Do badgers have ears?' she asks. I assure her that they do, though they are hard to picture – white along the tips, now I think of it. She believes he's blind in one eye too, but has been from the start.

'I'm pretty sure he's on another badger's turf,' I say. 'You must keep watching out for him, and adding the vitamins to his food. I'm told thinly spread Marmite works too.'

'That's good. We're always looking out for him.'

I don't tell her Martin isn't holding out much hope of the badger making it – news of the more recent open wound on his shoulder made him quite despondent, and his judgement is based on years of experience. This badger already seems the weaker party and he hasn't got the message yet about being unwelcome on this patch. One of them will have to win, and though they are unlikely to fight to the death he is looking increasingly vulnerable. But we have to let him take his chance, and moving him because of the odd scrape wouldn't be right. I like to think he'll find his place here before long.

3: *Getting along*

Our twentieth wedding anniversary and a bolt for freedom. Rupert and I eat in a local Italian restaurant overlooking a riverbank quay – the children's favourite choice of meal too, but we feel compelled to leave them at home. I tell them we're researching it on their behalf, that it could be really rough. It's not. We're home early and the eldest three are still up. 'You've got school tomorrow,' I say. 'Come on, time for bed.' Annie rolls her eyes and I know what she's thinking, any kid is suspicious of their parents at her age. 'Okay, you can stay up a bit longer,' I tell her as the others go upstairs, and sit down with her on the sofa. 'We're going out again in a minute,' I tell her. She looks surprised. It might be our most romantic night of the year but I have a yearning to see badgers, and we creep out of the house just after Maddy turns off her light.

As soon as we arrive at the sett and stop by the fence a female badger comes along the path, pauses, and then proceeds down the hole we're overlooking. The area is alive with badger sounds, there's playful keckering in the thicket and even in the wheat-field behind us. Then a cub goes down the hole, his markings as neat as any pedigree puppy's, his eyes as oversized and doleful. Seeing this little fellow, it's easy to understand why they were kept as pets years ago, though he's not showing his destructive powers right now. Rupert misses the cub as he's turned to look into the field, the noises there are so distracting by this point – we wonder if it's a fox. The ears of the wheat are moving and a badger head appears, as if coming up for air.

'Is it an adult?' I whisper.

'I can't see.'

Another cub goes down the hole in front of us, his ears up straight and turning to catch the evening sounds. We think they are coming through a tunnel leading from the hole we're watching and up into the field, though we can't be sure. Perhaps they are hunting their supper – a field mouse, a vole, a shrew – the ground is very dry and worms and leatherjackets must be hard to come by.

And then, in the very centre of the wooded area, a broad, ample, badger boar emerges, the size of a large, overweight Labrador. He sits at the top of a mound and observes, as if all that he surveys is his, and in a way it is. He has a dignity and slowness about him, as if the whole world should slow in his presence, as we would stand and wait for royalty or some self-important official. He commands our respect without even trying. I feel I should bow or something, but I just stand and watch until he's lost from sight.

The next day I walk the dog around the sett, dropping generous handfuls of peanuts in the enclosure. That evening we go out to watch, hoping for a similar spectacle to the night before. We hear them – there is the odd chirp, not constant enough for bird song, and then some corporate chittering. We wait. Has the mother warned the cubs not to come to the hole tonight? Were we seen after all?

Before now I had never stopped to notice the start of rainfall in a wood. It's disconcerting – it sounds like footsteps all around, as if animals are emerging en masse – and you don't know where to look. Then you realize that nothing is happening; or if it is, it's concealed by the prattling drops and you've no hope of hearing anything meaningful. But as always, you hang on a bit longer, just in case.

Sometimes you know you won't see anything, whether it's raining or not. Is that an intuitive understanding, an inherent ability as your psyche assesses the wind direction, the amount of light, the smells you're carrying, without engaging the brain? Do we transmit negative emotion when we've had a bad day, making us more detectable? Is that why, then, that badgers are more likely to appear when I've had a good day and everything's going well? Other times you know they're not coming, but then hear a noise – is it just a clumsy pigeon? You feel you must stay, to be absolutely sure.

I wonder if I'm missing something more profound here. I know we underestimate animals, that it's easier to minimize them and think they are way off from our own level of consciousness. But at times their ability is unquestionably superior to our own. Animals can predict imminent danger; accounts of the 2004 Asian tsunami tell of elephants running for safety at least half-an-hour before disaster struck, and of a mass exodus of many other creatures, from buffaloes to bats. In World War II pets were often ahead of air raid sirens, convincing owners to take cover. Although these reactions must be biological, or at least in part, their perceptive powers do make us question whether our own senses are dulled in comparison, and could with a little effort be heightened. Humans are not without intuitive ability – in the 1950s Ronald Rose's research concluded that Aborigines could communicate with each other over a distance of miles simply through the power of thought. Loren McIntyre's story, told by Petru Popescu in the book *Amazon Beaming,* covers his 1960s trip to locate a tribe in the Amazon rainforest. During this time he discovered the tribesmen's 'beaming' technique, or their 'other language', as they themselves referred to it. McIntyre stayed with them for two months due to missing his flight home.

In 1919 William J. Long asserted that wolves from the same pack connect with each other even when there are miles between them ,[4] but his research methods have come under fierce scrutiny. However, in recent times Rupert Sheldrake has taken up his ideas and applied them to domestic dogs. His study leads him to suggest

---

[4] Long, William J. 2005 [1919]. *How Animals Talk: And Other Pleasant Studies of Birds and Beasts.* Vermont: Bear and Company.

that pet dogs simply know their owners are on the way home, irrespective of factors such as daily routine and sounds. I wonder if this could work both ways, for our yearning for a deep connection needs listening to. In his poem *A Night with a Wolf* Bayard Taylor dwells on the possibility, suggesting that he's experienced a bond with the wild that some of us crave:

> His wet fur pressed against me;
> Each of us warmed the other;
> Each of us felt in the stormy dark
> That beast and man were brother.

Occasionally in our Western society a person claims they have the ability to transmit thought to animals, but this cross-species communication is lacking among most of us. Could we not just convey the message somehow that we mean no harm and they can get on with it, we won't be in their way?

Tonight we know for sure it's not going to happen and turn to head home. I spot headless wheat stalks along the field edge. There are little piles of husks beside the fence too. I can almost picture it happening – the reachable windblown heads are pulled off by the badgers and taken to a safe place. Here they nibble through them and spit out the husks, like children with cherry stones.

It's July 1st and Maddy and I are off badgering again. It has been a warm day with no obvious breeze and the conditions are perfect.

We hear cub chitterings as we approach and then it is quiet. I imagine there are two family groups living here. Maddy thought she saw four cubs the night they charged at us, and the fact we see them with such regularity suggests there is more than just one unit. Most litters contain two or three cubs. Those living in close proximity will play together and be on very familiar terms. We don't have long to wait before a cub appears at the usual hole and scuttles down. A couple of minutes, and then another. They're so keen to explore, like kids sent to the water's edge with buckets and spades, always quicker than their adult counterparts and chattering to themselves as they go. I step back to give Maddy a better view, but stand on a twig – the cub looks up at me and meets my eye before retreating down the hole. Next the turn of an inquisitive, mid-sized badger – a yearling female? She looks my way and I watch as her eyes travel from my feet to my head then stop. It's as if she's waiting for my next move to decide if I'm to be feared. Maddy adjusts her footing and the badger turns, showing us a fan-shaped tail. A female after all. Maddy hears noises in the wheat – she raises her shoulders at me and nods in that direction. I watch as she sees a small face appear, her smile in her eyes, too, and her small dimples appearing beside them. I see her follow the moving wheat stalks right up to the far corner. I had told her they may be in the field as we left the house, but didn't divulge just how I knew. She didn't ask.

Nothing happens for a while. All that activity must be half-an-hour ago by now and there is school tomorrow. We have been watching a slither of thumbnail moon appear and it's time to go home. All in all six sightings at the hole tonight and one in the field. Aeroplane trails trace a wide, open sky before the sunset deepens. We reach the village and football echoes from TVs in houses along the street, the images flashing golden light across the pavement. The moon is shining brightly as we reach our gate – 'It's a waning crescent, we're doing it in geography,' says Maddy. 'I wish I could remember them all.'

The term races ahead and the older girls are burdened with homework once more. Rupert and I agree on a quick round of badger surveillance before it gets dark. We're out again without Maddy noticing. In the thicket the badgers are roaming, but we can't see them. It's late July and the plants are towering and dense – grasses are as tall as me, and trees heavy with leaves lower their branches to meet the undergrowth. There's the sound of rubber shoes scuffing on a floor at speed – badger cubs enjoying themselves, making their sports hall noises. It's good just to listen to them and know they are okay – I feel like a parent checking on a newborn, listening for their breathing in the dark but anxious not to disturb. Soon I'm frustrated though and step over the fence and pull down an elderflower branch in the hope of seeing *something*. The rush of movement, a badger bounding towards us but I can't see it – then a cub at the hole as it pushes its way through.

Rupert catches my eye and nods in the direction of the field. It sounds like badgers fighting in a distant corner. We whisper exchanges. The noises move to another field that we'll need to walk through on our way home. I'm in no hurry to move, but Rupert nudges me, his eyes darting, his movements fast. 'Come on, let's go and look.'

We can hear them thrashing about as we draw nearer. What if we get caught up in it? Rupert is as close as he can be, overlooking a dense area of trees and brambles. 'They're in there!'

I take a wide path and make my way around the back to watch from a safe distance. The noise stops. Has one been killed? Injured badly? I wait a while but nothing seems to be happening. I wave at Rupert but he's not seeing me, or pretending not to at least. After a couple of minutes I wave again and he jogs towards me. 'We should get home,' I say.

'They must have heard us. A full-on scrap and they dropped it, just like that.'

The next day I revisit the scene with the dog once it's light. The grass is buzzing with insects, but there's no evidence of badgers having been here. I step into the longer grass to where Rupert stood last night. There's a puddle of red on the ground, a clump of three lords and ladies have been flattened and lay gleaming in the sun like spilt blood.

The weekend arrives again and I can hear the dog dealing with a rival outside. I realize the neighbours are probably still asleep. I pull on Rupert's wellies that are by the back door and make my way to the gate: Mrs Joss is there with her two Westies. The puppy and Tyn continue to bark at each other, but the old Westie simply stands and takes it all in.

'She has lung problems, just doesn't have the fight any more. In some ways it's easier, but others not.'

She tells me again how grateful she is for all my help. She's had more digging and I promise to come with Rupert as soon as he's on holiday to badger-proof the fence.

'They're vicious,' she says.

I rebuke Tyn again and listen as she repeats her theory about where they are getting in. I tell her I'd thought they'd come from Mrs Stephens' direction, until I saw where exactly her house was situated.

'Oh her – no, my house isn't on her side.'

'So whose land is it?' I say.

'It's old Charlie's, he turns a blind eye, though if the truth is known, I think there's more to it.'

'Oh?' I say. This should be funny. Charlie is in his nineties and probably the oldest member of the village. I see him walking down the road to the shop sometimes and I now think it's unkind to call out a greeting. It looks painful for him to move his back from horizontal to vertical, and then he's just plain confused, unsure of where the voice has come from.

'I think he's got a sett and has filled it in, so they're coming to me instead. It's obvious isn't it?'

'I can't imagine an old boy like him out shifting earth,' I say.

'He's got a son,' she says. 'They're *in league* you know.' She looks me hard in the face, as if this really is a serious matter. 'Do you think you might have a word? Just go and talk to him, see if he's been blocking holes on his side?'

I make my way round later, Maddy is tagging along and I feel a little like a Jehovah's Witness. I should probably have left her behind but she is persistent. A caged tawny owl greets us at the gate, like some kind of archaic warning system: 'Whu – hooo'. I don't think the bird wants us here, we have disturbed his peace at the very least. We stop to admire him but are within sight of the house so I nudge Maddy on. 'Come on, this isn't what we're here for.' The modern house is surrounded by high hedges, I guess the owl is used to his seclusion.

A younger man comes to the door and I explain I'm from the badger group and we're trying to establish where they are coming from. I don't take in his appearance, I'm so intent on making myself understood.

'I can tell you right now, you're wasting your time.' He's about to close the door on us, but then pauses and opens it wider. 'Hang on a minute, I'll go and ask him.'

Soon I'm waved through towards the back garden. Maddy's muttering things at me but I pretend not to notice as I feel we're being watched. Then a window opens and the old boy hangs out – 'Are you from the council? Did the council send you?' He has one tooth left in his lower jaw which makes him look both very young and very old.

I tell him we're trying to help Mrs Joss.

'Oh her, she worries 'bout everything. Probably thinks there's badgers under her pillow. I can tell you right now, you won't find anything.'

We're expecting to find evidence of a major cover up now, but it's exactly as they said. The ground is pitted with snuffle holes and it's another meadow for a back garden, but no holes filled in or badgers redirected. Not that I can find anyway.

The next day Maddy comes running into the house and finds me in the loo. 'Mum, Mum,' she says, banging on the door. 'I think I've found a badger hair in our garden.'

'Hang on,' I say. I unlock the door and she bounds inside. '*Here.*'

I dry my hands and take the hair, holding it up to the light. I tell her I think it belongs to the dog. The colouring looks exactly the same.

'It doesn't! It won't roll! Try it!'

She's right. Now she's running down the stairs and I'm following. We're at the bottom of the garden in less than a minute, in what Jemima calls 'the forest yard': a strip of tall trees – sycamore, leylandii, holly and plum – the width of the garden and just four metres deep. There has been digging under the rope swing and the roots of the old sycamore have been exposed. We're on our knees and together spot a gap under the metal mesh fence and more obvious holes under the one behind – the neighbours have tried to fill it in with bricks. I find a badger hair in the root hole and put it in Jemima's plastic cooker sink that's found its way down here.

We're on our feet now and Maddy high-fives me. 'We've got badgers!' she calls to Rupert. 'I was so jealous of the old ladies–'

'Keep it quiet,' I say. 'It looks like the neighbours don't want them.'

'Must be why the dog goes beserk at night,' says Rupert. 'It sounded like a right fight a few weeks ago, I thought he'd found a fox.'

Jemima has heard now and is attempting cartwheels in the garden. We run inside to tell Eliott and find Annie curled up on the sofa with her laptop.

'What, are they there now?' she asks.

'No,' says Maddy.'

'Then what's all the fuss about? I don't know why you're so excited, they'll eat the chickens in no time.'

'They'll be fine,' I say. 'Did you really think they'd be out in daylight?'

'I don't know.' Her eyes are back on the screen already. Conversation closed.

We think we know where the badger visitors are coming from. Our garden backs onto two properties, and behind them stands the Baptist Church in its generous grounds. The first of these houses was built in the Sixties and its neighbour within the last decade; a country meadow that we dreamt of owning saw the arrival of diggers one morning, to our then baby Eliott's delight and our dismay. He was transfixed when I held him at the window and in tears when I walked away.

The church was built in 1804 after a wealthy resident became increasingly annoyed by the sound of singing next to his house, and donated land in the centre of the village for a new building. We found badger holes just behind this church, where the woods meet the graveyard. Our first watching place. Perhaps they are merely bolt holes, a stopping point as they make their way in from other locations, but their base isn't far away.

Badgers and graveyards don't go well together, given the way badgers like to dig everything up, but the badgers were most likely here long before the church was built. And the houses. We are on their land, not they on ours. Some setts are mentioned in the Domesday Book of 1086, their presence alongside us is nothing new. Eliott and Jemima love to spot where new sticks have been wedged at the base of the church fence and point out each one, like it's another badger triumph. 'Look, they're getting through here, now!' 'And here!'

I keep a watchful eye on the patch of woodland behind the church, though strictly speaking it's private ground. I feel a conflict of interests here, having been told when joining the badger group that it's important to regularly visit a badger's home turf. It isn't fenced off though sometimes our dog 'wanders in', at which point I put him on the lead and walk through to the other side. I feel vindicated one day when Maddy and I can't find the badger holes behind the church any more.

'I'm sure they're over this way,' I tell her.

'No, I thought they were over here.'

I use an old stick to push away at the ivy on the woodland floor, but in vain. The dog is on his lead and getting himself tangled up with fallen branches and I let go for a moment. He runs to an area now covered with grass cuttings from the church grounds, a new compost heap. I pick up his lead and he tugs, sniffing the ground like a trained police detection dog.

I kick through the grass with my boots but it's well-compacted. As I investigate with the long stick I realize we've found the badger holes, now filled in.

Days after this discovery, Maddy, Jem and I are heading to the church flower room when we see Clive, an old fellow who looks after the grounds. He's always cheerful and happy to chat. I tell him I see there's been a lot of badger activity and that I'm part of a badger group, suggesting he contacts me if it gets out of hand. I don't mention the holes that have been filled in. He probably knows something about them – I know it won't stop the badgers, but want him to be aware these efforts are not invisible. Perhaps it wasn't him, I tell myself, trying to give him the benefit of the doubt, but he's always the person I see on the sit-on mower.

'They're a blooming menace. I'd shoot them if I had my way.'

'You can't do that,' I say. He has to be joking.

'I would, I mean it.'

'They're protected,' I say.

'I don't care.'

I put the bucket of flowers down on the ground and look him in the eye. I'm taller than him, which I quite like at moments like this.

'It's illegal.' He's not registering what he's saying here. I tell him that the police and RSPCA refer cases to us, and of how we're run by an experienced ecologist. To him we're just meddling do-gooders who make the job of maintaining a church property and its graves all the more difficult. We part amicably enough and I don't think he realizes what a big deal this is for me. 'He could be winding me up,' I say to the girls, trying to lighten the mood, 'he's known for his sense of humour.' I've no idea of what they just made of our conversation, I was too rattled to look at them. They must think he was being facetious but he really wasn't. I fill an empty bucket with cold water and drop in the flowers.

'Mum, why does Clive want to shoot the badgers?' asks Jem, her eyes full of tears.

'They dig where he doesn't want them to. But that's no excuse to shoot them,' I say. 'Anyway, he can't, he's not allowed to, he'd get himself into very big trouble.'

'I'm sure he wouldn't,' says Maddy.

'I know. Not everyone loves badgers like we do, especially when they cause them problems,' I tell them. 'I'm pretty sure the badgers are safe with him around.'

It would help if the badgers could learn a little discretion. In the field near our usual watching spot there's a flattened patch of wheat, the size of a large family car. Then there are other, smaller areas. 'Probably dogs,' we say, walking on. After all, we've seen them bounding through the edge of the crop. 'Just as likely,' I say, convincing neither of us.

'There's wheat in their poo,' Maddy announces with a certain pride one day when she peers into a badger latrine – that is, a shallow pit close to their enclosure. I'm not sure if she's more pleased with their deviance or her detective skills. The farmer must be aware of what's going on, but there's little he can do about it. 'He's not exactly short of it, it goes on for miles,' she says when I voice my small quota of sympathy. True, it won't affect his overall harvest, but I'm beginning to see why some farmers may feel slightly antagonized – even those whose work is solely arable. Like farmers Boggis, Bean and Bunce in *Fantastic Mr. Fox,* the conflict can become an obsession, with some finding the cull the perfect excuse for their troubles.

My neighbour Lisa likes to hear of our badger discoveries. A zoologist by training, she enjoys wildlife too and has been feeding a hedgehog in her garden, though all of that may have come to an end: 'I found this brown curled thing,' she tells me today in her Australian accent. She picked up the accent when she lived there for a few years; it suits her relaxed attitude to life. 'It was a completely empty hedgehog skin,' she says. It could be down to a badger but I'm not saying anything – I need to be sure, after all. Later I dig out my authoritative copy of *The Badger* and read Ernest Neal on the subject, who tells me in no uncertain terms that a hedgehog skin without contents can only be the work of a badger. Further research leaves me in no doubt. Though partial to a little hedgehog, foxes are not so tidy and struggle with the prickles, often resulting in injured and mangled hedgehogs, destined for wildlife rescue centres if they're lucky. A clean hedgehog jacket indicates the work of a badger, while clusters of spines and body parts the work of a fox. Lisa and her husband had a new fence installed recently and left a gap at the bottom to allow hedgehogs in. And a little more besides.

The summer holidays are stretching out before the children like a vast sea, and for Jemima I think it's unsettling. Perhaps that's why wantonness has set in. I know I need to leave her to play and nothing drastic has happened – as yet – but she could do with a tracking device. She's pulling books off the shelves in the playroom, 'Looking for old lost stuff,' she tells me. I walk in on her at the basin downstairs – I always know in the back of my mind when she's been there too long. 'Jem, what have you got there?'

She shows me a ball of soggy tissue.

'I want to squeeze it onto the flowers and make them smell nice.'

'But you can't make them smell any nicer, and that squirty soap smells of lemons.'

Then there was the 'help' with the gardening yesterday. It was well-meant, but hollyhock heads littered the front path. I told her that I liked them and wanted to keep them. Minutes later she'd cut a buddleia flower and sellotaped it to a hollyhock stem.

Perhaps I need to lighten up – I did at least laugh – but it's the increase in arguing and answering back that's especially wearing, and it's not yet August. 'If you don't want me to argue, just let me, it's the only way,' she said the other day. And then there's Annie. Annie. I catch her relaying news of a punishment to Maddy this evening:

'I paid for that phone with my own money and Dad's basically stealing it.'

She's crying and Maddy is consoling her with Polos.

'Why did he take it?' asks Maddy.

'He found me on it at half-past midnight. So what? It's the holidays. I can sleep in.'

'It *was* too late,' I say.

'Katie wouldn't leave me alone.'

'That's why we say no tech in your rooms at night.'

She looks at me like I've said no food or water for the next six weeks, her brow rumpled, her eyes staring and full of tears.

Eliott comes out of his bedroom and she calls him over. 'Do you know what room it's in?' she asks him. 'I'll give you gum. I've got a new packet.'

'That's not going to help,' I say.

'It's my phone.'

'Annie –'

'I'm just saying.'

I suggest she lets it blow over, but she's in bickering mode and thinks I should be the only one to discipline her, 'cos you're the more lenient of the two.' She doesn't know when to stop and has it all out of perspective. Rupert dares to pop upstairs for something – 'Dad, where did you actually put my phone?'

And so I am needing my badgers. 'I really have to get out,' I tell Rupert. 'I think I've got cabin fever, I don't mind a drenching.'

'I *know* you're missing your badgers, but it's far too wet tonight. You're still not better. You're way too obsessive, do you know that?'

Within the hour the rain eases and the birds start to sing again. I take off my glass beads – they might rattle – and pull on a fleece. Maddy knows my plan almost intuitively and is waiting at the bottom of the stairs. It's drizzling on Sandwich Road but we're not bothered. She stops to pick up all the rain-thirsty snails and puts them on the walls: 'Oh look, he's going to get trodden on,' and 'Ew, those two are mating, I think we'll leave them.'

In the woods, branches graze the ground with the weight of water, cupped in their fully extended leaves. There is mud everywhere, though only yesterday the ground was dry and cracked. In the field the grass has been flailed, the nettles flattened by wind and rain.

Just a glimpse of a badger tonight, but that's enough to restore my inner peace. He was hulking along at the back of the sett on our arrival, heading towards a light-filled exit. And now at eight-thirty the woodland is getting dark. A blackbird flies around the enclosure, shrieking its alarm call, then a fox leaps from the field and over the fence, swift and lithe. Maddy gives me eye contact, her mouth open wide. There is some noise in the undergrowth, a near-bark and a shriek – a fox-badger confrontation? Would a fox attack a cub on their territory? It quietens and we wait. But the action has passed and it's time to go home. We see the fox again on our way out, entering the enclosure from the side, as if coming from the teenage wood. A flash of amber trailing a white-dipped tail.

We settle into a holiday routine; in the mornings the house is quiet and I write before they surface. Or if they do, the TV helps out until I can stop. Eliott is practising for the Kent Test, the entry exam for grammar schools that still exist in our little corner of England. 'I hate this stuff,' he says. 'Have you ever used any of this in real life, Mum?'

'That's not the point. You have to try.'

He's not especially motivated and is always on the hunt for distractions. He reminds me that he wants to come badger watching, that there's no school tomorrow. I tell him that on one of Maddy's first outings, two spooked badgers charged at us. He says he's not scared and high-fives me his own consent.

We walk the dog around the badger sett later to decide where we'll wait. The harvest is half-in and butterflies seem to be drawn out by the heat today – we're comparing the Peacocks with the Tortoiseshells, and follow a Meadow Brown until it stops, hoping it will unfold its wings.

Evening arrives and Eliott appears early, wearing fleece, bodywarmer and trousers tucked into two pairs of socks. Rupert's not even home from work. 'Eliott Greville, proud to be a member of the East Kent Badger Group, at your service. Attention!' He salutes me. I tell him that we won't be going for another couple of hours, and it really won't get that cold.

Soon the sunset is reflected in Lisa's windows opposite and we emerge dressed in dark blues and greens, trying not to look conspicuous on a summer's eve. We pass Deb the hairdresser standing outside her salon with a group of friends, admiring a new car: 'That's the most girly colour for a car I have ever seen,' she says.

Thankfully the mint green car's arrival means she doesn't ask me where we're going. Tell a village hairdresser and you've told the whole community, and not everyone has good intentions towards our wildlife. Once out of earshot we begin to discuss our plan: Eliott and Rupert are to wait in the teenage wood, while Maddy and I will head for our usual spot. We've more chance of disturbing them if we're all together.

We feel more exposed without the usual wheat-backdrop and I break off an elder stem for Maddy to stand behind. The hole into the field has been uncovered now – it's massive, not dissimilar in size and shape to a toilet bowl, with only a very gradual narrowing inside.

It's a long wait tonight, but the wood is definitely active. We hear a whistling, whining noise – a badger cub? Maddy looks at me and raises her eyebrows. I nod back at her and she smiles so that her dimples show. Mice are in the nettles in front of us, and a tawny owl sends out his call. The wheat that's left is growing pale now, no longer golden but faded, looking sun-bleached and old. Moths are flitting in front of us, drawn out by the new Mead Moon.

The clock at Waldershare chimes nine and we see Rupert and Eliott coming along the field to join us. I think they've disturbed the badgers – perhaps they are heading for cover, for a thumping, cumbersome noise comes from the enclosure, and now a small badger face appears at the fence, next to the hole. I was beginning to think we'd only hear them tonight. Did this little creature really make all that noise? There is a playful glint in its eye, as if the chase is on. Another badger joins the first and sniffs its bottom. A third meets them at the hole, while a fourth emerges from the hole in the field. It must be his first time out since the harvest began, and he runs as fast as his little badger legs will carry him, to the standing wheat twenty metres away. 'It's like the Great Escape,' whispers Rupert.

I have pins and needles in my foot. A mouse is right beside me, another reason to stretch it – and a big male badger goes down the hole in front of us. He'd looked at us but didn't seem bothered.

'Can we go now?' whispers Eliott in a voice loud enough for any badger miles around to hear.

'We probably should,' I say. 'Annie has Jemima.'

'That big one we saw last of all didn't mind us being there,' says Maddy on our way out. '*Oh, it's them*, he thought.'

'They were fine with us because they had each other,' says Eliott. 'None of them were really alone. They kind of look out for each other, don't they?'

'It was a complete badger zoo,' says Rupert.

'It's not always like that,' I explain to Eliott. 'It's really not.'

'Why didn't they stick around a bit longer?' asks Eliott.

'They never stay still for long,' I tell him. 'Spotting them is half the fun.'

White flowers of the upright hedge-parsley light the path ahead as we step over a wire fence. We forgot our torches but the moon is growing bright.

We're riding a wave of badger activity and I'm checking the garden for evidence as soon as I'm up, pyjamas tucked into wellies, hair untouched – well no one's going to see me. The peanuts have all gone and the earth has been grubbed up. Maddy later finds hairs and we measure them: 5 centimetres of white, the suggestion of a very old badger according to Ernest Neal. Estimates vary, but no organization seems to suggest they live longer than 16 years. Jemima is becoming quite the detective too, and announces to the surrounding gardens we're 'collecting plums' when on our hands and knees, which is partly true. She rebukes me for using the word badger, having taken my advice about not telling everyone she knows a little too seriously: 'Mum, stop saying that word. It's b – a – d – jer.' To her it's an incredible secret. She's somehow okay with the fact we're not taking her with us tonight – for now. Being custodian of a secret seems enough.

In the fields the harvest is in completely – we have to see what they'll make of it. For so long it has provided the cover that they want. Eliott is changed early again. We pass the time looking at the garden birds and I teach them to distinguish house-sparrows from tree sparrows – grey heads to match the slate rooves, brown to blend in with the trees.

The badgers are out in the enclosure when we arrive. One young badger comes close to the hole in front of us and sits down, as if on sentry duty. He is alert and stretches his neck and then his back, sitting up tall and staring into the distance, before adjusting his gaze to look at us. He must think we're okay, as he takes the hole and emerges into the field near to where we are standing. When he reaches the crop a change comes over him: I wouldn't have believed that a wild animal could look bemused, but this one does. He's not sure what to think of his altered habitat and runs parallel with the rows of felled wheat stalks – up and down alongside the small heaps, as if trying to find a way through a maze – then up and over them, like hurdles. He returns home further along, not into his usual area where we're waiting.

Moths are out again and bats, fast and two-dimensional, dive in front of us, then up vertically and into the trees. Eliott is sniffing and fidgety. Maddy glares at him. He's shuffling in his body-warmer like it's a sleeping bag. Silence for a while, except for the itching and scratching. The cracking of twigs behind the green veil, but we can't see inside. Then a group of three cubs charge from the field towards the enclosure, following the path of the first. I was reading Ernest Neal again today, who writes of different badger clans in a neighbourhood frequently calling on each other before starting their nightly forage. He goes as far as to say the badger paths between setts are the most travelled. I wonder if the local cubs have learnt to do this independently already? I do know of a cluster of holes in that direction. We're building up a picture of their homes and bolt holes, though can't be sure of the permanent residences yet.

But soon a worsening cough forces me to spend time away from the badgers – I can't suppress it, and my voice is coming and going in waves. The children think it funny and get me to repeat sentences so they can mimic the high croak and loss of volume. We're home more and neighbourhood boys start to knock for Eliott. I guess Kent Test Practice is driving them all out of the house, but I'm not up for an invasion and never have been. I let him go to the park and then worry – his lack of road safety has been witnessed before by his sisters. But why do I really object?

He's only just ten, but I was free-range by that age, building dens out of straw bales and riding my bike to friends' houses. Perhaps it's the memory of kids ringing the doorbell for my brother when we were young, and my mum's desperation: 'Ignore it, we're having lunch. That's the fourth time today.' Or the fear of him turning feral and starting to hang out at the bus stop, just because the older kids do.

Jemima distracts me: 'There's a bird in there!' She is peering into the empty wood-burner.

'Not again,' I say. 'Keep it shut, wait for me to open the patio door.'

Too late. 'Jemima!'

The bird flies around the room and knocks itself out. Maddy comes in to see what all the noise is about. 'It's by the window, it's a *house* sparrow, Mum.'

It's on its feet now but clearly concussed, nodding its head like a Churchill dog in a car window. 'Aw,' says Maddy. We're probably too close, squatting so near to it like this. Maddy's hand comes towards it and it's flying again, into the kitchen and now the boot room. He hits the wall and falls, cartoon style. I open the back door and we wait for him to find his way outside.

It's the second week of August and already the evenings are darker. There is news about Sally and Glenn's wounded badger – or rather news of no news. He hasn't been seen since we last spoke about him climbing down from the bird table, and I fear he is no more. I bumped into Sally when shopping for groceries this afternoon and she told me the latest. The thought of it has stayed with me. When a badger is such a regular visitor and then disappears it doesn't look great. I am finding it hard to stay away from the badgers in our own village and am aware of being short-tempered without them. Three weeks have passed and I feel like I am on a fast, but I can at least contain my cough now. The family will all benefit, I tell myself as I get changed for another night walk.

We wait at the sett and we're relying on guesswork: is that a badger lumbering that we can hear, or just the wind? As the evening goes on the noises are louder and more distinct. Eliott points out a badger crossing the field, entering their fenced-off sett at a distant corner. Now on the alert, Maddy spots two more, but they are not up close and the badger bonanza seems to be over. We can hear the cubs playing in their cover of shadows, the wooded area reaching darkness long before the fields. *Ek, kek, kek, kek, kek.* Then the sounds of heavy badgers thrashing their way through the nettles – it could even be careless humans for all the noise they make. I'm feeling Eliott's frustration. He crouches down, apparently having given up. 'Mum, can we go to the teenage wood?' What makes him think it'll be any better there?

It is dark now, though a full moon means we can see where we are going. We stop to watch through a gap between these two badger camps. There's noise up ahead, it comes close to the fence – we stop still and hold our breath – are they going to come through? We look at each other and back to the badger path on the other side of the fence. Not a sound, they are not there now. That's that then.

I wonder if they are less drawn to the field now that the harvest is in. Perhaps we will need to wait elsewhere, but I'm not convinced that will be any better. It's hard to see into the enclosure now the nettles are so high and I'm not sure where else to go. It's a shame because given long enough I could start to make connections; I find it hard to tell them apart at this stage, and would love to get to know them as a clan.

Our attention turns to the garden – we put out peanuts and find they have gone the next morning, and collect hairs from the fence. I wonder how often they come – could we be on their nightly forage route? Perhaps we will be, with enough effort on my part. I spend several nights waiting in the garden and stay out longer than in the fields, but so far have not been rewarded. Maddy and Jem have started to count how many cherry plums litter their path in the evenings, and mix in some of the sour damsons from the other tree for good measure. The cherry plums are going – occasionally there's a stone that's been spat out – but the damsons aren't. There was one with large teeth marks this morning, someone had clearly thought better of it.

But I haven't given up on seeing them in the woods just yet. I still have a cough and a come-and-go voice, but there might not be many more opportunities left; badgers venture out less in the colder months and sightings are harder to come by. There's an autumn feel to the air already, I *need* to be there, and I dig out my warmest winter socks.

'They won't miss you,' Rupert tells me. Perhaps he means he's not missing them, and Maddy and I set out on our own. There has been more heavy rain today and the ground is muddy. We see a flock of small birds high in the sky as we reach the woods – it looks as if they're preparing to leave, trying out a quick run-through of flight formation. It could be a group of willow warblers, or just the resident chaffinches that share the badger enclosure and stay around all year. I have read that flocking happens when the new brood reach independence and the family units lose their importance.

We return to our usual spot, it's not time to abandon it altogether. I'm studying the oak tree in front of me: a clump of wispy shoots have all emerged from the same node as if it's sprouting facial hair. The coastline of beech and oak trees on the other side of the field is still reassuringly green, we are hanging on to summer for a bit longer.

We hear a cub noise behind us, and then badgers thumping around in amongst the trees. It's mating season, and a definite chase is going on in there, full-on badger testosterone now unleashed on the females. It sounds like this sow won't succumb that easily. I don't tell Maddy my theory straight away; she's still disappointed in them over Lisa's hedgehog, I'm not ready for more disdain. Maddy's face is animated now and I see her eyes follow the movement. The romping subsides and the cubs take to the floor, a puppy-like barking now the only sound that fills the air – it's as if the birds have stopped to listen to this attempt at maturity – before the high-pitched chimp-like noises start. It's dark very early: we hear the clock chime nine at Waldershare and decide to go. Summer lightning blazes across the sky as we walk through the field – no thunder or rain, just a wide silver flash and two figures hurrying home in the darkness.

We have to leave the badgers for a week's holiday in the Brecon Beacons. The journey is spent practising Welsh accents without much success. 'Is Fireman Sam Welsh?' pipes up Eliott once we've crossed the border, referring to his pre-school TV idol.

'He's as Welsh as they come,' I say.

Now he's launched, reliving an old episode in the voice of his old hero. 'Don't say it in front of the locals,' says Rupert. 'It sounds like you're taking the pee.'

'Why are all the signs in gobbledygook?' says Annie.

'*It's Welsh,*' we reply.

The cottage is at the base of Pen y Fan, the highest mountain peak in South Wales. June, the elderly owner, treats us like long-lost relatives, insisting 'You must knock whenever you need us.' Our dog leaps up at her in his shameful terrier way, but she seems to find it endearing. 'The salt and pepper is in this cupboard...' she tells us, giving us a tour of every conceivable space. It's an old barn conversion with dark rooms and heavily stained beams that creak as the temperature changes. There is a shared indoor pool, the inducement Annie needed to agree to such a rural spot.

We've turned up with art materials and books, and Rupert his compass. The next morning he's off to climb Pen y Fan with Maddy after an early breakfast. He picks up the lead and the dog is running around him in circles – fool, he has no idea what he's in for. I'm really not sure he'll keep up with them.

'We won't be long, I think we'll be back in an hour-and-a-half, but don't wait in for us.'

'Shorts?' I say.

'I'm on holiday.'

'In *Wales.* Take your coats.'

The sky darkens and brownish clouds sit just above the earth-scattered hilltops, looking as if they've risen out of them. We search for figures on the hillside but can't spot them yet. Annie emerges from her make-shift bed in the conservatory. 'Where is everybody?'

'Dad and Maddy are walking up the hill, Eliott and Jem have gone to the zip-wire.'

'So when can we swim?'

'Later, I need to talk to June.'

'The Wi-Fi isn't working,' she says. 'It's ridiculous. How many days've we got here?'

'We've only just arrived!'

'I could've stayed at home.' She's pouring herself a large glass of orange juice to compensate. 'I wish I had.'

'You're only just *fifteen.*'

'Katie's in Greece, Mum. Wait till she hears about this.'

The wanderers return soaking wet, Maddy with trousers muddy from the waist down, her new patterned canvas shoes now a uniform shade of brown. 'I fell over a few times,' she says.

'I told her those shoes wouldn't get her off a mountain,' Rupert tells me.

'They did the job. My laces did keep coming undone, but I didn't want to retie them. They were wet and covered in sheep poo.'

'We got a bit lost up there.'

'A *bit*?' says Maddy.

'There's no visibility. The fog just came in, we'd been round in a circle at the top and we lost our bearings. We came down a way we weren't expecting and had to ask for directions back to the farm.'

Did the dog just sigh? He's curled up on the doormat – his only refuge from the slate flagstone floor – and catching up on some much needed sleep. He hasn't had a walk like that in weeks.

'The views were amazing to start with,' says Maddy. 'You could see for miles. I'm really glad I've done it. I want to do it again before we go home.'

'You'd better get out of that gear,' I tell them. I take their dripping coats and wander through to make some tea. I'd like to make it up Pen y Fan too, though with Jemima in tow it'll take hours. I want to find the waterfalls closer to the cottage first, and we need to book some horses while the rain is holding off. Perhaps it will miss us here. I did at least find bats outside last night – I *heard* them, and headed around the house in the direction of the noise. They were flying over the trampoline, my point has been proven.

I return with a tray of mugs to find Rupert sitting in the middle of the sofa, holding his glasses in two pieces. They've broken on the bridge of the nose. He's calm about it, but blind as a bat, as the saying goes. Actually, if he could see like a bat it would be a huge improvement. 'I was cleaning them,' he says. 'So much for titanium being so durable.' He's lifting them up to the light, as if he's going to spot a way to fix them like this.

'Don't suppose you've brought any spares?'

He raises his eyebrows at me.

'We'll have to go into Brecon,' he says. 'This must happen all the time.'

Annie gives him the contact-lenses-are-best lecture he's heard so many times before, and I make a few wrong-number calls before remembering the optician's number correctly.

'You're just outside the guarantee,' I tell him. 'But you can have an appointment after work next Monday.'

'Are there shops in Brecon?' asks Annie.

'There are, that's why we're going.'

'Well that's something.'

We knock on June's door and she kindly produces an old pair of hers: 'To tide you over,' she tells him. *Put them on, Dad, you'll look amazing.* We find the opticians she recommends, and all the others in Brecon – it's a Sunday and they're shut. At least we can swim, you don't need to see for that. The next day we revisit and are turned away several times. Looks like I'm the sole driver for the week, and the long journey home. The last assistant has inspiration just as we're heading for the door. 'Leave them with me for an hour, I'll see what I can do.'

'You're going to have a great holiday, Dad,' says Eliott.

'Yeah, you're going to miss most of it,' says Annie.

We return to find she's fitted the lenses in some new frames, and the holiday is back on. We take a narrow boat tour up the river, and watch an old man pulling onions from his garden. He lays them out on the table in a neat line, as if presenting them at some horticultural show. 'This is just like Rosie and Jim's,' says Jemima, bouncing in her seat.

Ducks are swimming alongside us and oversized ripe blackberries line the riverbank. Eliott opens his window and stretches out a hand, but he can't quite reach.

'They look like badger holes over there,' I say. 'At the edge of the wood, can you see?'

Jemima comes over to my side and she and Maddy press their noses against the window. 'There's one!' says Jem.

'Doesn't it go any faster?' says Annie, looking up from her phone. 'We're being overtaken by those walkers.'

'There's a speed limit of four miles per hour,' says Rupert. 'I think it has something to do with the wildlife.'

'Great,' says Annie rolling her eyes. 'When can we swim?'

Swallows are nesting in the open garage where we're staying, and are my badger substitute for the week. Even Annie comes outside to watch them: 'Well, it's not badgers, I draw the line at that.'

The parents return to the nests every few seconds to feed their young. They swing wide when they see us, drawing an exaggerated circle into the air. The semi-fledged line up and seem to wait on a beam for days. I'm out in the garage sorting the washing and Annie and Eliott come running inside. Three fat swallows bulging from a nest fly up and away. By lunchtime they are back in the nest again, and others wait on the beam. 'It's what they do,' says June. 'They climb back into the nest until they're well and truly gone.'

Our last day, and the swallows mass on the roof of the white cottage in the courtyard. We all go outside to watch. June and her frail husband Bob are outside with the other family who are staying. 'They haven't done this for several years,' says June. 'It's really special. We've never had so many as this year. But it does mean they'll be off very soon.'

The car is packed and we're ready to go, too. 'I don't like to think of you leaving,' she says, taking my hand. 'Sometimes we can't wait for our guests to leave.' I tell her we'll be back. She crosses her fingers on both hands. 'I hope you will.'

'Well I won't,' comes a quiet voice from the back.

We're home and I'm quick to see if the badgers have been coming in our absence. A new hole has been made at the bottom of the garden, an alternative way in through the other neighbour's property. They have resorted to sour damsons now, and a trail of plum stones leads up to the base of the damson tree itself, half-way up the garden. I provide a peanut feast for them to signal the usual menu is back on.

I set up camp in the garden that night, sheltering under the playhouse porch with an umbrella. All is quiet, and the peanuts are still there in the morning. Frustration sets in. Rupert has to work evenings and Eliott, Maddy and I head to the woods without him. A nagging voice tells me I'm being irresponsible. *It'll be dark soon. It's bad enough you wandering out on your own at night, but taking the children? And what sort of example are you setting? Think of the risks they'll take when they're older if they get used to roaming around at all hours.* A dog launches itself on the other side of the fence as we take the path from the street, causing it to shake. 'It can't get through, don't worry,' I say.

We reach the field and find a glut of conkers on the ground – they weren't here a week ago – and stuff them into our pockets. Maddy picks up a crushed one that has large teeth marks – the work of a clueless cub? Another has been hollowed out from the top, and tiny teeth marks like scratches suggest to us wood mice, or perhaps squirrels. They are said to be poisonous to some wildlife, but there is something irresistible about them, and not only to us. I tell the kids the word conker has its origins in the word conch, for the conker game was first played with snail shells.

We pick at the blackberries as we make our way down, still feeling the smooth conkers in our pockets. It's just gone eight but an owl is hooting already, telling us our daylight hours are limited. We walk across the stubble and it shifts beneath our feet, before reaching our usual spot. Soon we can hear them, but they don't come in our direction.

'I saw one,' says Eliott on the way out.

'No you didn't,' says Maddy. 'They must've smelt you.'

'I did see it, it came to the hole.'

'We were looking the whole time,' I say to him.

We're home by nine without mishap, and I make myself an apple and rhubarb tea and wait in the garden. Rustling noises come from amongst the trees. Eliott runs out to say goodnight, and sensor lights flick on and off in a neighbouring garden. All is quiet. Then a voice, *'Nigey!'* A cat miaows its response, a door slams, followed by nothing. The guinea pigs emit the occasional random squeak, like the bleep of a fire alarm needing a new battery. I think the wind is blowing the wrong way. I think I need some night-vision equipment. My throat hurts and it's hard to speak, but at least outside in the dark nothing's expected of me. I sit on the arbour a while before making my way inside.

I don't know what's driving me – perhaps it's the knowledge they are out there, and the thought that if I just hold out a little longer I may be rewarded. The peanuts went last night –

eventually – and they'd left the shelter of the trees and wandered into the garden as far as the playhouse.

I suspect spotting them is do-able, but I'm lacking in insight or something. Jim Corbett, who in 1926 killed a leopard said to have been responsible for 125 deaths, wrote in *The Man-Eating Leopard of Rudraprayag*, 'Wrong estimation of the intelligence of animals, and the inability to sit without making any sound or movement for the required length of time, is the cause of all failures when sitting up for animals.'

Our walk a few nights later reminds me that there is a broader purpose in our coming out here. I'm out with Maddy, and once at our usual spot we hear voices. Some young lads with dogs are in the field beyond the trees – now much of the undergrowth has fallen away we can see a lot more. We are looking in at the centre where I saw the proud boar emerge a couple of months ago, and through to the other side. Will they keep going up towards Waldershare?

'Chavs,' says Maddy.

Now they are coming the other way and loud voices are up alongside the enclosure. In a moment they are behind us – four lads with large dogs, I spot an Alsatian but I'm trying not to look. They have stopped talking. I'm not sure if they are meaning to intimidate, but I get the feeling they are. I crouch down and pretend to search for something and then find it, before we head for the exit. We say nothing until we've crossed the field and are nearing the streetlamp that marks the pavement.

'They didn't come out you know,' I say. 'They didn't, I kept looking back over my shoulder. What are they going to do in there? Yobbos.'

'*Chavs*, Mum.'

'You know I don't like you using that word.'

We are walking up The Street and past the pub. The shops on this hill are long gone, and lights shine from the houses that now line the road, a mix of old and new.

'Well, we haven't seen much of them lately, but it always seems to be on a Saturday night. Guess we should be glad they're not usually there.'

'Did you see that man in the pub, Mum? He was so large he covered the whole window!'

We reach the turning for the footpath again. 'We could watch the badger holes at the end of the track, we don't have to go all the way in. It's got to be worth a try.' We look around us – no one – and cross over. The path is very dark now and seems to go on much further than before. I stop when we've gone a little way and look at Maddy.

'I don't mind,' she says. 'We can keep going.'

'I don't think so. Those boys're still knocking around. We'll look a bit suspicious if they see us coming in again. Let's go home.'

We settle ourselves on the trampoline, me with my green-lidded mug of tea and packet of throat sweets, Maddy with her phone. We try to keep still and to avoid making the springs creak. There's definitely noise on the path and behind the compost heap, a slow shuffling, a rummaging. The neighbours behind open their back door and music starts – it sounds like the Bee Gees. That's just great. Maddy looks at me and shrugs her shoulders. 'I'm tired, Mum. I'm going in.'

Soon I hear the gate open and the car pulls in. Annie must be back from the party she was going to, I may as well call it a day. I'll just give it a minute longer, that badger – if that's what it was – has to move sooner or later. *The inability to sit without making any sound or movement* as Corbett said – well, that might be the kids, but not me. Time passes and the seventies greatest hits continue. I head inside. Annie is watching singing reality show The X Factor and taking up a whole sofa, her legs stretched out in front of her, laptop open. I sit down to join her on the other sofa. She raises her eyes at me as I pull off my scarf.

'Saw the best badger I'd seen in ages today,' she says. 'In Canterbury of all places.'

'Really?'

'It was stuffed, in the Beaney museum.'

'Very funny. You know, you miss out on a lot.'

'You reckon? At least I'm not ill. Anyway, it's just a bit weird.'

I want to protest, but her earphones are in already. I'm not sure if she's watching the TV at all.

AUTUMN

4: New beginnings

The holidays are coming to a close. Change is everywhere, and I think our badger watching is doomed. We try to forget the reason we're out, telling ourselves that the sight of badgers would be an added bonus, but there's still therapy to be had here. The teenage boys with the Alsatian are far from our thoughts; it's rare to see anyone in the woods, and I'm convinced they are harmless enough, only wanting to intimidate so they have the place to themselves. For today it seems the place is all ours. Autumn leaves crunch under foot for the first time, and Maddy and I collect seeds from the common lime up near the sett, the small beads wrapped in close velvet like the buds of antlers. 'Feel that, Mum,' she says. She puts her fingers inside beech mast husks too, and picks the fluff of Old Man's Beard from the hedge. It is the most tactile season, when we all wrap our fists around perfect acorns and the smallest pinecones.

Tonight it's the last badger walk of the holidays, though I think Maddy's ready for a break. She sways as she stands by the sett – she doesn't realize she's doing it. 'Stand still,' I say, and she does, briefly, and then she's off again. We move back and crouch at the field edge, hoping they won't sense our presence now. My toe goes numb. I adjust my footing and kneel on a nettle.

Every five minutes or so we hear *something*. An excited badger. Brief badger interaction. Heavy movement. The sound of one coming close and I'm up on my knees, peering. Tawny owls are out, stringing sentences together, each trying to add one more syllable than the last.

Silence again. I ponder using my torch – this is surely pretty close to what marksmen will soon be doing in the cull zones in Dorset, Somerset and Gloucestershire in an attempt to control bovine TB. I wonder how my internet searches would look to an outsider – as if I'm some dodgy self-appointed culler who needs night-vision. At least the badgers are still here; Ernest Neal writes of how they can abandon their main sett for a month in September. It's very dark now. Minutes ago I looked into the sunset and back into the enclosure and that blast of light has somehow made me see less.

Maddy is fed up, I can feel it. We need to leave anyway. Now she's gallumping in the field badger-style and I hiss at her to be quiet – we don't want to jeopardize our future chances. Soon we are away from the sett. It's closet-dark in no time and I want to say, 'Speed up, *run,*' but I don't want to frighten her.

'I won't come when it's school the next day,' she says to me when we're home. I kind of knew that.

Annie is resigned to school the next morning and as soon as the blazer is on she sinks her hands into the pockets. 'Eugh, there's a boiled sweet from last term.' The gym kit is assembled, footwear found in the boot room: 'Mu-um, there's poo on my trainers. Can you clean them, please?'

'No, *you* clean them.'

There is a beautiful, obscuring mist this morning and dew-laden spiders' webs lace the apple trees. Annie's is the first school back, and the rest of us cling to the holidays for one more day, walking through the fields as usual. Redshank flowers are everywhere – not red at all, but pink, clusters of berry-like buds, each the size of a swollen grain of rice. It is part of the knotweed family and considered a nuisance by many, destined for the silage heap; each plant can produce up to 800 seeds in a year. We pick some to take home – the farmer isn't going to miss it.

I'm trying to decide where we could loiter at night now that the harvest is in. I think the only option is to climb the wire fence and stand in amongst the trees, close to where the badgers emerge. I find an easy way in before we walk back through the teenage wood. 'The floor is sinking, Mum,' says Maddy.

I come over to where she is standing, and have to agree – it feels as if the badgers' ceiling could give way in places. Is it really that thin? I like to think of their tunnels coming very close to the surface, but they are probably at least sixty centimetres deep – I think this is the work of moles.

At home the children are content with a mass of fledgling robins that fly from an overgrown rose bush in the front garden. Mothy is the word used most often to describe them, closely followed by cute. Jemima watches from the playroom window and Eliott his bedroom at the front of the house. They flit around the garden and visit the bird table, as familiar to us at the moment as sparrows.

Annie arrives home with a transformed air about her, a dishevelled ponytail and the look of a hard day done.

'Did you have a good day, Annie?'

'Spose. In science Alice and me put our hair under the microscope and I barely had any split ends!'

She's wired, and dare I say it, invigorated by a day at school. Eliott is at the table working on his Kent Test practice and she sits down to help. He's distracted by the birds again, and now a dragonfly: 'It's like a helicopter sideways on.'

'Come on, Eliott, focus,' I say. 'A couple of weeks and it'll all be over.' I'm trying to prepare a class here but not getting very far. I start teaching adult education classes soon after they're back at school.

Now we're both gripped by a baby sparrow that can't stop flapping its wings, like it's shaking off raindrops or shivering with cold. It's cheeping continually and flitting from one place to the next. The father flies in and begins to feed it on the wall, then breaks off to feed himself at the bird table. The mother comes in and takes over. She looks skinny, like she's been feeding this baby at the expense of herself; it is far bigger than she is.

'This is actually quite fun, EJ,' says Annie. She's looking at his book, not bothered by the activity outside.

'You reckon?' Eliott picks up his pencil again and chips at the yellow and black paint with his thumbnail.

'Just put the effort in, you don't want to end up at my school. Seriously.'

'I am trying.'

'You don't have a clue at your age, you're too young to know. Look – that's *wrong.*'

He's scribbling over another potential answer with a yellow crayon.

'Why that one?' asks Annie.

'It's a bit of a guess. I don't know. It's the hatching.'

'It's going *the wrong way,* you muppet.'

'Why?'

'*Can't you see?* I should give up now.'

'It's alright,' I say to him, giving Annie a hard stare. I come over to look at his page. 'Don't get it,' he's written next to a grid of nine squares with a random sequence of shapes that are supposedly doing something. On the question below are the words 'Could be' in his scrawling hand, with question marks beside three out of four options. I pick up his book and flick. 'DIDDN'T UNDERSTAND' he's written. What a nightmare. All this after weeks of patient explaining, of step-by-step unravelling of every sequence. I've briefed him on how they may be trying to trip them up: *Look, three answers with an 'F' starting the code, it's likely to be one of them. They won't make it too easy. Do you get the psychology?* Have we got anywhere?

'Can we see the badgers tonight?' he asks.

'You've got school tomorrow,' I say. 'Perhaps at the weekend. You can watch the bats, though.'

Our bats. As I've read more about them I've kept a watchful eye and have been rewarded. Jemima and I have heard the pipistrelles squeaking before dusk, throat-clearing for a few minutes before they fly out of the trees at the bottom of the garden. They skim up to the house, around the gardens and back down in a well-rehearsed circuit. Jem has put on a hat, scarf, poncho and earmuffs. 'You won't hear them,' I say. 'And you don't need any of that stuff – it's over a lot quicker than badger watching.'

I find Annie with her laptop on her favourite sofa and ask if she'd like to come and watch – 'They're amazing, Maddy had one fly right up to her face last time!'

'Might as well. I've got nothing better to do.'

There are no bats to start with and I think she won't stay, but she does. Trying to win back her phone after her latest fall out with Rupert, perhaps. The solar garden lights have come on, but I realize we're twenty minutes too early. And then it starts. 'There! There!' say the younger three, jumping up and down and pointing out their path with outstretched hands.

'How do you say it, Mum?' says Jem.

'Pip-i-strelles,' I say.

'Pipsy stels.'

'Where do they come from?' asks a voice behind me. I turn just to check it really is Annie seeming interested. 'What do they do during the day? Did you see that one?' I didn't, I was too busy studying her face for signs of irony but there are none. Perhaps she'll warm to the badgers after all, give it time, I say to myself.

'Maple!' A near neighbour is calling in her multitude of cats. Annie joins in with her batty voice, calling our chickens by name.

'Annie, you can't do that!' I say. 'Cynthia must've heard.'

'Here chickens, time to go in,' she continues, loudly.

'Jacob! Rosie! Maple!'

Annie copies again. 'No!' I say, pushing her back up the garden. It's all quiet. 'Jacob!' she calls in the lull. We're all laughing but trying not to. 'Come on, Jem, school tomorrow, let's get you ready for bed.'

A quick attempt at badger watching tonight. I sit on the top playhouse step and wait, tea in hand. I hear a loud thud behind me and turn my head – a pie-worthy Bramley has fallen to the ground. Another bat flits past me, diving erratically, oblivious to my presence. This one looks larger than the others. The sound of bleating sheep is carried on the wind, and then the closer sound of a dog barking. Now it starts to yelp. It sounds like a set-to – with a badger? I wait a while but the excitement has passed. Cars come and go on the surrounding roads, lights flick on and off in the houses behind the trees.

My offering of peanuts does seem a little tame. Could there be a treat that's more enticing? I have come across recipes for 'badger cake', which consists mainly of lard, peanuts, Sugar Puffs and raisins. The ingredients are mixed together and cooked in a pan, then put into the fridge to harden. I can just imagine the kids helping themselves, thinking it's some variation on chocolate fridge cake. It sounds an unnecessary faff, though perhaps I'll scatter some cereal with the peanuts next time, just as an experiment. There was a news story recently of a badger who'd entered a house via a cat-flap and helped himself to the contents of the fridge. You can watch footage of him devouring a family-sized Bakewell tart until he's rudely disturbed. The cat-flap badger ate six eggs from the same fridge the night before.

I wonder if I'd be doing this with my evening if it wasn't for my badger experience as a young child. We could hear his claws as they scraped the back door – it sounded hollow to me. Was he baring his teeth? We hadn't put any food out, but Mum had said it was too late. Would he keep going till he'd made a way in?

We soon grew to love our holiday cottage badgers, and followed the advice in the hand-worn 'sightings' book, turning off lights, putting out scraps and talking in hushed voices. We watched from the window each night as they shuffled up the path in single file, their noses fixed to the ground. Even my brother was entranced, no elbows in the ribs or antagonistic comments in my direction, just perfect harmony between us. Perhaps that's why my parents loved the badgers so much too.

It's strange how childhood shapes us, gives us things to cling to and own long after the experience has gone. Those badgers are all I remember of our Dorset holiday, though the family album reminds me of wading in the river in my red wellies and green and white checked dress. Badgers were far less common in England in the 1970s, so there was the feeling of being let into a special secret if you saw one. Holidays always carry with them the expectation of adventure, and the knowledge that you are out to make memories. This combination has created one lifelong devotee, the fascination really won't leave me alone.

Another thud as an apple lands behind me; my cue to go inside, I've been out here for nearly an hour. Slugs are sliming their way into the guinea pig run as I walk back up the garden.

Rupert and Annie are ensconced in the snug, the small TV room in the house. School documentary Educating Yorkshire is on for Annie's benefit, though she doesn't look interested. 'You're not watching that,' I say to her now. 'Look at you.'

'I am watching it.'

'I haven't seen your eyes on the screen once.'

'Well I have been. When you were watching *badgers*.'

'Why don't you put your laptop away?'

'Is it on just in case something big happens?' asks Rupert. 'Something everyone's talking about and you need to have an opinion on.'

'Course not,' she says. 'It's just like my school, no one notices anything odd about this, it's just normal to them.'

'It can't be as bad as this,' says Rupert.

'It's probably worse. You're weird if you're not dysfunctional. They think I'm *posh* because I come from a *village*. I hope you get Eliott through that test,' she says, turning her head away.

It's Sunday afternoon and the younger three are at the table sorting through their blackberry haul. 'There's a maggot,' says Rupert, looking over Jemima's shoulder. He reaches for it, finger and thumb poised.

'Dad, put it outside,' says Maddy. 'Don't kill it!' She says she hasn't eaten a blackberry since last autumn when he ate a maggot to provoke her.

'I'm having it,' says Jem. 'I'm calling it Maggie.' At bedtime it's in a small container with a collection of leaves for bedding. 'Maggie's house can go on my dressing-up box.'

'Annie, you're in charge for a bit. Dad and I are just going for a quick walk in the woods.'

'Don't get lost,' she says.

'Don't raid the cupboards,' I reply.

I'm excited, we're heading for the enclosure and this time we'll be right inside it. I'd be amazed if we don't see anything tonight. I have in my pocket a night-vision flashlight – just a small red light from Amazon while I research the more serious equipment. We're on the woodland path now and Rupert is walking in front of me. 'Why are you wearing your favourite trousers?' I look down at my snagged badger-watching ones. 'We're climbing fences tonight.'

'I thought you were in a hurry to get out. We needn't have

worried though, it's still light.'

'We'll make noise. There needs to be a time of quiet before the badgers will come out,' I say. 'Besides, the light is fading.'

It is four weeks since we've seen any badgers out here, three since we've heard them and I'm determined not to miss out this time. Our new approach has to pay off and it feels like a new beginning. The field has been harrowed now, autumn's arrival has been confirmed and the golden crop is but a memory. We reach the sett and climb over the fence – every step reverberates as the brittle twigs and branches crack beneath our feet.

We choose a near spot behind a beech tree and wait. It darkens quickly amongst the trees, though the sky still holds its blue beyond. Before long we hear badgers come close – they're no more than ten metres away, but concealed by trees and ground cover. The tree I'm leaning on is damp and mossy and I move my hands – eugh, that's disgusting, I've landed them on a slug. A fallen tree in front of me is soon lost to sight, its bare, badger-stripped trunk invisible in the darkness. Sniffing noises as badgers, noses to the ground, dig for worms, and then the sound of a badger clearing its throat. I never knew they did that, it sounds so human.

Owls hoot beyond the enclosure but we can see nothing at all, it's so dark. A badger could be at my feet and I wouldn't see it. I shine the night-vision torch and a moth flies into the light and up my sleeve. I yelp, *yelp*, how stupid! I'm not frightened of moths, I must just be on edge. The badgers are still stomping around, despite the light and my little outburst. Then a noise behind us – I turn with the torch to hear a badger crashing off at speed.

My pulse is racing. What a fool. Are we biologically wired to be on edge in complete darkness? I'm not afraid of badgers, this is all perfectly fine. This really isn't like me at all.

'Should we go?' says Rupert.

'Why?' I whisper.

'I think we spooked him.'

'Do you think he'll attack us? He won't, he's long gone.'

'No.'

'Give me a bit longer.'

We're silent again. A couple of minutes pass. 'We should go,' I say.

As we head out it's impossible to conceal our movements. There's noise coming from the teenage wood, perhaps they've legged it from here to there. I can hear cubs playing as we head that way, keckering like antagonistic children and chasing each other at speed. The sounds stop as we enter, I feel like a school teacher re-entering a classroom. I prop the torch in the fork of a tree and we each choose a trunk to stand behind but nothing happens. We're too blundering, we won't see anything by moving around like this. I take the torch from the tree and we turn to leave.

When we're home I take peanuts down the garden and see Rupert poised, statue-like. 'I can hear badgers – in next door's garden,' he says. 'Let's go closer.'

It's 9.15 p.m. and they're out in the village already. There *is* hope. A three-rail fence divides the gardens at the bottom here and I squeeze past the chicken house to stand beside it.

I hear a chittering noise. Then Austen opens his back door and comes out. Well that's blown it. There's a noise from a garden further along. *'It's in the black bag,'* comes a voice, 'The *black* one.'

We wait a few minutes before heading in. 'They probably won't come to our garden till one in the morning,' says Rupert.

'Perhaps we should start growing veg like Austen,' I say.

'What, just for the badgers to come and eat it?'

We're definitely getting closer and the next night I'm out just before nine. The badger cull began again this week and I can't help dwelling on it whenever I'm out here. It sickens me to think of those waiting for badgers with the purpose of killing them. It will be just like this: in the quiet a loitering presence standing behind the trees, trying not to move for fear of being spotted. A robin sings from the fir tree above me, spouting its optimism. Cynthia calls in her cats. And then I hear a badger arrive: it is stumbling through the undergrowth and I can hear it eating peanuts, sloshing with its mouth open like a small child. I'm shining my infra-red light and see a badger's head come and go in amongst the plants. It's a slow eater.

'Lola,' calls Cynthia. *Shut up woman.* I'm sure she's called that cat in three times now. But the badger continues to eat. I see several flashes of its head, I can't work out how big it is. Then she emerges into the garden, nose down, following the trail of nuts and cereal and eating them one by one. It must be a she – it's not an enormous badger, though it could be a cub from last year. Tyn, our Border terrier, is about the same length, and I think last year's males could be much larger than this. The slim face and overall delicacy of this badger convince me finally that it's a girl.

She turns towards me and I see her grey, Dougal-like coat draping onto the floor, an oversized bedspread that hangs lower than it should. I watch her for a few minutes, mesmerized. For some strange reason I start to feel slightly nervous – but what would she do if she smelt my foot and realized I was here? I am less than half a metre away, closer to a badger than I have ever been before. I edge myself up onto the trampoline, and she withdraws into the darkness.

I'm back in the house, it's nine-thirty. 'Guess what I saw!' I call.

'Could it have been a badger?' comes a sarcastic voice. I find Rupert sitting in the snug, he's the only one still up. 'I don't think we need filming equipment for now,' I say between stilted breaths, more from excitement than exertion.

'Filming equipment,' he says, 'who ever said anything about filming equipment?'

It's the day of the Kent Test and Eliott is up early. 'You'll be fine,' I tell him. 'Your levels are great. It was only that code cracking we had to work on, and you've come a long way.'

'Good luck EJ,' says Annie as she packs her bag. 'You'll do great, and if you don't there's always my school. Not that I'll still be there,' she says.

'Don't worry,' says Maddy. 'You're better at maths than the rest of us, Mum and Dad included.' She ruffles his hair and he winces at her. 'Girl germs,' he says. Then he smiles a broad grin and puffs out his chest. 'You should all learn the cornet. It did it for me. That's what Dad says.'

He has *no idea* how many duff notes we've suffered, how many random screeches as he's learnt to play a respectable tune. I watch him piling into his cereal with none of the exam nerves Maddy experienced when it was her turn. I don't think I could go through that again. It's true, his cornet playing has corresponded with a steady increase in academic ability, but we've been here before: a child who is keen to pass and really should...

The afternoon arrives, and his class come out under a tangible cloud of relief. The tension has left them and they're looking pale and tired, shirts hanging out, bags trailing, shoe laces undone. Shells of their former selves, as if they've undergone some life-changing rite of passage.

'How was it?'

He waits for his friends to walk on ahead before he will talk. 'Well, near the end I realized I'd missed a maths question so I'd put all the answers in the wrong place. I had to rub loads out and put the answers back in again. I'm not sure if I've done it right.'

'Don't worry,' I say. 'You've probably done better than you

think.'

Saturday sees the test at the Dover Boys' school, an alternative entry route, and he comes out of this one feeling far more confident. 'It was really easy,' he says. His energy is back and he's bounding round the kitchen as I watch the grill. 'And Nathan and Sacha were in the same room as me. We could be in the same class and everything, it was in alphabetical order.'

'We'll see,' I say. 'But really well done. We're going to eat out to celebrate all your hard work. You choose where we go.'

'McDonalds.'

'*Eliott,*' says Annie, appearing at the first mention of food. 'Come on, we could go somewhere decent.'

'Nope, McDonalds, please.'

The parents are stressing more than the kids. The mums are talking as we wait for assembly to start the following Friday. 'I've told her, if she doesn't get into grammar school we're moving out of the county. My family are in Devon. There's no other reason to stay.' No pressure there, then. 'If she doesn't get in there's something wrong with her.'

She can't mean it, not really.

'Does she like Dover Girls?' I hear myself asking. 'I mean, where does she want to go?'

'What's not to like?'

'They're too young to choose,' comes the voice of another parent behind.

Do I tell them that I worry grammar may be too full-on? That I've seen Maddy in tears with the homework load, that I want Eliott to enjoy being a child for a little longer? I choose not to.

The badgers are making their presence felt now. I have noticed a badger pathway through the grass – imagine the course of a small tank that's repeatedly taken – and it leads to Austen's vegetable garden, which runs parallel to ours. He has banged in a couple of metal poles to block their route, but that won't last. He's an easy-going neighbour to have though and is unlikely to make an enemy of wildlife. I don't feel the need to tell him, it's easier not to at the moment, just in case he's unimpressed. Rupert tells me he's often heard badgers on that side, that he's been out for the last few nights when I'm fast asleep and caught their chittering. So the bug's got him too, then.

The weeks continue with stealth-watching. Maddy and Eliott are keen to try, and most nights I have some company outside for a while. We endure music and wind and cold, but no more sightings, at home or in the woods. At times I think they're coming, but some noise of ours spooks them, for all we hear is their clumsy exit, concealed by the thick curtain of trees. Rupert likens it to gambling – 'There's just enough hope to keep you going, some little signal that makes you think you should hold out.' We know all the cacophony of neighbourhood noises: chickens scraping their beaks on the inside of their coup; the names of Cynthia's cats; the protests of the one confined to a cage, and its toy with a bell; the shrieking of Sal at the care home near the church. And then, just sometimes, the survival stampede of badgers when they know they've been sprung.

Perhaps I should just content myself with the evidence that they've been. And very soon there is more. Eliott has dug himself a pit at the bottom of the garden, a holiday-boredom induced exercise, and this morning we see something large has started to burrow into it. Perhaps it's early days, but it's not looking very expertly done, though it has most definitely been claimed. I like to imagine it as training ground for the cubs. Roots are hanging out and a little mound of chalk fragments lies to the side. As long as they don't tunnel towards the chicken run I don't mind.

Rupert is constructing a new platform in the trees 'for the children' as the old one was unsafe. 'Are you going to go up there?' Jem asks me, 'To watch the badgers?'

'I might do.'

'Can I come up there with you? I want to see them.'

'It would be late. And dark. You'll see them sometime.'

'*When?*'

She's soon satisfied with a live cam feed that follows four orphaned cubs, courtesy of broadcaster Simon King's website. A tangle of badgers that sleep together during the day, even though three small chambers are available to them. Cameras monitor them inside the sett. There's a pile of feet in the centre, heads lolloping, rising and falling bellies (these are well-fed badgers), the occasional yawn, stretch, nibble or itch, and then a crashing down again onto the mattress of each other. They are so easy in this makeshift clan, the picture of a contented family unit; the three boars and a sow were all found separately but moved in here together. If only they knew how many eyes were on them.

We like to watch them when they wake in the evenings, and our thoughts turn to 'our' badgers nearby, and how they must be stirring, too. Maddy, Jem and I are watching now. They all grow restless, stretch, yawn and wake up. One listens at the hole, then drags in some more bedding. He climbs directly onto his resting friend and sits down. No response. Three leave the sett by seven-thirty. The fourth has crashed again, like some irritated teenager who doesn't want to be turfed out of bed. We're laughing loudly and Annie comes in, hearing the noise.

'Oh my *goodness*,' she says, with none of the meekness of the word. 'Whatever next! I thought something good was on.'

Rupert pokes his head round the door. 'I'm going to get Eliott. Anyone coming?'

Eliott is at his first ever St. John Ambulance meeting, a first aid charity who train and make use of volunteers. He's always had this instinct to comfort and rescue, first seen on a beach when he was two and another child was crying. For a long time it was a firefighting obsession, with visits to station open days and waving at fire-engines (I didn't mind). But the gift of an Action-Man-sized human model with detachable organs changed all that. He quickly learnt to put them back inside in order, and this new activity feels like a natural progression.

'It was amazing,' he says when he's home. 'I'm glad I chose that and not football.' Most of the boys in his class tried for the school team this week and he felt pressured to by his friends. He backed out when he realized this was on the same night.

'We learnt to resuscitate. And there was a line of broken crash helmets from Lydden race track. They've confiscated them you see.'

He's leaping about the family room, making my laptop shake and the floor creak. He high-fives me, then knocks my terracotta bell that hangs from the hop-framed archway. Small fragments of hops drift down to the floor.

'And what were the people like?'

'Okay.' He's less impressed with the company. 'It was all girls.'

5: Badger strife

It's a warm September, though the signs of autumn are everywhere. Early morning mists, squashed squirrels on the school journey through the leaf-darkened lanes, and a broken down combine that we pass on the side of the road for days. The tyres crunch over beech nut shells like gravel, and conkers drop onto the car roof near the school. At home, Jemima likes pointing out the cobwebs in the garden – they are stretched out like washing on the line. In places they resemble hammocks for resting in the sun. She finds them in the house, too. Crane flies slumber on the windows and doors – 'harvest spiders or harvestmen', larvae from the leatherjackets the badgers find so palatable. I discover sycamore helicopters that have somehow found their way into my bag, and sit amongst crumpled receipts and half-filled notebooks. Large black dragonflies are out, southern hawkers perhaps, though they're quick and I can rarely see them close up. It's a season I usually love, but the thought of not seeing badgers for months makes me feel like I'm entering a very small, cramped space, a glass room that's filling up with water. It's a fact they will be less active soon, and won't be visible at all in the daylight hours as the nights draw in. And so the summer is passing, and ahead the long nights and barren landscapes. I order some real night vision equipment and wait.

*

There is screaming in the darkness; twenty hysterical children – mostly boys – their unbroken voices at glass-shattering pitch. This is youth club in the village for Eliott and friends. 'Get into twos!' I shout over them, pausing before flicking back on the lights. 'You're out, you too, sit over there. Into fours!' Soon we're down to a winning pair of boys who cheer and run around the hall in a victory lap. 'Losers,' one of them shouts.

It's nearly time for them to be collected, though they could go on all evening. The group is full of the local year sixes and they know each other well. 'Can we have the lights off again?' asks one. They want to play tag with glow sticks in the dark. Now the silver band has started practising in the room above the church, across the car park from here.

I imagine our badgers loitering just metres from where I'm standing. They won't be out for hours tonight; in fact, I'm surprised they've stuck around for so long, what with youth club twice a month and hall bookings for parties. Do they find all this strangely reassuring – the noises of home, like the clunk of the boiler and the squeak of a floorboard? The band music could be the refrain for several generations of badgers, an old English lullaby early on a Sunday morning, and a wake-up call on a Friday night.

We're the last to leave, and I close off the kitchen hatch. 'We'll go home the long way tonight,' I tell Eliott and his friend Alfie. 'I left the torch at home. Let's save that dark footpath for another night.'

The next morning we discover the badgers have been – the disturbance of last night didn't put them off. The peanuts have all gone, and in their place is a length of old blue gnawed rope fraying at one end. It has several knots, and the appearance of something a dog might play with. Had they dragged it in from a neighbour's garden, or dug it up? There are badger footprints in Eliott's boredom-pit, too.

The post arrives, and with it my night-vision monocular. I can't wait to use it, but it mustn't be turned on during the day or it won't work. It's the span of my hand and rests in it comfortably, the weight of a heavy shoe. Eliott walks into the kitchen and finds me looking at it.

'What's that, Mum?'

'It's my night vision. *My* night vision.'

'Cool. Can I see you in infra-red, Mum? Can I hold it?'

'You mustn't play with it,' I begin to tell him. 'If it's dropped it's useless, and we can't turn it on during the –'

'You can actually see through clothes with it, EJ,' says Rupert, emerging from the boot room.

'Can you?' he says in his impressed voice. 'Actually, that's not good is it?'

Later I take the night vision on its first outing to the bottom of the garden. I'm not that wowed to start with – it's far from the footage I saw online and more like underwater vision. I adjust the focus and am able to zoom in on the chicken wire that's attached to the fence. That's better. It's just not too good up close, the bushes and trees have a lurid glare about them. I'm not likely to see anything tonight anyway – there is a concert on at the church in aid of First Responders, a community service provided by St John Ambulance volunteers. Eliott is down there playing his cornet, and the Mission Impossible music is reaching me, the beat steady and repetitive. A neighbour between us and the church comes out and drops recycling in the bin. I'm getting head-pain from this thing but it's addictive. I'm resigned to the badgers lying low tonight while hope niggles at the back of my brain.

I hear car doors slam and voices calling, 'See you tomorrow,' 'Laters,' 'Well done, guys.'

When I head inside they're back already. 'We crept in, didn't want to disturb you.'

'Where's EJ?' I say, placing the night vision carefully on the worktop.

'He was shattered, he's probably already asleep.'

The new week starts, and I take a call from Martin. 'Ed's in your village, sorting out that problem I told you about.' He gives me the name of a lane I've never heard of. 'It's a sunken lane, you won't miss it.'

My friend Lisa is at the door with three-year-old James in his off-road pushchair. 'I've got to go out,' I tell her. 'But you might like to come. James likes diggers doesn't he?'

We reach the banker-mansion end of the village and scan each turning for the resemblance of a sunken lane. We take one – 'Just round the next bend,' says Lisa, 'It's got to be.' We find ourselves in a field behind a padlocked gate and make our way back to the main road. A young man stops us – he's black and looks out of place in our ethnically undiverse village. 'I looking for police station,' he tells us. 'A phone.' Is he an asylum seeker? In Eythorne? But he has no bag, nothing, and he's dressed up for the occasion, wearing a suit jacket with his jeans. 'There's a train station,' I tell him. 'Take the next main turning to the left. You'll see it. Some men work there, have a phone, could make you a cup of tea.'

Rupert is home today and I call him. 'You might want to come out and find him, he looks like he needs a friend. I can't help right now, Ed's expecting me.'

'Did he look Sudanese?'

'Yes.'

'He wanted the police and a phone? He's going to turn himself in. He'll probably be in my class tomorrow.'

'But he wasn't dressed like it. He could've been going to work.'

'That'll be right. They give them new clothes at Calais before sending them on their way. So, haven't you got there yet?'

'Nope. We're not lost exactly, we just can't find it.'

Lisa has a gut-instinct and we take a lane that we've already passed. 'Can you hear that?' she says. There's the rumble of heavy machinery nearby. James is kicking his legs in anticipation while finishing his mini-breadsticks. 'It's them,' I say as we turn a corner. The digger stops and the driver calls for Ed, who walks down the lane to meet us. 'This is Sam,' he says. His friend waves as he wanders off to take a break. I introduce Lisa and James, too. 'This is what we do for a living,' says Ed, pointing at the high banks on either side; they have covered them in a strong wire mesh, and the base of the lane itself.

'They couldn't get their cars out, some mornings,' Ed tells us. 'The badgers had chucked so much earth across the lane. Natural England granted a licence.'

'A bit like being snowed in,' I say with a smile. There's something about the deviance of badgers that appeals; I'm not sure why, it's quite perverse really. Perhaps it's not so questionable – we love the underdog in literature, the longsuffering endurance of characters such as Diggory Venn in Hardy's *Return of the Native* and Gabriel Oak in *Far From the Madding Crowd*. When difficulties are piled on them we wonder how they will cope – it's why we are drawn to Dickens' Oliver Twist, David Copperfield and the Cratchit family, and from infancy the Bible stories of David and Goliath, and Daniel in the lion's den. We respect characters with the good sense to do things their way – and not get caught – and when they win out we share in the triumph. There is something in us that likes to speak up for the voiceless, and these underdogs in the natural world have enough opposition. James is now seated inside the mini-digger and being shown the controls. Three little doors have been placed in the bank, the size of cat-flaps and with the appearance of garage doors. These hatches allow the badgers through but not back again, forcing them round to the other side of the bank and away from the lane. 'It's not a problem for them,' says Ed. 'They're just being sent a different way.'

The doors can be blocked off after twenty-three days as the badgers will have to emerge for food by then. Just occasionally they don't appear for twenty-one days and the counting has to begin all over again. 'I've taught the owners to monitor movement with sticks,' says Ed. 'If the sticks are still in place, the badgers haven't been through.'

I ask who bears the expense of this whole operation. 'The owners,' I'm told. And I've always dreamt of living at the end of a lane like this one.

I read Jemima her choice of school book at bedtime, *A Bad Day for Badger,* while watching the sun set over the trees at the bottom of the garden, and the church beyond. She is sitting up in bed and showing her toy badger the pictures. Soon she's yawning and snuggling under the covers as I read. She is still, I don't really think she's listening and I stop reading – 'Go on,' she says, and she brings her round face up close to mine, as she does when she tells me things. 'You can't stop now.' Her big brown eyes are now showing no trace of tiredness.

'I'll just finish the chapter,' I say.

She lies down again and rolls onto her side while I read on a few pages.

'You've stopped.'

'That's the end of the chapter.'

'Show me.'

I do, and as I kiss her goodnight she clings with her arms around my neck.

'Come on, Mum,' says Maddy. 'You've taken ages.' We have agreed on a badger mission, and Rupert says he'll put the chickens away and help with Annie's homework – her algebra is beyond me anyway.

I place the small night vision torch around Maddy's neck and, tucking the new monocular under my arm, we set off. She points out a fresh badger hole just off the street, and I shine a torch over the creeping tree roots as we pick our way through the woods. We make our way to the field edge as before, but now there's so much debris from the beech and oak above that it's hard to make a quiet entrance. We haven't deterred the badgers though, for soon they start crashing around behind the fence. One walks into my lurid field of vision – a medium sized badger, perhaps a female – and then another, who stops to sniff the air.

Have we been detected now? This larger badger pauses, as if trying to grasp a profound thought that was almost fully formulated but has gone. He's about his business once more, bumbling through the undergrowth, behind a tree, and now stopping in a clearing to inspect himself for fleas.

We should be glad of the badger's heightened instincts, for they are of course crucial to his survival, even if this ability to outwit means most people never get to see a living one. It makes the quest all the more fun. Smell is the badger's main means of communication, his primary sense, needed for drawing up boundaries, establishing a social hierarchy, registering members of a sett and determining general peace or unease. A badger's skull contains many turbinals – or intricate scroll bones – that point to his acute sense of smell. These, combined with an excellent sense of hearing, mean the badger is well kitted-out for a life on the run. I have to let Maddy try out the monocular and whisper some instructions whilst passing it to her but she struggles to see anything. I point to the outline of trees that line the field behind us and she manages to see them – I think she's just not tall enough to see into the enclosure in the dark.

'Do you want to go to the teenage wood, you'll see more there.'

'I don't mind.'

'Do you want to? Really?'

She nods and we set off. A few steps inside and we've spooked them. I don't know what I was thinking. Since when did they stay out when we've walked in on them?

'I feel bad that you didn't see anything,' I say as we head home.

'That's okay. I still got that high, that kind of buzz. This red torch is amazing, it's the best one I've ever had.'

October arrives, and with it a new challenge. I'm out early as usual, to re-block the hole the badgers use to access our garden – I open it up for them every night. If I didn't block it Tyn would be through it at the first opportunity, but he won't emerge from his bed until Rupert comes downstairs. Peanuts remain where I scattered them, in the pit and in amongst the trees. I crouch down at the hole beneath our wire fence and reach for the sticks that the sycamore stores for me in an encompassing umbrella stand arrangement; its overactive growth has sent several gnarled branches around sideways before their spurt upwards towards the light. I study the hole beyond ours, where the badgers come under our neighbour Malcolm's solid wooden fence – it doesn't look right, I think in my early-morning state, before realizing that it's been filled in with bricks and soil. I check on their other entrance hole alongside the first; an even better job has been made of this one.

I tell Maddy when she's up. 'They've done what? Can you unblock it?' She slams the fridge extra hard and pulls open the cutlery draw so that the contents shake.

'They'll find a way through, just wait and see.'

'That's just great,' she says, looking at her new timetable on the inside of the cupboard. 'As soon as we're back at school all the fun stops. We can't see them in the woods and they can't come here. *And* I've got German today. That teacher hates me.'

'I doubt it.'

'She does, she really has it in for me and Alice. I want to drop German but I've got to do it for two whole years.'

Annie comes into the kitchen, still in her pyjamas. 'I need a school shirt, you seen any?'

'Try the laundry basket, it's in the family room.'

'Why's Madeline looking so stressed?'

There's no response from either of us and Maddy steps over to the back door. Annie waits for her to turn around. 'You look like you're going to cry,' she says to her.

Maddy is silent. 'School, life,' I say for her. 'You know. Usual stuff.'

'They've blocked it,' she says.

'Blocked what?' asks Annie.

'The badger hole at the bottom of the garden.'

'Good,' says Annie. 'At least they won't get the chickens. You really need to get a grip, Maddy. Do you want the chickens eaten?'

'And you need to shut up… I hate you sometimes.'

She stomps off up the stairs and Annie is shrugging her shoulders at me – 'What? I haven't done anything. She needs to lighten up. And did you hear that – she says she *hates* me – are you going to let her get away with that?'

The primary school drop off takes forever, a bin lorry blocks the lane at Coldred and I come home the long way, doubling back past the school. I sit down to write but can't concentrate. I could just give the badgers a little helping hand – we're getting into a pattern now, it can't come to an end. And besides, soon there'll be less for them to eat in the wild.

I find a small trowel and the yellow-handled secateurs and wander down to the bottom of the garden. No sign of anyone next door, I think to myself, peering over at the garden on my left. I could be visible if Austen were out pulling veggies, he's much taller than me and it's better to be safe than sorry. I place the implements on the ground and climb onto the platform on the sycamore tree to have a look – it's as I thought, they've filled in the main hole with soil and bricks. The other is covered with an upturned planter and weighed down with stones – well, at least that one will be easy for them. Back down, I hack at the holly and climb over the wire fence. If I can make a level surface on our side they'll get through without a problem – I was amazed when Martin first showed me the gap they can manage – a cat would struggle to get underneath.

Strictly speaking, our boundary is the wire fence I've just climbed over, but several trees have grown on the line and would need to come down if we were to observe it correctly. The large sycamore has absorbed the fence and grown around it, so that part of the fence is hidden inside the tree itself. I did raise the question of the tall trees with the neighbours once – before the badgers came – and discovered they like the screen the trees provide. Long may that last.

Three china chickens are grouped in front of their water-butt – even that looks like it's made from terracotta. I can see they wouldn't want it knocked over by a blundering badger. If only the badgers had chosen to dig behind those tall ornamental grasses to the side. The garden looks like it's been manicured obsessively, and any measures taken by me or the badgers will no doubt be rectified in the warmer months.

I move a good bucket or two of earth and chuck it further along. I could be doing this from my side of the boundary, to be fair, but it's easier to get to from here, just behind their tall fence – I'm not actually in their garden, just poking the trowel underneath. The trowel hits chalk and stones, scraping as it goes; they'll hear this from the house if their back door is open. Stories are only now emerging about Annie and Maddy's formative dares at the bottom of the garden. They would take turns climbing the fence – a smaller one in those days – running in and touching flowerpots, each one further away than the last. They were caught on one occasion – '*What* do you think you're doing? I'll tell your parents if you do that again.' Soon after Simon, then the owner of the property, appeared on the doorstep. 'We could see him from the snug, we were so frightened,' said Annie. 'We hid behind the sofa till he'd gone. Grumpy old git.'

'I was sitting there with Josh the hamster in my hand,' said Maddy. 'He could have bitten me but I didn't dare move.'

This couple owned the neighbouring meadow and built the aforementioned second house that Eliott obsessed over when he was small. The new owners of the first property are mostly agreeable, but not so keen on the dog. 'Can you come and get your *dog*,' he'd said on the phone a few months ago, before we knew the badgers were around. It wasn't a warm welcome we received. We drove round with the car, me in posh frock and heels ready to go out, Maddy in the front passenger seat. 'I don't want to miss this,' she said.

He was sitting outside his grey brick house when we arrived, hanging onto the dog's collar like he was some canine criminal, the lowest form of all dog-life. It was lucky I'd decided not to walk, the ten minutes it would have taken would have been too much for his limited patience, judging by the look of him. Although we share a boundary at the bottom of our garden, our houses are situated on different roads.

'I don't know how he got through,' I said, apologising. I fumbled with the clip on the lead before attaching it to Tyn's collar. It was true, I genuinely didn't back then.

'You need to block them, I'm fed up with it.'

'Has it happened before?' He raised his eyebrows at me in an exasperated, sarcastic expression. If he'd had a cigarette he would have been drawing on it, hard. Well, I wasn't aware of it happening before, but then we're somehow used to Tyn's Houdini routine, taking the front gate when it's left open and any hole that appears in the hedge. We don't object to the neighbourhood cats who choose to stroll across our lawn, though I suppose they take themselves home.

'It's those *holes* he keeps digging.' He was standing up now, a wide stance, hands on hips, really not prepared to let this thing go. Do they seriously still think all this is the work of one small Border terrier? If you're going to build houses on meadowland it comes with the territory. Our own house here used to stand at the top of an orchard that spread to the left and right, covering several acres. Previous owners sold off portions of land, and now the only nod to its apple-growing past is two small apple trees near the bottom of the garden. The community may have forgotten what the land was originally used for, but generations of badgers apparently haven't.

Eliott and friends developed a game throwing grass cuttings into the garden of the red brick house. That wasn't popular either, but now he's moved on to adventures further afield. 'Can I go up to Sun Valley Way?' he asked yesterday, dog on lead before I'd even got out of the car. 'I've got my DS this time,' he said. Two of his good friends live up there, and it's just a short walk from home. The dog looked complicit and I let them go.

I gather some fallen sycamore leaves and push them under the fence, scattering some more on our side. This disguises my efforts for now and they should be none the wiser. But Maddy and Jem will be pleased.

A few days later I hear a chainsaw at the front of the grey brick property. I call the dog from his strip of sunshine on the family room floor and attach his lead. We need to walk to the church grounds and see what he's up to – I'm worried Malcolm's tackling the badgers' access from the other side. We run rather than walk, and slow to a nonchalant stroll as soon as we're within sight of the house. The sound is coming from where I thought, but this isn't a big ground-clearing operation, it's just a tidy-up. I'd envisaged him installing fences that the badgers can't get under, but that's not happening – at least, not yet.

While I'm here I need to check on what the church have been doing with the holes. I make sure no one is looking and enter the grove of trees behind the church hall. The holes are still covered with grass cuttings, the badgers haven't attempted to reopen them and I don't blame them. I visit the holes further inside this little patch of woodland; they also look disused, and are filling up with twigs and leaves. A piece of broken mirror is lying on the ground and I pick it up and lightly wrap my hand around it – it has a sharp edge and would injure any wildlife that happed to tread on it. I have lost my bearings, we should be near the footpath by now, but I can see the graves near the edge of the wood, and we emerge behind the hall again. The guy with the chainsaw doesn't seem to have noticed us anyway. Yew berries have dropped to the ground and lie squished on the path – unlike humans, the badgers can eat these without being poisoned – the toxins held in the seeds that are digested whole. I look into the tree and see there are plenty more for them. We follow the line of graves to the cast-iron gate at the back of the field.

The post arrives while I'm home and the dog barks, jumping onto the porch door, knocking it open – there's a letter from Dad, I recognize his handwriting and tear open the envelope. 'Thought you might enjoy the enclosed, it sounds like that refugee you told me you'd seen.'

I read the headline: 'Mother's biscuits help detain illegal immigrant' – but he wanted help, he wasn't going anywhere! And I think 'refugee' was the word they were after. There's a photo half-way down the article and I recognize him straight away. I wish I'd been the one to help him. I wonder who took the photo. He has his back to the camera and the mother of six children (how is that relevant – are we meant to fear for their safety?) is sitting a metre away from him, an embarrassed smile on her face. "The police asked us to stop him running away, so I gave him a Penguin and a packet of Hula Hoops."

Talk about an agenda – I wonder if the other papers have reported it any differently. Has anyone asked him for his account? I read on. He's an Eritrean science graduate, and covered 3,500 miles on foot before hiding under a lorry in Calais. I suppose it's nothing compared to the challenges he's been used to at home.

There isn't much time to dwell on it as Martin phones me about another anxious elderly lady. A Mrs Hickson from Dover. Could I do a visit for the group? A badger is under her shed and she's frightened, he says. I phone her straight away.

'I'm really worried,' she tells me. 'Can you catch anything from it all? What about this TB they're talking about? In cats now, too?' I want to tell her it was nothing more than scaremongering when the cull was found to be 'ineffective and inhumane', but I stop myself. The cull failed on the government's own humaneness grounds, with up to 22% taking more than five minutes to die, which would have caused them 'marked pain'. Targets of 70% of the badger population in cull zones were not met, while disturbed badgers caused the 'perturbation effect', leaving their home ground and finding another and so spreading the disease. Would a cat stay anywhere near a badger? Not according to Martin, they'd flee at the first whiff of anything larger than themselves. If a cat catches TB it has most likely eaten an infected rodent, but it was an idea that caught the imagination of some.[5] The story took off early in March 2014 when the cull was understood to be a failure. Mrs Hickson is still talking. '… she's really frightened –'

'Sorry, who's really frightened?'

'My elderly neighbour, she's eighty-four. She had someone come over and use some creosote for her, then fill it in. She's petrified.'

I tell her I can come tomorrow to take a look.

I arrive just after nine the next morning and park with half the car on the pavement, as the residents have done. Mrs Hickson is waiting already with the front door open. 'That's right,' she calls. 'We get these giant lorries come through, there really isn't the space for them, and they won't care if they take the side off your car.'

She stands in her doorway in a lemon short-sleeved jumper. 'I

---

[5] The disease has been found in domestic animals such as cats and dogs, and wild animals including deer, foxes, rats and squirrels. It is thought the most common route of transmission is, however, between cattle themselves.

don't feel the cold,' she tells me as she leads me through the house and out the back door. 'You know, it's very good of you to come.' As we climb the steep concrete steps to her back garden seagulls keow above us, flying up to a deserted hill beyond the houses and back. The lawn is pitted and badgers have obviously been at work. A small blue boat rests on its side and she points out some scratch marks on the underside. 'Is that *them*?'

'It could be,' I reply.

She opens a small gate at the back and we walk along the 'alleyway' – an overgrown grassy path – and into her neighbour's garden. 'The neighbours won't mind,' she says. 'The badgers are getting under our shed from here.' A wire fence has a gap at the bottom and it's clear they are coming through this way. 'They probably lure the badgers in,' she tells me. 'My husband took a seagull's nest down for them once, but they usually encourage the wildlife.'

She has a son who lives on the same road, and I suggest that she asks him to put stakes at the base as a temporary measure, and digs in a more sturdy fence when she can afford it. Now she shows me her neighbour's garden on the other side, the steps that belong to the property alongside her own. 'It was a hole next to *that* step where we heard something. We thought it was baby foxes. I'm worried they have a path from under my shed that'll come out *there*,' she says, pointing at the neighbour's garden again.

I tell her that I don't think it could be anything more than a bolt-hole. This is a built-up residential area after all. 'I imagine that's where they are coming from,' I say, pointing at the wooded hill that shadows these houses below. 'This is much too heavily populated for their liking.' She frowns at me. 'I mean, they like things very quiet, an occupied terrace like this really isn't rural enough for them. I'm sure your shed is only a bolt-hole, you know, a place to lie low for a minute or two when on route home.'

'I've heard they can leap up to four feet,' she says. 'In a garden like mine, you've got nowhere to turn.'

I tell her that she's perfectly safe. That if there were a badger in her back garden it would run away as soon as she opened the back door. 'But look, you could put some solar lights in the beds next to your steps, and some more near the back door, there's no way they'd come close if it's lit.'

I think she's reassured. She takes me inside and invites me into her sitting room. 'It's just so stressful,' she says. 'My husband has just gone into a home, he's deteriorated very rapidly. He has dementia, you see. He banged his head and it wouldn't stop bleeding.'

'I'm sorry,' I say. I can see the badger issue is one layer of stress too many. The sympathy is more than she can cope with and she quickly changes the subject. 'Jamie can come on Saturday to make the fence secure,' she says, but I can tell it's really too long for her to wait.

'Do you have any bricks?' I ask her.

'I've got a whole pile.'

'I'll do what I can today,' I say. 'Just as a temporary measure.

Make sure your son sorts out something more permanent, won't you?'

'We will, but I've read on the internet that you can put in some badger gates, that they can be relocated to somewhere new. That's what we really need, wouldn't you say?'

*

'You wouldn't believe what my maths teacher was wearing today,' says Annie at supper.

'Go on then,' I say.

'It's this black *thing*, it just hangs on her. She's lost inside it. I'm not even joking.'

'Is it a top, dress or what?'

'Dress. And her arms and back are really hairy and she has this short haircut that she doesn't know how to style. Not surprising she hasn't got a boyfriend.'

'But is she explaining stuff any better now?' asks Rupert.

'Not really. But that's not the problem. We have to look at her like this. It's so distracting. It doesn't help. She wears dog-tooth leggings with a stripy –'

'Is the homework okay tonight? Only I was going to go out with your mum.'

'Oh really?' I say.

'It's Cubs,' says Eliott.

'We'll drop you first. I need a go with this night vision,' he says.

Annie sighs and concentrates on twiddling spaghetti around her fork. 'The homework's okay, but you two should get a grip.'

Rupert smiles at me, like that was a challenge to rile her even more.

'I'm tired but I'll hear Jemima read,' says Maddy.

'That's that sorted then,' says Rupert.

I return from Cubs to find Rupert pulling on his boots. 'We going on this badger walk? It'll be dark before we know it.'

I catch a glimpse of black and white in the undergrowth almost as soon as we're inside the wood. This stretch has been cut off by a fallen holly tree and I suspect nature is a little bolder and a little wilder in there now. 'I could use my chainsaw on that,' says Rupert. 'I'd be doing the community a service, and besides, I could use the wood on my lathe.' I'd rather he left it alone. He'll probably forget about it in a day or two anyway.

We reach our usual spot along the field edge. I use the night-vision and see a badger straight away – it stops for a scratch and then casually moves on. There's a stampede noise, nettles are waving and now a cub is at the hole in front of us. Rupert nudges me – in seconds the badger has emerged from their field crater. He's in reverse, pulling more earth out into the field as he goes. He is joined by another, larger badger. 'Where did that one come from? I didn't see.'

'Out of the hole,' says Rupert. 'Stop looking through that and you'll see a lot more.'

'You want a go, don't you?' I say.

'Wouldn't mind.' I pass the night vision monocular over and he takes it from me with great care, as if it's a communion goblet filled to the brim. Now cub chitterings are coming from the enclosure, there should be lots for him to see.

Minutes later I can hear them in the field again, though I can't see anything; darkness has swaddled the scene quickly. One comes close – I can just make it out. Rupert whispers to me, 'He's watching us but he's not really bothered,' and a blackened shape ambles towards the hole.

Now I have the night vision again and can see three sets of eyes behind a tree in the enclosure, Scooby-doo style. Then we hear movement. What *do* they make of our presence?

'We'd see more if we were in there,' says Rupert.

Well that was hardly great last time.

'We're best off here,' I say. 'We're not frightening them, it feels like we're here on their terms.'

It's seven-thirty and we start the walk home, Eliott will need collecting from Cubs. Maddy will wish she'd come – it's been like an August midnight – perhaps tomorrow. The local Dalmatian is out with his owner, walking the field in the darkness. He's off the lead and comes over to us, barking. We must look conspicuous, why would a grown couple be out in the countryside after dark? We hardly look like we're courting. The badgers are still in the field – I hope they make their way across to the other side before the dog sees them and gives chase.

Eliott comes home smelling of bonfire and excitement. His Cubs leader wants him to play the Last Post for Shepherdswell in just three weeks' time. 'Do you want to do it?' I say. Stupid question. He's riding high on the honour of it for now, doing that leaping thing where he can't seem to stand still but is going nowhere in particular.

'Of course he should,' says Rupert.

'I'll give it a try,' he says, reaching in the cupboard for a glass. 'Can you pour me some milk? Will you come and watch, Mum?'

'I wouldn't miss it for the world. Just remember, it's not about you. You're leading people into a time of quiet.'

'Not something you're known for,' says Maddy, coming into the kitchen and adjusting his neckerchief, then giving it a playful tug.

'Get off.'

'Everyone's going to be there. Rather you than me, Eliott,' and she lifts him from under his arms.

'You couldn't do it with your guitar anyway,' he says. 'That would be funny.'

The next morning he finds the music Rupert must have printed for him and pegs it to his stand. He begins to play – the first few attempts are pretty rough, but he soon has the hang of it. It's making me feel really morose, and I find myself staring out of the window and fixing my eyes at a random space, as if grieving. It is raining outside beneath an ash grey sky. The dog joins me at the window and watches; this attentiveness isn't his usual style, but it's as if the music is in some way affecting his mood, too. A magpie breaks the calm outside with its football rattle click, and Jem comes to the table with a plate of toast made for her by Maddy: 'One side chocolate spread, the other side jam,' she says, and dips it in her tea.

Are we the only beings to feel sorrow? I think it's unlikely. Badgers are familiar with grief, if the books I have been reading are to be believed. Among their sixteen different vocal sounds is a death-wail, verging on a scream, said to accompany their burial of dead comrades. On a June night in 1941, naturalist Vesey-Fitzgerald witnessed a dead badger being brought to a hole by a boar and sow and apparently buried. Both badgers grieved audibly, with a sound somewhere between a wail and a whimper. Vesey thought it was their father, the old boar, that they buried. He was profoundly moved by the sight and was in no doubt about what he had seen.

If a badger dies underground it is usual for members of its clan to bring it to an unused alcove that they seal, a burial chamber made within the sett's own boundaries. This is not only for the adult badgers; many cubs don't survive the early weeks to venture into the world above, with less than half making it to adulthood. And if a mother dies then her young cubs will also, unless, of course, they are weaned.

The Last Post music becomes the tune of the moment and soon

loses its melancholic edge. Eliott's an early riser, and his playing wakes Annie with regularity – 'Mum, can you tell him he can't play that thing before school?'

'It's not that early. Besides, you need to be up.'

'Eliott, you little git,' she calls down the stairs.

I go into the snug to open the curtains behind him. He's now listening to the Last Post on Rupert's laptop. I catch sight of the screen; he's playing a skateboard game at the same time. He realizes that I've seen and turns the laptop away from me. 'It's fine with me, Eliott,' I say. 'You need to get familiar with the timing, it can't do any harm, playing a game as you listen.'

The autumn rain continues all day, but I need to get out – we haven't had a badger walk in ages. Maddy wants to come, too. Rupert tells her it's good for the two of us to have some time alone together, but she somehow persuades me. She's laughing at Rupert as he struggles to get his hood up whilst walking along the road. 'Dad, you'd probably have to sit on the friendship bench at school,' she says. 'Do you need Mum to help you?'

It's dark when we enter the woods and we stumble along, half-blind. At last we find our usual waiting place, like falling into bed and finding the familiar dips. The night vision needs refocusing but I can smell them, they are definitely here; it is not a strong odour, like that of the fox, and it's not often I can sniff them out at all. Perhaps it's a combination of rotting leaves and anticipation, but I like to think it's something more. The trees are dripping on us and Rupert is cleaning his glasses, though it's not going to make much difference. I can see a large badger at the back of the enclosure – I have the night vision monocular and pass it to him, now he's tucked back in his shirt. He has a go and then passes it on to Maddy – 'I can't see anything,' she says in a hoarse faggy whisper.

'Adjust the focus,' says Rupert.

'I've tried, it's not working.'

'Give it here,' I say. I look into the far distance across the fields and back. It's useless, I don't know what she's done to it, I can't see anything at all. We're getting wetter and I'm getting crosser by the moment. The minutes are passing and I can't sort it. I step over the fence and start to head home, Rupert and Maddy trailing on behind.

'I told her she could adjust it,' says Rupert.

'She doesn't know what she's doing,' I say, turning back. 'I've told her before not to change the setting.' I catch her eye. 'You don't always have to come, you know.' She's crying now, which really irritates me. 'Look, it's dark already, we'd got here too late. Maddy, have the infra-red torch next time, okay?'

She says nothing. That's just so infuriating, she takes after her dad when she's feeling wounded and just *sulks*. How does that help anyone? It's so superior, and then they can't let go, they brood for hours.

'We're here now,' says Rupert. 'Couldn't we stay a bit longer?'

'And see what? She's stuffed up the equipment.' I unzip my coat as I walk and push at my sleeves.

'I could sort it if you'd let me try.'

'We've frightened them off by now, what's the point? Here, have it anyway.'

Soon I climb over the wrong bit of fence and can't find the path. The small red torch isn't up to much. 'Rup's where *are* you,' I call. The moonlight seems to be non-existent tonight.

He shines the torch and they emerge out of the darkness.

The next day I buy Maddy some badger socks and place them on her bed as an apology. I had lost it, I was totally unreasonable. I do enjoy her company, I tell her, I didn't mean what I said. She seems to have forgiven me, but is all the happier for a discovery at the bottom of the garden: 'The badgers have found another way in,' I tell her. 'They're coming through Simon and Louise's now, too.'

She laughs. 'I want to see,' she says, reaching for her wellies. 'He snitches on us, I don't like him. Serves him right.'

'I just need to get my glow stick,' says Jemima. 'Wait for me.'

They run out of the house, leaving the back door wide open behind them. I shut it, then follow on. Jem heads the wrong way along the path at the bottom. 'I can see, underneath that holly,' she says. 'I have to get in there with my glow stick.'

'It's over here,' I say. 'You can't miss it.'

'I want another badger mission,' says Maddy. 'This is great and everything, but I want to be out rescuing badgers, or rescuing old ladies from badgers anyway.'

'It's the wrong season,' I say. We are at the beginning of November and the badgers tend to behave themselves at this time of year, sleeping more and emerging only when it's very dark. The male cubs are yet to be evicted from the sett – the main cause of badger fatalities on the roads – and their lives are in a state of equilibrium.

Hollyhocks are waving near the house as we return up the garden; they are fizzling out like damp fireworks, only the last pale blooms remaining at the top of each stem. Summer has finally lost its grip. The radio's on in the kitchen and I hear that the ozone layer currently covers an area the size of North America. Hopes it would shrink with the banning of chlorine emissions have been slow to materialize. It's said to be 'healing', though I suspect this is wishful thinking.

My thoughts turn to Mrs Hickson after my conversation with Maddy and I wonder how she's doing. I will give her a call – all part of the badger group service.

'You've just caught me,' she says. 'I'm going up to the care home to see my husband.'

'So how are things? Are the badgers leaving you alone now?'

'I think so,' she says. 'The lawn looks fine. To be honest I haven't been thinking about it much. My husband can't speak now, he has breathing difficulties. We thought he was in a coma earlier this week. He does sleep such a lot.'

'I'm sorry to hear that,' I say.

'Not much we can do about it. He's only going to get worse.'

There's a tapping on the kitchen door in the afternoon; it's the chickens, their soft pecking telling me they want to be put to bed. It's where they always loiter when it starts to get dark. I lead them down the garden with a crust of bread and Jemima follows, staying behind to collect the eggs from the nesting box. 'This one's from Roxy, I saw her lay it,' she says when she's back inside, her grin wide. She places it on the counter and it rolls onto the floor. I take the other one from her hand and crouch down to clear up the mess.

Badger watching is getting difficult now that it's dark by six o'clock – I should be cooking for the family then, rather than climbing fences, and we save our adventures for the weekends. Our walks are more out of habit than expectation but I'm determined not to give in. Fireworks sound, though it's not yet November 5th – they've been heard every night in the village since Hallowe'en. I try texting Annie in the dark: 'We're still in the woods, won't be long. Help yourself to jackets from oven, toppings all ready in fridge. Mum xx.' The text won't go and we turn to leave. Water is pooling in the exposed tree roots, a convenient find for the wildlife anyway, and the woods are characterized by mud and slime, felt rather than seen. After supper I try waiting in the garden again. I hear the odd noise that speaks of them – I can imagine them just sitting it out, waiting for silence. That line about the ship keeps coming to me from Hardy's *The Convergence of the* Twain', 'stilly couches she' – I'm sure that's what they're doing, just loitering with intent. The peanuts are going, they are leaving footprints and old unearthed china in their wake, it's not like I'm imagining it. This is so depressing. I'm going to go in and join the family again, it's just not worth it. The garden is in total darkness, the solar lights that I've dotted about the place don't come on, there's not been enough sun for days.

It's Remembrance Sunday and Eliott has been up since six, practising hard. He's perfected his piece and I'm feeling so proud. He has been attempting it without the music this week, and that's when he hits the duff notes, so he's playing safe and taking it with him today. 'We're off to Shepherdswell in ten minutes,' I call up the stairs.

Annie's door opens. 'What? I haven't got any make-up on.'

'Put it on in the car and I'll wait with you. Not that you need any, but I do understand. We'll catch them up, okay?'

Soon the vicar leads the congregation out of the church and onto the village green, where we wait beneath the stone cross. Eliott stands in the middle as the crowd assembles around him, filling the road outside the pub and on two sides of the green. It's eleven o'clock. A red car pulls up and waits, its engine running, driver tapping his thumb on the steering wheel. Disapproving looks are shared, quiet comments made. Now the crowd are silent and the vicar nods at Eliott to start. He plays a few duff notes and pauses. Then a few more. 'He's nervous,' says an old lady's voice behind me, rather too loudly. She's obviously not quite deaf enough. The car driver turns off the ignition and I avoid looking in his direction.

There's a shuffling of feet and a low mumble of voices. Eliott tries again and can't make a sound. I want to run up and hug him, lead him away from the crowd and tell them all just to get on without him. It was a lot to ask of a ten year old, after all.

I watch as the vicar lays a large hand on his shoulder from behind. All is silent again. Now he's off, a few wobbly notes and he's away, playing as it's meant to be heard. The hand is still there but it seems to be doing some good. I imagine what it must be like for him – half the height of many present, looking up into their faces, all sombre and without a smile. Old men in suits and medals. Ladies in heels and coats with brooches. School friends, fellow Cubs, Brownies – or the dark side, as the boys call them – parents he recognizes, teachers, flags to be raised, wreaths to be placed. And everyone expecting that he'll deliver. Now we wait and pray and ponder. This frightened, laid bare feeling – I wonder if it's how a badger feels when it's spotted? Fingernails are inspected, nudges shared between children, stern glances given. I watch as the vicar nods at him for the rouse. He plays this flawlessly and lowers his cornet, looking straight at me, a smile twitching at the corner of his mouth.

Afterwards both Cub leaders come up and hug him – Akela is ex-military, and he and his wife say they shed tears as he played. The vicar steps over and smiles at him warmly. 'I want you to play next year,' he says, shaking his hand. 'That's a demand, not a request.' There are pats on the back and words of praise from many as we make our way back to the car.

'I'd rather not,' he tells me on the way home. His eyes have glazed over and are fixed on something way off in the distance. I'm not convinced, but we'll know in time.

'You'd never get a chance in Eythorne,' I say. 'Not with the Silver Band being so full of capable people.'

'It was my fault,' says Rupert. 'I should have warmed up your cornet. How could anyone be expected to play that from cold? I am sorry, Eliott, so sorry.'

'It's okay, Dad,' he says, but I can tell it's really not.

'You got there in the end,' I say, turning round again to look at him. 'You'll know if you do it again.'

'That's not going to happen,' he says.

WINTER

6: Fixations

Winter is setting in, though I think I'm in denial. Frozen leaves lie on the morning grass, their serrated edges sharpened with rigidity. The first holly berries have appeared at the bottom of the garden, blush-coloured now, but suggesting Christmas all the same. It's too soon, I'm not ready to be boxed in just yet.

After school I persuade Eliott and Jem to come on a walk to the woods – the days are getting shorter but there will still be daylight now for the next few weeks. Some days it rains and they are confined to the school building till home-time. Eliott skids through the mud and the slimy paper mache of brown, wet leaves like a newly released otter from an animal shelter. Nettles are still around in the woods, ankle deep and dying back. But self-heal, or prunella, is hanging on, its indigo-blue flowers out of place among the other languishing plants. The North American Nuxalk tribe used the roots and plant itself to make a tea. It was said to heighten their observational powers; I think I could do with some this winter. A squirrel startles me as it runs across its branch infrastructure above, causing the few remaining leaves to fall to the woodland floor beneath.

The children's faces have some colour again and they select weapons from the ground, fallen branches to thwack at the remaining undergrowth. But Jemima is so slow, the school day has taken it out of her and pink clouds are already passing in front of an early moon. We keep turning back for her, taking turns to call her on. Annie and Maddy will be home before us and wondering where we are.

Back in the village, starlings mimic the sounds of computer games on their high wires, loitering as always around The Old Bakery where friends live with their teenage children. I suspect the birds have sat close to an open window once or twice. We can see our house now, the lights shining from every window – they have to be home, we decide as we walk along the pavement. Annie is in the kitchen and tosses her phone on the counter as I close the door.

'Hi love, what's the matter?' I say, giving her a kiss.

She kisses the air in a distracted, agitated way. 'They've stopped my Snapchat.'

'Why?' I ask, filling the kettle. 'There must be a reason, you haven't broken any rules?'

'Like I'd do that. No, they say a third party set up is no longer allowed.'

The rain is hammering now and I concede. 'I'm coming tomorrow,' I say. 'Maddy's turn, EJ. So how's your special torch?'

'It's good but my thumb ached using it. Yours is better.'

Walking out of the wood, I'm starting to feel wet on the elbows. 'Let's go through the teenage wood,' I say, 'It won't be so bad in there, the canopy's denser.' That was wishful thinking. I unzip my coat and tuck the night vision inside – it is meant to be waterproof, but I don't want to risk it. Now the rain is coming down the back of my neck and I pull my coat across me. As we walk along the field I can feel the wet soaking into my jeans, at the back of my knees and then all over. So Rupert had a point. I know he did, but they did wimp out a little too quickly.

Once home, I drip my way up the stairs and peel off my trousers – they cling to me with devotion, I think my legs have swollen with the cold. I trample them into a heap on the bedroom floor and fling open the wardrobe doors. My jumper and t-shirt are wet through, and I remove more layers than I'd thought I'd need to. My feet start to tingle, then burn; I didn't know I was that cold. I look at my reflection in the long mirror: my hair has taken on the appearance of a sheep's fleece, a mass of frizz and no curl. I smirk at the sight of myself, then look away – that's not even worth tackling tonight, and I want to be with the children.

For every badger sighting there are a few failed attempts, though the last success story is already weeks ago. I pull back the curtains and look out of the window before going downstairs – the rain is easing off now, perhaps we should have stayed out after all. I enjoy the feeling of warm, dry clothes and land myself on a sofa with Eliott and Jem. 'Fun was it?' says Annie, raising an eyebrow.

Jem hugs me her forgiveness and climbs onto my lap.

'My turn tomorrow,' says Maddy to Eliott.

'But we didn't get to see anything, we were only there a few minutes.'

'That's how it goes, little bro.' She throws a cushion at him and smiles.

Later, as I head down to our own private watching place, I hear a flock of geese flying low across the garden. They pass over so quickly I can't see them, even with the torch, but their comical chatter lingers in the air. I stuff the torch in my pocket and wander with the monocular to my face, carefully so as not to disturb anything, or lose my balance in a new badger-made rut. As soon as I'm there I can see two sets of flashing eyes. I stand very still. The eyes come and go four times – *finally I'm going to see something* – then a flash of colour in front of the trees. I press the infrared button so that I can see everything: it's a fox. He starts to eat the peanuts and I move the night vision camera over him. He's seen me and flees. That's what I wanted, at least I now know not to use the infrared if a badger comes close. I've wondered whether wildlife can see infrared for a while. There is some debate about it, but if a fox has responded in this way, what's to say a badger would be any different? The manufacturers want you to believe it's invisible to them, but I'm sure it's not the case.

I think about the fox and wonder where he's gone. I feel pleased and then guilty. Why am I being selective here? What's my motivation? I suppose I think the badgers are less likely to come if he scoffs the lot, but is that really a problem? I think it's been too long since I've seen them and I'm starting to go mildly insane.

I hear something squealing after that – it sounds like something small in great pain – has the fox caught a rabbit? It's a horrible noise, full of suffering. One long high-pitched note that turns a corner as it ends, perhaps in one final writhe – an unpleasant death for sure. Would it have survived if I'd let the fox eat the peanuts? I'll never know.

I talk to Rupert about the noise when I'm inside. He's in the snug with his laptop on, cocooned in his own little world. I don't want to intrude on his calm but feel I must. 'A strange question, but have you ever heard a rabbit die?'

'I might have, in my misspent youth.' He looks up and flashes a guilty smile, and then back at the screen.

'But from a gunshot, presumably? They're silent creatures anyway, and that would be instant.'

I explain to him what I've heard.

He looks at me with an apologetic expression and talks quietly. 'I went out with some local lads once, ferreting. The ferret brought the rabbit out.' He's chewing on his lip, though he's probably not even aware of it.

'How did it die?'

'It wasn't me that did it. This bloke we were with wrung its neck. It kind of screams.'

I'm reading about Secret World before I go to sleep, the wildlife rescue centre in Somerset, but my mind is still on the fox. Is there any food I can put down that won't interest him, that will only attract the badgers? But soon my attention is caught by a statistic – a dog fox will on average live for 15 months in the wild, a vixen for 18. I'm feeling bad about my selective care for wildlife. What makes me think I have the right to discriminate?

Some would say that wildlife is exactly that and we should leave it to its own devices, or risk upsetting the sensitive balance as creatures muddle on through together. But is giving a little helping hand really so bad? There is the old advice about putting out water for birds in hot weather, and breaking ice for them in the cold. To do none of this would be neglectful, so where do we draw the line? The badger cull wades right into the middle of this debate: data from 2007 suggests culling badgers brings with it a rise in fox numbers, which is damaging for ground-nesting birds and hares. And then there is the loss of hedgehogs nationwide, with a possible increase in cull zones – could badgers be responsible for this? The answer, it seems, can be found in a badger's business; a recent study conducted in Poland found hedgehog in 'fewer than 1% of faecal samples', leading The Wildlife Trusts to state there is 'little evidence to suggest that badgers are the principle driver of UK hedgehog decline'. But if the data was indisputable would there be a case?

I have to conclude that Secret World is right in its acceptance of all wildlife, for every other argument I consider seems forced. I try to picture what's going on at the bottom of the garden as I put out the light, and give the foxes a mental welcome.

Maddy taps on the door gently the next morning. She must have seen the glow of the bedside light from under the door. 'Look at this,' she says, carrying her laptop through and standing over me while I sit up in bed. *'This top quality, wonderfully soft real Badger Hair Shaving Brush –'* her eyebrows are moving expressively as she reads – 'is reasonably priced for luxurious badger hair and has a rigid case to protect the brush when travelling.' She looks up at me with betrayal in her eyes, unable to comprehend that the world could be so cruel. 'Is it legal?'

'It must be in some places round the world,' I say.

I'll leave her to discover for herself some of the other badger products out there. I'm sure she will in due course. There are badger items to be found at The Dapper Dead, a shop owned by Emma Willats, a vegan taxidermist who makes all her sporrans from roadkill and finds no conflict with her beliefs. 'The way I look at it is that if something has been killed for me then that's wrong,' she says. 'But if it's something that's died naturally or been run over then we should try to preserve it in some way.'

A badger sporran with badger face sells for £750. And for me, it's hard to feel anything other than unease as those two black beady eyes stare back at you. I don't see how they can be appreciated in quite the same way when they are dead, and I wonder what the intention would be of the wearer – to win admiration or the reflected glory of a ferocious fighter, when he is, of course, provoked? The shop's Twitter feed makes interesting reading: 'I've cut my hands so much doing taxidermy I'm pretty sure my blood is now 50% human, 25% Fox and 25% badger. Do I get a superpower?'

Badger teeth were once used as buttons in Scottish ceremonial dress, and can be sourced online with a bit of searching, although you may end up with the teeth or claws of an American honey badger. Tie pins made of badger penis bones were a known gift in Victorian times, presented by a bride's father to son-in-law, then a symbol of fertility and a male equivalent to the old new borrowed and blue, though not as commonplace. At least Maddy won't be coming across these items by accident.

The school week begins again and Rupert has left for Dover with Annie and Maddy. I clear away the breakfast things and begin on another round of packed lunches.

'Jem's got my school fleece on,' says Eliott, coming into the kitchen.

Jemima is on badger duty when she's home, and places her toy badger in a shoe box, which she rests on top of the radiator in the family room. 'You have to give them water and keep them warm,' she says.

It's dark and I take the stairs in slow motion, rolling my foot, waiting to hear if it creaks before transferring my weight. There's a pile of clutter near the bottom. I make it down in near silence and hope Jemima is still asleep. The dog sits up in his bed under the staircase and stretches his neck, keen for a greeting.

'Hi, Tyn,' I whisper, stroking his head before lifting the door latch into the kitchen. Five-fifty says the kitchen clock. It's warm in here already and the washing is dry on the ceiling, hanging from an airer on one of the beams.

There's noise on the stairs. Jemima finds me and presents me with her wide gappy grin.

'It's not up time,' I say to her.

'I can't sleep.'

'I'll be going back to bed myself in a minute,' I say as she heads back up the stairs. That's a lie but I just need some time alone.

She pauses on the stair. 'My wrist still hurts.' She fell off her bike into some nettles yesterday, and sting marks covered her hand, wrist and the side of her face. The dog injured his paw at much the same time and limped home, Jemima wailing most of the way as she held my hand and Maddy pushed her bike. It didn't help that she'd had to abandon a handful of chestnuts that she'd collected underneath Churchill's tree – they were way too small and best left for the squirrels.

'You'll be okay,' I say, reiterating the mantra from yesterday. 'Don't wake Maddy.'

It's quiet again and I grab a notebook and pen. I first saw the time at 4.30 this morning, thinking it must nearly be time to get up. I know I'm anxious about Dad, but I don't want to talk about it in front of the kids. He has further tests this week – an MRI tomorrow and a bone scan on Thursday. I wish they both could tell me how they feel, but I suppose they are already in 'positive thinking mode', an approach to 'outwit the cancer', from what I've read. I don't believe in it myself. I've got to stop doing my own research online, it's not helping.

There's something new on the dresser – Rupert has finished a beech-wood bowl for them. I walk over and pick it up. It's heavier than it looks and curvaceous, like a clay pot that's been squashed down, but altogether perfect. Their garden hosts three large copper beech trees, giants from my childhood. Back then, the tallest held a rope swing and we'd launch ourselves from the top of the steep bank, feeling like we were flying over the sheer drop below. It was rigged up by my brother Paul, a tree climber almost from birth. Now he's a tree surgeon and keeps an eye on them, occasionally lopping a branch to allow some more light into the bungalow.

On our last visit to Suffolk Dad had told me that the trees were showing signs of stress. 'There'll come a time when they have to come down and it could be in my lifetime.' I couldn't quite believe it. Paul has planted a Himalayan birch in front of the middle one, a lame excuse for a tree, spindly and pathetic in the shadows of the towering beech. He hopes it will be well established by the time the beeches fail.

In Celtic mythology the beech is said to be the 'tree of wishes', and wishing rods were once tied to its branches. I have wishes attached to those old trees, but I've said enough. I'm finding myself way too preoccupied with Dad's health and need the badgers to distract me. I have decided I need a filming device for our badger at home, that will trip in when anything comes close. This way I should be able to identify wildlife visiting the garden, and hopefully get to know it. Our garden's central position in the village does mean wildlife is cautious about visiting too early, but hopefully this will give me some idea about when and where to wait. A Bushnell NatureView Camera is put on order, a Christmas present chosen and ordered by me, a necessity for my mental well-being of course.

December arrives with a blast of cold air. We're indoors more and it's almost dark when the girls arrive back from secondary. Our neighbours Lisa and Mike are home with their new baby. Maddy has sewn some felt booties and Annie is now baking them a chocolate cake. I leave her to it and head down to my intended spot for the nature cam, torch in hand. It smells strongly of fox here now, it did this morning too, some marking of territory has been going on.

I have worked out that the digging down here in Eliott's pit isn't the work of the badgers, but a fox. This has to be disputed ground. It did look like a beginner's effort and we'd decided that a badger cub had been putting in some practice. Since then we've been finding the hole blocked and then unblocked, with lumps of chalk left to one side, and now I can see peanuts inside, stashed away for the depth of winter. This is typical fox behaviour. I can't fault his resourcefulness – the supply isn't going to run out, but he doesn't know that. I'm aware that at least one badger is taking them, too, and I want more than ever to see it. I think a few late nights are in order, and perhaps a sneaky test run of the cam before Christmas Day.

Dad has his MRI this morning. I compose a text to him in my head while driving back from school first thing – ridiculous really, but I don't want to come across as too worried, or as neglectful either. I imagine Mum alone in the waiting room, holding onto his keys, coins and phone and I start to cry.

I do text, and I phone later in the week when it's all over. Dad is out playing snooker, but it's Mum who really needs the chat anyway. 'The bone scan was fine,' she says. 'A quiet machine, it just passes over and under you. The MRI was altogether different. I was waiting for Dad and this annoying idiot came out, they should've led him out of a different doorway. "The noise in there's like a jumbo jet right up close. I hope you're not claustrophobic," he said. Some poor lady was waiting. "Well yes, I am a little bit," she said to him.'

There's some vulnerability in Mum's voice when I asked how she is with it all and the sadness stays with me. I guess it will remain until we hear the results next week. I start baking for the primary school fair, there's a cake tax tomorrow in exchange for the children being allowed to wear their own clothes. We can buy it all back at the fair, but this time I'm making a huge surplus for the family. I'd rather not go as there's no room to breathe, but the children really want to. We should be glad it's still happening. Ofsted arrived this week with little warning and decorations morning was postponed. Then came a letter in Jemima's bookbag: 'Father Christmas will not be able to meet the children during the day on Friday due to the inspection but he has agreed to come back into school on Monday.' Don't let them be seen to be having any fun, let's just put life on hold and pretend that this is normal.

The weekend arrives with the first real frost of the year. I watch from the bathroom window as Jemima runs into the garden without a coat, excitement level equal to finding several inches of snow. I head downstairs – the door is wide open and winter chill fills the room.

'Come in, shut the door!'

She's back with a bundle of frozen leaves, 'Look, they're all hard! Look at this one!'

'Put them outside, they won't stay like that.'

I open her book-bag again for the remains of Friday. 'Your child is an angel,' reads a note from the teacher. 'Please find the appropriate costume for next week.'

Rupert and I make it to the woods in the evening. Dusk is so early that now the only opportunity is at weekends. The grass is hard underfoot with just a crisp layer on the surface, like it's been set with hairspray. We step into the enclosure to wait. Rupert climbs the fallen tree that I lean against. I look up to see how it's all changed from last time – the trees have lost most of their leaves and the canopy is an angry scribble, a jumble of harsh black lines. There is just a small gap that's still framed with leaves, and the moonlight is coming through.

A young badger scoots around the edge of the enclosure, squeaking as it goes. We can't see it but I'm certain that's what I'm hearing. It sounds het up and a little desperate, its verbal outpouring at times shrill and plaintive. This is the usual sound a cub makes when parted from its mother, but surely she can't be far away, not at this hour. There is a different edge to it this time, it's not a cub at play as I think it has been in the past. The Santa train on the village railway is sounding its horn, blasting its optimism for miles around. Children will be queuing on the platform, sure that this Santa is the real deal, that he's worth the wait. The carriages will be lit with fairy lights and a man in a bear costume will walk up and down, entertaining the children as he goes. I just hope Santa can remember the children's names this year and doesn't look quite so fed up.

The cub is out of earshot now; he has either returned to the sett or accepted his solitude. There is little activity tonight and I don't want to give in, but it's so cold out here. I look up at Rupert and nod and he climbs back down. The moon is low over the trees as we walk across the field, full and golden, like a heavy Christmas decoration that hangs low. I'm reminded of the old glass patinaed baubles that would grace my grandparents' tree. It is the full moon of December, the Oak Moon or Long Night's Moon, said to be a time for 'hope and healing' – the idea being that soon the days will get longer, and by implication it will all get better from here.

I wonder if part of the moon's beauty is its permanence, its enduring presence through time. It must be why some are driven to want to touch it. Perhaps that's why I'm drawn to watch badgers too – they are a continuous, abiding part of my story, though in some ways they will always be unattainable: we are watching them on their terms, not ours. The pet dog can be stroked whenever I choose, and he receives lots of attention, but that's effortless, acceptance easily won. A badger might decide to watch us, may be just a little curious about what we are, but there it ends. It's hard to push beyond that, unless they are being rescued and rehabilitated. Perhaps that's why some people stray into infidelity, just to see what lies beyond the ordinary, to see if the unreachable may in fact be within their grasp.

The days pass and I prepare myself for news of Dad. I'm out to collect the children again, and the weather isn't exactly encouraging optimism. An uncompromising wind has stripped almost every tree of its leaves, even the resistant beech. Only in the hedges does that umber glow remain. Some movement up ahead – a grey horse is troubled by the car and tries to buck its rider. I stop and wait for her to gain control. She's flustered and the horse is looking like he'd rather be running free, that he might just bolt. A thick band of silver tinsel is looped around his neck from a more obliging moment. He calms now and she takes him into a driveway to let me pass.

We arrive home to be greeted by the chickens, as usual. Eliott shuts the gate and chases them away from the car. One is missing: Ruby, the leader of the flock, a feisty red hen. I find a crust indoors to lead them back down to their house – they usually wait on our back step and peck at the glass door at this time of day, as if asking for their evening routine. The chicken doesn't appear. I shut the others away and search the garden, then walk up to the house and around the front. Eliott comes outside and says he'll take over. 'It's alright Mum, you go inside.'

He's back in minutes. 'Well, my detective skills have worked it out. It's not looking good, Mum.' He's standing in the doorway with such a serious expression, trying hard not to cry. 'See, there was this smell of fox poo and I followed it. He'd got her, there's a pile of her orange feathers.'

'Hang on, I'm coming.'

He leads me into Jemima's 'forest yard', the area where we see wildlife come and go. I pull back a trailing bramble and place it in the fork of a tree before pushing my way through the holly bushes. There in the far corner lie the remains of the much-loved chicken.

I tell the girls when they're home.

'Really?' says Annie. She looks a little shocked.

'Don't tell Jemima, not yet.'

Maddy is crying.

'It's a *chicken*,' says Rupert.

'Don't be so ridiculous,' Annie says to her.

'You thought she was a bully,' I tell her, my voice quiet and low.

'Yeah, but still–'

'Did you find Ruby?' asks Jem after supper.

How exactly *do* you explain this one? 'Eliott did. The fox had come in the day. I'm sorry, love.'

She starts to sob and sits down in the armchair that's too big for her, hand over her eyes. Annie is singing the *Circle of Life*, altogether lost on Jemima but not the rest of them.

'She was my favourite chicken.'

'I thought that was Amy,' I say unhelpfully. Well it's true. Amy lets her pick her up and follows her everywhere.

'No, Ruby was.'

'She was mine too.'

A good time for the Advent house I think. Annie hides a bar of chocolate for me and writes a clue that she puts in the small drawer. They find it no trouble and the tears subside.

Chocolate consumed, Jemima is back in the chair, crying quietly.

'Do you want to sit on my lap, Jem?' asks Maddy.

'We could always call one of the other chickens Ruby,' says Eliott.

'And how's that going to help?' I say.

I decide to ring Dad when Jemima's gone to bed. I figure that even with waiting room delays, they must be home by now. The phone is engaged – is it off the hook? It's gone eight o'clock, the appointment was at five.

The phone rings as I stand above it. It's Dad. He starts to tell me about how they were there late, how they thought they'd be locked in the hospital, miss the last Park and Ride bus out of town.

'Did you get your results?' I say.

He says that it's treatable, contained. I'm shocked and surprised both at once. *Early prostate cancer usually causes no problems...* that's been going round in my head for days. They have accepted that he won't have surgery – he has glaucoma and is worried about losing his sight, but there are other options to consider. He'll be around for a good few years yet. What a relief. I know that I've inherited the worry gene – if it can happen it probably will.

Jem finds me downstairs the next morning, fixing the tree lights. 'Look, I've got them working again.'

She comes over to sit next to me on the floor. 'Mum, cos it's the dress rehearsal today, should I pretend to be happy even though I'm sad?'

'Yes, you must. You don't need to be sad though. Why are you sad?'

Like I don't know. We've had the chickens as long as she can remember and they're a part of her existence.

'She could just be lost in the garden,' she says.

'Come on,' I say to her. 'Let's go and see if the badgers have been.'

7: *Welcome guests*

Maddy has a day trip to France and I'm awake early, listening to a gale whip round the house. The ferries won't be running. She'll be fine. They'll know whether it's safe, and besides, it's not far. She can't go. It's ridiculous. What kind of kill-joy am I? She'd always remember if I said no.

I must get up, we have to be at the school by six o'clock.

'It's okay, Mum,' she tells me when I wake her. 'We're going through the tunnel.'

Annie's artwork is all over the table, and I stand in the kitchen, eating bowls of cereal and drinking too-hot tea. I get Maddy there safely, driving at forty on the dual-carriageway. Girls have started to congregate outside the school entrance. 'Don't forget to use your French,' I say as the door slams in the wind.

'Where's Maddy?' says Annie at breakfast.

'On her way to France.'

'Ha!' she replies, stirring sugar into her tea. 'In this?'

'She's taking the tunnel.'

'That must be so weird. Can you really see the sea-bed? I don't think I'd like it.'

Even Eliott is laughing.

'What's funny?'

'You're in a train,' says Rupert. 'You can't see the sea at all.'

'Well that's just dumb. Anyway, I didn't really think–'

'Yes you did,' says Eliott.

She says she's preoccupied. It's her art mock today and she's ready to paint an A2 sized portrait of Jemima from an 'in-character' photo she had to take – blue dungarees, red coat, gappy teeth showing through a wide grin as she stands beneath the willow tree. Jemima's not smiling now though, and mentions the chicken again.

'You eat chicken,' Annie tells her.

'But I don't want to any more,' she whispers in my ear.

'Do you think Maddy will bring you back a present?' asks Annie. 'I reckon she'll have bought one for everyone and nothing for herself.'

The bed-time story doesn't help. Jemima can't quite believe it. I'm reading her *Charlotte's Web* – her request – and the old sheep has news for Wilbur the pig: "There's a regular conspiracy around here to kill you at Christmastime."

'It'll end happily,' I tell her. 'Don't worry.' But right now the world is a shocking place.

I leave Rupert to deal with it – he's the meat-eater – and take

Eliott to his last ever Cubs meeting. He's quiet. 'What's the matter?' I say, as we drive past the wood yard.

'I'm not sure I want to leave.'

'Tell them,' I say. 'It's really up to you.'

'But I'll be too old if I stay much longer. They say there's a waiting list and I think I'm holding some little kid up.'

Annie had wanted to go late-night shopping, but with Maddy and Eliott to collect later she's persuaded to do some virtual shopping instead. Soon we're side by side on a sofa with a laptop each and she leads me around New Look, Accessorize and the Body Shop. I favourite her choices and let her finish the chocolates that I'd shared with my students, and even give her the smallest glass of wine. I think she's appeased. Maddy returns with French mints to share – they're voted 'boring' – and some nougat for Christmas. Eliott is collected last and I ask if he's said anything. 'Balloo shook me by the left hand,' he says. 'Oh, well, that's that then,' I say.

We continue to find badger evidence in the garden, but they don't seem to be out whenever I'm loitering with night-vision. We find more pieces of unearthed china – presumably from the days before rubbish collections – bits of unrecognizable plastic, and green furled sycamore shoots. This morning it's a piece of old brown teapot spout, and some half-eaten peanuts with teeth marks; something had startled them for sure. This has been happening a lot lately, and we compare it to the chocolate game, where children throw on hat, scarf and gloves to eat chocolate with a knife and fork. The object of the game is to pile in as much as possible until someone throws a six with the dice. The badgers have as long as it takes before something worries them. Perhaps it's down to the neighbour a few doors along who's been building his workshop in the dark.

I lift the lid on the chicken's nesting box. Daisy looks up at me, unimpressed that she's been disturbed. I feel as if I've walked in on someone on the loo and place the lid down with care. I find I'm doing a chicken head-count all the time at the moment.

I've received a text from Mum. Dad's had a serious nosebleed again and went to hospital at two in the morning. Sometimes they won't stop and he needs medical intervention. Perhaps his blood pressure is up and he's feeling stressed.

Then a call from the primary school. Eliott has passed out whilst visiting a retirement home with his class. Can I come and collect him? I find him looking red-eyed and paler than his white-blond hair. 'I started to sway and I couldn't stop it,' he says. 'I remember singing the first bit of It was on a Starry Night, but that's it.'

The female teaching assistants are flocking round him and send me off to find his bag and coat. 'You can put your feet up, Eliott, watch lots of telly. Wish I could.'

'We did have trouble rousing him,' one says to me in a hushed voice. 'We carried him through and put his legs up, we had to slap him on the face several times.'

He tells me he's glad to be home before his big sisters – secondary school finishes at lunchtime today. Soon he has a fever and I'm feeling relieved. A bird is singing from the rooftop above his window as he sleeps, and a short poem by Oliver Hertford comes in to my mind:

> I heard a bird sing
> In the dark of December.
> A magical thing
> And sweet to remember.
>
> "We are nearer to Spring
> Than we were in September,"
> I heard a bird sing
> In the dark of December.
>
> *I Heard a Bird Sing.*

I'm trying to keep hold of this little bird the next day, when Rupert is determined to do the Christmas holidays visit to his sister's in Ross-on-Wye. Eliott has the back row of the car to himself and is looking decidedly rough. The girls are fussing over him – especially Maddy. There's nothing like a bit of illness to stir family affection. Mistletoe balls are high in the branches like nests, the fields receding in varying shades of brown. 'Are we nearly there, yet?' asks Jemima. It's going to be a long journey – we're still in Kent.

Eliott rests for most of the journey and doesn't seem to mind that we've taken him away from home. In Ross he's less bothered by the abundance of girl cousins than usual – four more than he has to deal with at home – and finds quiet corners for himself while chaos reigns in the rest of the house. Perhaps being the odd one out makes him stronger and is teaching him self-reliance. Before long he's seeking out company and eating again.

Yet as Eliott begins to brighten, I receive another text from Mum – Dad has been back to hospital in an ambulance. Soon we're home and Eliott is almost back to normal, but Dad is getting progressively worse. He clocks up four major bleeds before Christmas, and several ambulance rides and cauterizations. They are worn out with it all, and concerned about why it's happening – could it be related to the cancer, I try to ask them, but the question isn't getting through. More blood tests and appointments.

At last Christmas comes, and with it the nature cam I've been resisting bringing down from the top of the wardrobe for weeks. Having set it up on Christmas Day, I surface early on Boxing Day morning, out to retrieve it while it's still dark, the frozen grass sparkling in the torchlight as I head down the garden.

"Let me see, let me see,' says Jem as I come in through the back door.

'Hold on,' I tell her, and we sit down on the top kitchen step together. 'Wow, that was easy,' I say as we access the clips on the small integral screen straight away. The dog climbs out of his bed and nuzzles his face in between us. There's footage of him chasing something away. Then neighbourhood cats taking a turn.

'Oh Jem, it looks like we've missed most of the action, we'd placed the cam just a little too high up the tree. The peanuts have gone, though.'

I set the cam at the perfect height later and I know it's going to be a success this time. There's lots to scan over. Robins. Mice. Blackbirds, thrushes, dunnocks. But no badgers – the memory card runs out as the wind sets it off repeatedly. This isn't surprising. We woke this morning to a crashing noise: one of our fence panels had lifted out of its footing and landed in the middle of the road.

I clear the memory card and reset the device. And then, the following morning, badgers. Frame after frame. I sit down to play the footage and Jemima joins me again. Eliott rushes downstairs to see what all the whooping is about. 'Look at this,' I say to him. 'It's a male.'

'Badger boy,' he says, coming to stand behind me at the table.

'*Wilbur,*' says Jemima with authority. 'He's massive.'

'The biggest badger for miles around,' says Eliott.

'And in our garden!' says Jem.

'He needs to bring his friends,' I say. 'He looks old. Are you sitting on the table, Jem?'

'Yes,' she answers with a huge grin.

Wilbur is so named because Jem is reading *Charlotte's Web,* and the needy pig has won her affection. I'm not sure how much maternal instinct will kick in over this badger, set to be her latest animal obsession. Wilbur the badger has scars above both eyes – probably from old fights, and some on both sides of his neck – perhaps a previous snare injury. His face is impossibly broad, exaggeratedly masculine and in the shape of an old bicycle saddle that widens out towards the top. He has leaves hanging from his undercarriage as he makes his way through the peanutted path, stopping to munch every few paces. It's 4.10 am and he stays for over half-an-hour.

It's Wilbur again the following night, New Year's Eve – or should I say New Year's Day, by the time he reaches us. Fireworks were going off in the village from 9 o'clock and the badgers would have felt sett-bound for hours, but at 5.27 a.m. he appears. Will he always come alone? An old badger like him must be head of a clan, and won't be living by himself. I imagine they're all out there, visiting the same places at different stages through the night. In the footage I've watched online badgers often feast in groups, and I look forward to seeing several come at once. I get the feeling we're the after-dinner-mints-course of the moving supper party. But perhaps it's better to be an afterthought – at least they're not depending on us.

'What are you going to do with this after a few days?' asks Rupert. 'You can't store it all and it's looking a bit repetitive.'

Doesn't he get that it's just fascinating? I tell him that I want to see whether there are more of them coming to us, to see when they arrive and leave and how they behave. I wonder if we can tell them apart. I may move the camera to a different spot at some point, but this is so amazing. The unfamiliar becoming familiar. The truth behind all those hairs we found – the one we measured that indicated an old badger – the digging, the sloshing sounds in amongst the trees through the summer, though I'd only once seen one emerge.

Wilbur is our most regular visitor, although not the only one. In less than a week two more have appeared. We start to tell just from their arrival who's who – Wilbur shirks the wire metal fence from over his head, like he's tossing aside a duvet. The others struggle, and so I've dug the hole deeper as we've witnessed their trouble. A long-faced badger has been named Georgie (we're not sure of the gender yet), and the third, called Robin (for the same reason) is distinctive for its strong, neat markings. Everything's in black and white, but we can see Wilbur is wearing a paler coat in his older years. These three are easy to tell apart, though they are never seen together. One evening both Wilbur and Robin visit, with fifteen minutes between them. Wilbur is the one who's out latest, sometimes going home at nearly six in the morning.

The badgers don't come every night. Strong wind and rain keep them away, and then there's the job of gathering the peanuts so the chickens don't stray into the wilderness. The weather keeps the fox away, too. He has been filmed several times, and now I've seen him up close he's forgiven – by me, anyway. 'He's evil,' says Eliott.

'Come and look,' I say. 'I don't think he is.' There's an innocence that resides in his wide, open eyes. At times he closes them to eat, a sure sign of contentment. He's a young one, sharp in his appearance and mannerisms, wary of what may be around. He looks into the trees and all about him. There is tension in his brush, held out straight behind him rather than at ease, or even wagging as the badgers' tails sometimes appear to do. He approaches the old Wensleydale and apricot cheese with caution and backs off before consuming the peanuts again. Soon they are stuck in his teeth and he grimaces and opens his mouth wide, his ears flat against his head as he concentrates. He hears something and he's off, the plush velvet legs now more than decoration.

'He's gone,' I say.

'Good,' says Eliott.

'He's only doing what he's been programmed to do. Surviving like the rest of us.'

Term is underway again, and a quick flit through the new footage is now part of the before-school routine. The full-moon may be deterring them, I think. And perhaps Rupert's bonfire. He burnt the wind-damaged fence panels with the old ones that lined the badgers' wooded area. It no longer looks like a shaded tunnel down there and I objected. 'I wasn't going to burn them all one at a time, just for the badgers.'

'I think it may be keeping them away.'

'I doubt it. We can always put something else up.'

I wonder if they hear the fox sometimes too, or another badger sloshing, and feel it's not their turn. It's the start of a cold spell and the first day of dodgy roads – on the school run we pass two cars that have collided just past the wood yard. I don't know if the accident happened by the stable, or if they've moved to one side. Jem hears the roads are dangerous and tries to stop arguing with me, but it's hard. She wants to wear her green coat like her best friend Isabella's today. 'But yours is too small,' I told her as we left. I checked the label – age four to five. The next ten minutes were spent with her explaining to me why she's right and I'm wrong. 'You can't chuck it out,' she says now. 'It's not yours to throw away.'

'Your red one is lovely,' I say, steering us out of a skid. 'Just be quiet now.'

She runs into school without a kiss – I follow her in, I'm still holding her book-bag besides. But at the end of the school day she launches herself at me so I nearly fall over, and gives me a big enthusiastic embrace.

We're blocked in near the school, but Jemima, Eliott and friends are just pleased to be free again and the car rocks with their excitement. I doubt they've even noticed we're still here. I wait for the school mum who's had the new CD for Christmas and wants to share it with us all. Doors slam. Ignition. Her music sounds and we're off.

'You've been shopping,' says Eliott.

'It was Maddy's last day of holiday.'

The boys are all battling with Jemima to talk the loudest. And so the routine starts again. A guy was scrubbing snowflake transfers from a shop window in town today and we must take our decorations down tonight – when these two are in bed; perhaps they won't notice.

There is blood on the nature cam the next morning. I don't want Jemima to see anything gruesome and vet the footage first. It's the fox as I'd suspected, but he doesn't look wounded, or have blood dripping from his jowls. He must have had his fill of rabbit or such like, and brushed the cam on his way past. Then some windy nights, and an absence of foxes and badgers. Mice are thrown by the wind and bounce off each other like hares, high off the ground. Or are they just hyped by the wind like dogs and horses, its wildness touching them? Perhaps it's both.

I check on our summer badger watching spot with Jem at the weekend. All is quiet, though the sett looks vulnerable now the vegetation has died back. The holes are so exposed on the dog-walking route that you wonder how the badgers survive. Jem stamps over the crop to admire the hole in the field. Tyn is pulling on the leash and I step between the rows of green shoots with him. 'It's huge, Mum! Look, you can see right inside! Do you think they can hear me?'

'I bet they can. Come on, let's let them sleep. They can probably hear us stomping across their ceiling right now.'

We walk to the teenage wood and step over the fallen tree that forms a threshold, wound about with ivy, like the work of an over-zealous spider. This area seems to have been abandoned as a youth hang-out for now and the holes are not obvious from a distance. Rupert thinks I should set up the cam here for a night but I worry it'll get stolen. They start at around £150, more, if like me, you want the red light to be invisible to wildlife.

The wind is penetrating and we turn to go. Jemima wants to walk along the exposed field edge. She lingers behind and keeps calling me back: 'Look, this looks like a really small horseshoe print.'

'Yes, you're right.'

'This footprint here, what is it? Is it a badger?'

'No, just a dog. *Come on.* My ears hurt. Let's go home.'

'You can borrow my earmuffs if you like. They will fit, I've still got my hat.'

'No, you're okay.'

The dog is excitable now as he sees a spaniel running towards him. We see flashes of our friends Neil and Mandy through the trees and meet where the field runs out.

'Hi Caroline. Meet Dixie.'

Dixie is very well-behaved and stands close to Neil, her back to Tyn as he leaps up and muddies his trousers. She is predominantly white, but sensible enough to cope with that.

'How long have you had her?'

'Just a few weeks. She's seven already. Her owner moved into a retirement flat in Canterbury.'

I feel the need to explain Tyn's lead. 'He knows where all the badger holes are and pulls like crazy.'

'It's in his nature,' says Neil. 'You can't blame him.'

'I think he'd come off worse.'

'I don't know, could be a close call,' laughs Neil.

The cold weather is taking its toll. Eliott goes outside to feed the guinea pigs and comes in to tell me that Madeline's is dead.

'Can I see?' says Jemima.

'Best not to,' I say. Last time it happened she went outside for the burial. She was so traumatized that I had to explain to her teacher why she was upset the next morning.

Eliott's eyes are watering and I tell him we'll sort it all out later. I hate dealing with dead creatures. When they're at school I walk down the garden to let out the chickens, and force myself to look in on the female guinea pig run. She'd taken herself into a quiet corner, tucking herself in beside a large piece of wood, apparently a kind of purpose-made death chamber. It will need to be sorted before Maddy is home from school.

Rupert returns home from work at ten – he was ill yesterday and had gone back too soon. Apparently the female staff were cross with him. 'You need at least two days for a sick bug,' he was told. He'll sort the guinea pig. He encourages them to have all these little creatures and knows how I feel about dealing with them. I won't clean them out either – 'I have the house to muck out,' I tell them.

Eliott is glad the younger female guinea pigs are still okay. He has an entrepreneurial plan: in the summer he bought two male guinea pigs with his birthday money – Bilbo and Frodo Baggins.

He'll breed them in the spring (should be interesting) and will sell them on for £5 each. That's the theory anyway.

The badger filming continues, with a success at least once every other night. I'm just beginning to realize that Wilbur is in fact very old. In the latest footage he places his rear on the floor to eat and seems quite lethargic. It's twenty-past-five in the morning and he's probably been foraging all night, but there must be more to it. He even manages to eat lying down for a few minutes, paws in front of him, stretching his neck as he reaches for the peanuts. As he walks around his bottom keeps dropping to the floor, as if he's lacking strength in his legs. Rupert suggests I buy him some cat food or something a bit more hearty. 'He's an old boy. We need to look after him.'

'I think the peanuts are good enough.'

'I suppose we don't want to encourage rats, anyway,' he says.

I'm alone now, watching the last of the new clips on my laptop before deleting what's on the card and setting the device for the night. Annie comes in to join me. 'Is that in our garden?' she says, taking a look at the screen.

'It is, usual place, down at the bottom.'

'You should deck it out down there as badger heaven.' No sarcastic smile even. I read her face closely but there's not a trace.

'What do you mean?'

'I don't know, what do they like?'

I know she loves interior design programmes, but for the badgers? She wouldn't like to think she's taking an interest, but she really is. If only for a few brief seconds, and not in front of anyone else.

The next night Rupert asks me for a badger update while we're all eating supper.

'Well, we had two last night. Wilbur came first, and then a second one, the younger one the kids are calling–'

'What, do they have names?' Annie has woken up. 'You'll see one dead out on the road and you'll say, *Oh, no, it's Wilbur.*' A dramatic, batty voice now takes over. 'It's *Wilbur!* I can tell from the markings. *Oh, Wilbur.*'

I smile at her and get up to clear the table. Rupert follows me into the kitchen. 'Wilbur might be an evil badger,' he says. 'He might have got his scars from being violent. Have you thought of that?'

Wilbur looks like the gentlest creature on earth, though he might not always have been – perhaps it's down to ill health and resigned submission more than anything else. Any past fighting would have been to become the dominant male and to defend his territory, rather than for the sake of sheer aggression. I've recently seen footage of him up close and he has a large chunk missing from the tip of his nose. I felt the need to back-track, and it's there in all the earlier images too. Annie aside, the affection for him is increasing in the household. Perhaps it's because he's so easily recognizable, with that softened aging profile as everything goes slack, and the worn fur on his neck, like a loved teddy bear. He continues to drop his rear to eat, even when he's only visiting for a few minutes because most of the peanuts have gone. There is that human desire to help, but nothing we can do – just watch and feel powerless.

Annie returns from a sleepover at her best friend's. It hasn't done her any favours and she's short with everyone. She has another French oral to revise for and numerous pieces of homework backing up, but she's hard to motivate. She's painting at the table and I stay away. By four in the afternoon I brave a conversation with her. On the table in amongst her paints is a notebook: 'Annie's fab journal for getting motivated and doing work,' it says on the front. I pick it up – there's nothing inside.

'Careful, it's wet.'

'Is this all you've been doing?'

'Yeah, but I'm just so tired. Katie kept me up until one thirty.'

'One thirty?'

'We were watching this film she wanted to see.'

'I don't want you having sleepovers in term-time if you're going to be like this.'

'We won't be so late again. We were knackered this morning. We were too tired to walk out of Deal, we were out of breath! We needed benches all the way along the road.'

'You need to get something done now.'

'I *know*.'

'We're having a take-away later, just get going and you've something to look forward to.'

'Tonight? I'm feeling a bit ill. We've eaten nothing but chocolate and junk all weekend.'

Jemima finds me early the next morning when she comes downstairs. I'm huddled over the nature cam and have been for some time, looking at new badger footage. It's dark outside but I went out with a torch to retrieve it and to block the hole for Tyn – at least the neighbours behind won't have seen me; I worry about being witnessed from their upstairs window at this time of year.

'Is that Wilbur?' she says, clambering onto the sofa next to me.

'It is.'

She's peering at the screen a little too closely, but I have seen it all already. 'Why does he keep sniffing the ground and moving around like that?'

'He's looking for peanuts but they've all gone. Two younger badgers came earlier and ate them all up. It's the usual story.'

'That's sad,' she says. 'We can draw them a picture with a badger with scars above its eyes looking down on them, looking upset. I'll pin it up on one of the trees. That'll make them think. How will he survive?' she says, glancing up at me and away from the screen.

I tell her that he's an old badger, that he's lasted this long, that he knows where to look. But it does seem unfair that the younger, fitter badgers come early and eat whatever's out. Georgie works the ground, pushing her long nose into the earth so that it moves as she eats her fill. Robin pads around on his young fleshy feet with the surplus energy of a small child. I'm pretty sure of the gender of these two now. Next we watch a thin-faced vixen with oversized ears. She looks up and around as she grazes, flinching at each imagined sound, her brush curled protectively around her legs.

For the next few nights I start to dot the nuts round in the dips and hollows so they take longer to find. Wilbur visits and revisits some nights, in the hope of finding *something*. He is always the last to arrive. I decide to put out more for them, and he comes almost every night, even when it's raining and the foxes and other badgers tend to stay away. Late January and he arrives looking filthy, his markings no longer distinct but hidden under a layer of dirt from his nose upwards. I've never seen such a filthy badger, but then it's not a face that would sell well on greetings cards and mugs. Though it's raining heavily he is relaxed and contented, shutting his eyes as he eats, looking up when his mouth is full every now and then. I can see moisture in the corner of his eye, his vulnerability evident as I get closer to him, in this virtual kind of way. I wonder if his jawline is softened due to missing teeth. He moves away from the screen now; peanuts cover the floor but he prefers to rummage in the hard-to-reach corners where he has to work for them. I wonder why I find this scene so satisfying; I suppose it's because I'm having a positive effect on his life. An indirect interaction in feeding him. I've handled the peanuts as I've scattered them and my scent is on them – would they run away now if they smelt me lurking outside? It's out of the question now anyway, they are coming in the small hours at this time of year.

It's the weekend and Maddy and I bake a pile of scones and whip up some cream – the Christmas party is on at the Baptist Church this afternoon, always a month after Christmas so that people are free to come. There will be the usual ludicrous games that involve finding the person with the longest arms, passing spoons underneath chins and eating a jelly baby from the top of a pile of flour, but the children urge us to come along. Many of us adults are content just to observe, it's far safer that way. Soon tables laden with food are carried in and children jostle in line for first pickings while the adults sit back and watch. 'Wish they'd let us go first for desserts instead,' says Annie. The noise dies down as everyone eats. Small china plates are piled with pyramids of food, an art perfected by children and dads.

'You got enough, Eliott?' I say.

'I couldn't choose so I had it all.'

The children land food on our plates when they discover they don't like something. Old china teacups filled with tea rattle in their matching saucers as they're carried around on trays. They will be grouped into patterns later by the elderly ladies before being stashed away in the cupboard for the next occasion. Do they think this tradition will continue when they are gone? The kitchen is cramped with the old overseeing the young, just making sure everything's done as it should be.

Rupert's plate of party food causes him something of a guilt trip, he tells me later. He sat next to the pastor, who updated him on the Indian slum programme the church is involved in. The daily feeding programme for the children had gone down to just four days a week recently, as the funds the church has been sending just weren't been enough. 'I'd been wondering about it when I was on my lathe earlier,' Rupert says. 'That's why I asked. I want to find out what's needed, see what we can do to help.'

It's the very end of January and I see two badgers eat together for the first time. At 3 a.m. Wilbur is eating his peanuts when a head appears to his right. He barely seems to notice but he must've smelt the new arrival before ambling off with his loutish walk. Soon he thinks better of it and comes back to the hole. Now he realizes it's Georgie and exits into our garden again, perhaps to give her some space. It reminds me of the early-morning unspoken courtesy of our family bathroom – we won't loiter when the younger ones are on the toilet, but grab a toothbrush and make our way to the downstairs loo. The older girls have the sense to lock themselves in.

Georgie is looking decidedly pregnant. I'm guessing Wilbur is the father, considering how indifferent he was to her arrival. All sows will be pregnant at the same time due to the delayed implanting of embryos, and each litter may contain cubs from different fathers. They are usually born from mid to late February, though occasionally as late as March or even April, and as early as December. These are the exceptions to the rule, however, and the reasons are unclear. What is known is that February gives them the strongest chance of survival. It has its advantages for the mother too; the winter is a sedentary time for all badgers, and no one wants a strenuous existence when they're pregnant. And that built-in incubator has to be helpful in the colder months.

The next night only brings us footage of a fox. Jemima is first down as usual and comes to take a look. 'Aw, *sweet,*' she says.

Eliott joins us in the family room. 'It's the skinny vixen,' I tell him.

'Mum, are you going to name the foxes?' he says.

'I wasn't planning to.'

'I can think of plenty of evil names.'

'You know they're not evil,' I say. 'We've been through this.'

'Yes they are,' says Jem.

Eliott starts running through his list of 'git kids' with fox-worthy names.

'You can't do that,' I tell him.

'What about Sam?' asks Jemima.

'He's half fox, half badger,' he replies. 'You don't know where you are with him.'

In his book *Minding Animals: Awareness, Emotions and Heart,* Marc Bekoff suggest the naming of animals automatically alters the human response to them; we view them differently because of this one small involvement. Describing the sentiment felt for named animals during the foot-and-mouth cull of 2001, he tells of Phoenix the white calf, discovered at the side of her slaughtered mother five days after she was dispatched. Then there was 'Porky' the Vietnamese Pot-Bellied Pig, saved from slaughter by Tony Blair.

Our fox is on edge as usual, moving her head constantly, a sideways walk with legs crossed. She sits for a rare moment of calm and I realize how like an Alsatian she is, now that she's still. She's on her feet again. As she turns to go she stops and pulls back. Is she frightened by the wind? People? The dog? She can't be afraid of the badgers or she wouldn't keep coming to their hole, unless of course she's very hungry. She has nothing to fear. Despite that elegant turnout and those Bambi-like legs she's a killing machine and that is why I don't want to name her.

There is a dusting of snow this morning. The children hope it's enough to keep them off school, but that's wishful thinking. Eliott is distracted by a delivery during breakfast – his laser gun for his 'dog walks' around Sun Valley Way. 'This is war,' he says. 'Wait till Nathan sees this.' Apparently *all* the boys in his class have them. I don't really like it, but then he did buy it with his own money. I hope the old folk don't feel terrorized.

His free time before school just isn't long enough – 'Oh Mum, I've forgotten the guinea pigs,' he says as they pile into the car.

'It's okay, I'll do it,' I say. I've got to go to work first but I don't mention that, and they are never short of food. The day is chaotic, Annie has a Sixth Form interview in Sandwich and Rupert has to take her in his lunch break, returning her to school for a French oral.

She arrives home in tears, something has gone very wrong.

'I blanked it,' she says.

'What, in the interview?'

'No, that was okay. The French exam, I completely forgot everything. It was too much, the interview and then that. My brain just gave in.'

'You must've done some of it.'

'Well, a bit. He said I can have another go tomorrow. Other people did badly too. He's calling it a practice run. But I've got a place at Manwood's.'

'If you get the grades.'

'Yeah, I know. I just need Bs in what I want to study. It should be fine.'

There is a strong smell of fox at the hole the next morning, far stronger than I've ever smelt before. Most of the peanut offering is still on the ground; the badgers haven't been anywhere near. There is no badger footage, just the nervy vixen eating alone. She is looking about her in every direction as she chews, when a blur of fox flies through the hole and straight towards her in an unmistakable attack. She's away, into the garden and beyond the camera's reach. The fence continues to shake, no doubt trembling in time with her Bambi legs. Foxes urinate the most malodorous smell when they're frightened, and I'm sure that's what happened here. It is the smell of fear. The badgers now stay away for days, there's not even a clip of a mouse or a passing bird at dawn. Nothing has been. Nothing. A no-go zone, understood by all wildlife until every trace of danger is rinsed clean of the earth.

Annie returns to school and I spend the day worrying about her. If she crumples under a simple oral exam, what will she be like when they really get going? I shouldn't have bothered. 'I did it,' she calls as she comes through the door.

'Did what?' Like I don't know. It wouldn't do to let them know how I fret over them.

'I got another A* in my French. Dad's cross with me, he doesn't think it's fair,' she says, dropping her bag in the middle of the kitchen floor.

'He'll be in in a minute,' I say. 'Be careful. But well done.'

'He doesn't think I worked for it. Most people got a second go anyway, we had to memorize a lot more this time. Sir said my accent is beyond GCSE standard, he's really pleased with me. I couldn't look at him, though. I stared at my feet right the way through. It worked so I'm not bothered.'

A reclining silver moon rests in the sky tonight and the wind has dropped. The badgers usually come out on a calm night. I'm hoping they can put the fox intrusion behind them, I can't believe it will unsettle them for much longer. I'm thinking about them when I wake the next morning and get up early to retrieve the device.

Soon I'm on the sofa, cam in hand and pressing replay. A badger with a sore eye is coming up under the fence. It looks like Robin, the smooth sleek head a giveaway, and soon I see his narrow tail. He keeps his left eye shut the whole time – I wonder even if he still has it, the surrounding area looks so gunked with blood. I've always suspected that Robin is one of last year's cubs, and perhaps this is evidence. When a new litter is born, the remaining male cubs from last year are banished from the sett. Perhaps Robin didn't go willingly. But he sticks around here for ten minutes before heading off, presumably to a new home in the ground. Georgie arrives soon afterwards at nearly four in the morning. She is looking heavily pregnant and lies down to eat. I struggled to tell these two apart for a while, but now the distinctions are obvious, even aside from her fanned tail and elongated snout.

The badgers continue to take advantage of the free peanuts and come most nights. They have dug deeper a hole between the tree roots and Wilbur sinks into it like it's a warm bath, his muscles visibly relaxing. He lingers long enough for the bathwater to turn cold. As he steps up and out he displays his tackle – he was always undoubtedly male with that broad face of his, but now there really is no question. Robin arrives after he's gone, and performs the same revealing manoeuvre. His eye is starting to recover a little, and an occasional glint of green shines between the closed lids.

The next day Maddy and I take an early walk to Wilbur and friends' suspected home. The old holes have been filled in again and covered with a layer of leaves. 'But where there's a badger will, there's a badger way,' Maddy reminds me, and we follow a badger trail that leads into an inaccessible part of the small wood. I feel sure they have relocated down there; only some heavy garden shears and some close monitoring would confirm the suspicion, and I'm not about to try. My curiosity would expose their path and any holes, only making them more vulnerable, and besides, I'm not worried for them. A couple of holes have been filled, but I'm confident the tunnel has other routes and exits. The fact that they keep appearing on our nightly footage is reassurance enough.

The weather is typical of February and snow showers come and go, turning the country lanes white for an hour or two at a time, before clearing again. It's too desolate for most dog walkers and Tyn and I feel we own the woods and fields. Puddles are still frozen at lunchtime, though children can still be heard shrieking from the playground half a mile away, wild excited shrieks of abandon, echoes of running into the sea and finding that it hurts. The next morning it's so cold I leave no footprints in the new layer of frozen snow.

Our badgers are undeterred, and forage along our enclosed little path every night. Perhaps the hard frosts make digging for worms difficult and this is a ready-meal of sorts. Wilbur arrives with a limp, keeping his rear right leg off the ground. He cannot live far away if he can make it to us in this condition. Later the young dog fox takes his turn. At first he appears to be salivating over the peanuts – not the usual dish to make him drool. He turns and I see a cross-section of his mouth, a complete row of fangs with no skin to cover them. The close up on the next clip forces me to look away. Could Wilbur have taken off the side of his face? Wilbur's cheek has looked swollen and encrusted for days, as if recovering from a gash. Perhaps Annie was right about him after all. But it's not for me to know whether they are the cause of each other's injuries.

Wilbur keeps up his visits, lying down to eat, front paws tucked beneath him. It's not an easy pose to get out of in a hurry. I'm watching him on the cam's own screen, a small rectangle the size of a book of stamps – is that a smudge on the glass or yet another injury? I run my thumb over him and it comes away. His ears wiggle in time as he eats, his head the only part of him moving – he's flat to the ground like a bear rug with head intact.

8: Badger therapy

A beautiful clear winter morning at last *and* it's a Saturday. For once the dog is out of his bed without waiting for Rupert to surface, and attempts to sit on my feet as I lace up my boots. Maddy appears ready-dressed, as if she also can read my thoughts, though that wouldn't be hard on a morning like this one. We set off for the woods at half-past seven under a snow-globe dome of blue. Lilac-hued clouds are dotted low on the horizon, just above the roof-tops, while aeroplane trails gleam beyond, as if planes have taken off at whim, lured by the brilliant sky. Into the woods and we hear a woodpecker drumming, the sound reverberating off the trees as we walk. They always seem to be out on late winter mornings like this. There is a warm glowing light in amongst the bare trunks, and the fields without aren't dull this morning but lit with a pinkish glow. Though the ground has frozen hard there are fresh badger snuffle holes. They have dug determinedly and deep.

We walk the circuit, checking on the badger holes in the teenage wood, and further on in the enclosure. The dog tugs on the lead every time his picks up a badger's scent, which is often. Maddy wants to find the woodpecker and we walk towards the sound. She stops underneath a tall beech tree containing several holes at the top. It is plausible. This is where the badgers fought in the summer, knocking over the lords and ladies. A dog walker stops to watch us and I feel conspicuous. 'We're trying to spot the woodpecker,' I say. Tyn looks up into the tree as if to support me.

'I've never seen it,' replies the man from underneath his scarf, his breath visible as he speaks. 'I've been coming this way for years.'

That's decided it. As he walks away Maddy crosses her legs and folds her arms, staring into the higher branches. We won't be off until she's found it. We don't have to wait for long – 'I think I can see it,' she says. She does have very sharp sight and I'm inclined to believe her. Something leaves the tree. 'That's it!' she calls, and we watch it go, a red underbelly blazing through the sky before it lands in a tree a hundred metres away. The great spotted woodpecker, as I expected. Green woodpeckers don't do the drumroll very often, preferring to 'yaffle', hence the name of the wooden bookend in the children's programme 'Bagpuss', Professor Augustus Barclay Yaffle. It is unlikely to be the lesser spotted woodpecker either, for this bird is now rare in the UK. The drumming starts again, tapping out a beat as we leave the wood.

Dad is too tired to talk to me this weekend and comes to the phone just as our hour is up. His radiotherapy is really taking it out of him and it's a struggle to keep up any semblance of routine; the weekly Sunday phone call that we've had since I left home is one of many things to suffer, but I don't blame him. I simply want him back to his old self, if that's possible. 'Don't worry,' he says. 'Mum'll update me. I'm sleeping such a lot at the moment.' Sunday starts beneath a milk-of-magnesia sky, and we stay under it all week; there are no shadows, just opaque grey above us. It set in soon after our walk that day and we feel glad that we had it.

The children have to be at primary school early this morning, it's Science Focus Week and Jemima has a trip to London. 'Have you got any boiled eggs?' says Eliott, ten minutes before we're due to leave. 'I need a boiled egg, Mum.'

'What? What do you need that for?'

'It's our parachute experiment today, don't you remember?'

I put one on to boil and soon it's ready and Eliott is knocking for his friend. We're in the car and on our way, Eliott complaining that the egg is hot in his hand.

'Did I turn that ring off?'

'I don't know,' he says.

A quick swing round the roundabout and back home. It's off. To Sheperdswell and a close encounter with a Stagecoach bus. It's coming through regardless, and as I wind down the window for some air I take in the multi-coloured corner, decorated with different shades of paint from the cars it has scraped. The children deposited, I relax into my journey to work, and in the next village a family of ducks are crossing the road from the pond. No hassles for them this morning, the world is going to have to wait. I put on the hazard lights and stop to watch.

There is a dead badger in the road on my way through Alkham village and on my way back at lunchtime it resembles a bag of spilt mince. I arrive home to an answer message from Martin: 'There's a dead badger one hundred metres north of the Swingate Inn on the Dover to Deal road. I'm wondering if you could go and have a look at it and move it off the carriageway before it gets dark. Make sure you take your fluorescent jacket.'

That jacket I really should have bought by now, I think to myself as I look over the notes I've taken. I'm ill-prepared for this. And I know I'm meant to have the gear, but I always thought it was to go to injured animals, not dead ones. I'm glad I haven't had time to give him the grid reference of the one I've just seen or he'd probably want me to move that one as well. It's not looking easy tonight. Anyway, I tell myself, Jemima has parents' evening. I'll see how it goes.

Jemima's coach is in very late and there's no time after school. Then it's Annie's dance performance – Rupert is going on from work to watch, but it does mean I'm needed at home. I leave a message for Martin telling him I'll go tomorrow.

I'm awake early the next morning thinking about it all. I dealt with a dying guinea pig the other day – that was horrible, but this is much harder. So how will I move it? I'll need a shovel. And a strong stomach, as strong as the shovel itself. I'm preoccupied as I go about my morning routine and find myself telling Jemima about it.

'What – do you like badgers more than you like our guinea pigs?' she asks as I put a bowl back in the cupboard.

'No. I'm just not looking forward to this.'

Once the children are in school I stop off to buy some high-visibility vests – Rupert should have one too – and drive on to the Swingate Inn to take a look. I wonder if I'm in for more of these calls, now that last year's males are relocating. I turn the radio off; I need to psyche myself up for this. Nothing. Did I miss it? I'll drive on, there are other pubs along here, perhaps he meant one of those. But there is nothing to see and relief starts to set in. This is a very busy road anyway, I think I'll cause a bigger disruption than the dead badger if I have to stop. I turn the car around and head back through. Then I see it – a small dead badger on the side of the road: someone has already moved it. A feeling of calm fills me. Never has a dead badger filled me with such joy.

*

We are seeing fewer badgers at home now that the frosts have gone. Perhaps the muddy ground is making it easier for them to fill up closer to their sett. Robin and Wilbur are out, but the females are staying away. The cubs are likely to have been born by now – it's half-term, mid-February and I suspect the mothers feel they cannot leave their young.

It's a dull, cheerless day and even Jemima is reluctant to come out for a walk. She'd watch TV all day if she could, and we need to keep an eye on the sett. 'But I'm hungry,' she says – we've just had lunch – and that swings it for me. 'You're coming. I'll arrange for Isabella to come soon if you can just start to be helpful.' We walk around the sett and find bedding around the main exit hole – a sure sign those living a little further from us are nesting.

Isabella comes to play the next day, and her mum Hannah has a quiet word with me at the door. 'Harry is gravely ill. He's in hospital in London. It's not looking good, I think they're preparing for the worst.'

'That's awful,' I say. 'Let's hope it's not so bad as they think.' Hannah doesn't look convinced. 'What's wrong with him?'

'They think it's meningitis. He was fine last week, and then overnight, this.'

'Do you want to come in?' I say, pulling open the porch door.

'I can't stop. We'll catch up later, though.'

And so I'm left alone to ponder the news and run through the autopilot procedure of making myself tea, my mind in places I'd rather not be, lurking in previously unseen hospital rooms, imagining the anxieties of my friend and her loved ones, only beginning to understand the pressures they are facing. Harry is the big brother of Jessica, who is a classmate of Jemima and Isabella. He's in the year above them at their close-knit village primary school of just two hundred students. The girls are playing together upstairs and I barely see them all afternoon. Maddy is creating outfits for their Sylvanian animal figures and doing the big sister thing, and I settle down to watch some badger footage with the bedroom door shut.

Robin is something of a clumsy badger. He knocks the filming device and runs away from it, then stops and gives it an over-the-shoulder glare before making his exit. A wood mouse is running up and down a sycamore tree, its headlight eyes revealing its erratic path. Then Wilbur is back, in fact he makes two visits. The second is just drawing to a close now: a hop and he lands his bottom on the floor before leaving via the hole. He's a happy badger, and his foot is looking better.

'*Muum!'* comes a voice from downstairs.

'Leave Mum alone, Jem,' Annie calls to her. 'She's having a quiet moment. '*Badger therapy,* she calls it.'

The holiday week is nearly over, to be rounded off with a surprise baby-shower for a friend. I'm out shopping with the girls on Saturday, buying spring flowers and sugared almonds and choosing neutral-coloured baby clothes. Annie bakes cakes and we head down early to the hall, to fill kettles and light tea-lights inside cream lanterns.

Word filters round at the party that Harry has passed away – that he's simply being kept alive until a team can come in to take his organs. There will be a service at the Shepherdswell church tomorrow to pray for a miracle. We're wiping tears from our eyes as we try to celebrate this new life that's coming. Harry isn't known to all the mums and we don't want to spoil Liaan's day, but it feels all wrong. So wrong.

I have to tell Jemima before it's her bedtime. Exactly how do I go about this? I'm rehearsing it in my head, aware it's not going to make sense to her. How can it? It makes no sense to me, either. I find her in her bedroom, sitting on the floor with her Sylvanian animals all around her.

'I have some sad news,' I tell her. I explain what's happened, as best as I can. She turns her head from me and adjusts the tiny shirt her beaver is wearing.

'Are you okay? We should talk about it. It doesn't normally happen, it's very very rare,' I say. 'Jessica's really going to need you all.' I put my arm around her but she turns from me some more. I walk from her room and start to cry.

I take an early walk on Sunday morning, just me and the dog. I need it if I'm to have any hope of getting through the day. I can hear a woodpecker from the front gate, the sound getting louder as I walk down the road to the woods. Tyn launches at a squirrel, though he's still on his lead. It shoots along the footpath and under a fence. I find the woodpecker noise is coming from the enclosure and follow the sound – the bird flies further along, but I don't see it go. I stand by the badgers' hole at the back of the sett and pause – Well, they are still here, sleeping beneath my feet, their lives are carrying on as normal. The sun is shining and I look up into a bare tree, an August-blue sky behind.

There is more bird song in the woods now. I see a robin and a wren – of course they would have stayed for the winter anyway, but nature is telling me that spring's on its way. I'm trying to identify the birdsong, beyond the usual blackbirds and woodpigeons. I think some of the finches have returned. It's amazing they choose to come back here at all.

I follow a wagtail from one end of Sandwich Road until I'm nearly home. It doesn't seem to realize that it can fly off to the side, that I'm not pursuing it. A mass of sparrows burst out of the fuchsia bush and away as I lift the garden gate latch.

The service for Harry is in the afternoon. I knock for Lisa and we gather a few more friends as we make our way there. We pass the headmistress as we find a parking space. She looks upset too, this is going to change the feel of our school community for a very long time. The church is almost full and we walk down the aisle to a pew near the front and sit down together. The vicar stands and confirms that Harry is being kept alive on a machine. He speaks of him as such a wonderful, likeable child, and we all know it's true, though I want his mischief to receive a mention. It's all the more tragic in that he was a child with flaws, like all of ours, causing his mum at times to shout and shake her head. He was real and knowable, a boy who was totally human, not angelic, a boy who was vulnerable and loved. He still is, and that's why we're here. We're invited to light tea-lights at the front and to say a prayer. His classmates form a long line and go up with their parents, one at a time. I don't want to look at them, it feels like an intrusion. It's hard not to cry now but I mustn't, this is bad enough for them without the mums all crying too. The vicar fetches more tea-lights, batch after batch. Everyone present lights a candle and the flames flicker as the wind picks up around the church.

'See that you do not despise one of these little ones. For I tell you that in heaven their angels always see the face of my Father who is in heaven,' reads the vicar. Outside, his classmates are each given a blue balloon as they assemble on the village green. They chase each other, balloons in hand, as if Harry were still with them. A few minutes spent just being children, the pain still inside them but now a part of them, something that will at times cause them to ache and wonder, but not to slow down. This grief has to be channelled through running and climbing, and occasionally through laughter. Some things need to stay the same. A parent calls them over and they release the balloons as a group, then look to the sky. They drift along in the direction of Harry's house, before rising swiftly upwards together, a band of blue rising higher and higher in the sky until out of sight.

Back home, the family argue over chocolate at supper time. 'Dad, have you eaten all that chocolate with nuts in?' says Annie. 'I bought you that with my own money... I could cry.' *That's you and me both, Annie.* I start to clear the table on my own. Don't they feel it? Can't they see how lucky we are, how pointless their stupid squabbles?

Jemima has tummy ache the next morning and says she doesn't feel well enough for school. She's sitting at the table, making a card for Jessica, snippets of coloured tissue paper all around her, felt tip pens with their lids off scattered across the table. I tell her that I'll put the card through her door later, but that the tummy ache will pass, that I used to get them when I was her age.

'Should I invite Jessica to my party?' she says.

'I wonder if it's too soon,' I tell her. 'She's going to feel wobbly for a while.'

I polish Eliott's school shoes and think of my friend Alex and what she'll be confronted with at home. The shoes, the school uniform. Evidence of him everywhere, things that he has no use for now. It's just too sad for words. Should we even be celebrating Jemima's birthday with her friends? But they have to function as normal, life can't stop. Jem has been sent upstairs to get dressed and I clear up behind her. A scrap of bright orange tissue paper with a perfect heart cut from the centre is lying on the floor.

Rupert has 'pruned' my favourite rose in the front garden. There's barely any of it left, I'm not sure it will recover from such savagery. I settle with the badger cam once they are all out, pushing aside the remains of Jemima's craft time at the table. I see Robin come early with the impatience of youth, and finish his supper by 9.40 p.m. We have a new badger that arrives an hour later. She makes several attempts at getting under the fence, an indicator that she isn't a regular. She is nervy, jerky, but soon relaxes into her feast. I watch her now, a pregnant sow, distinctive for her right ear that's somewhat unusual – it has been injured in the past and though healed, a gap is visible down the middle. Her eyes seem a long way down her face. Not the prettiest badger, but I'm glad she's come.

Another badger I am pretty sure is Wilbur arrives after she's gone – it has an injury, a badly torn ear. I flick back to the pictures of our newcomer, but they are not the same. This is Wilbur, with his broad face and dented nose, and with his ear, yet another battle wound.

*

'It's half-past six, see?' Jemima is holding her new watch so close to my eyes that I can't focus. Now she kisses me and clings tightly round my neck. 'Thank you, Mummy, it's just what I wanted.' She makes her way over to Rupert to thank him too, and he attaches it to her wrist. She is seven today and the ongoing tummy-ache has been momentarily forgotten while she tears open parcels and cards. She has her very own pink binoculars from her grandparents, and from us a rucksack with wrapped presents inside every pocket.

Yet she's not herself and doesn't want to play after school. The birthday tea is of no interest to her and she's early to bed. Rupert comes with me to a badger meeting at a local pub and sits round behind the bar, close to the fire. I'm over-tired and glad of my chauffeur, feeling worried about Jem and sad about Harry – sleep won't come without a nightcap these days and Maddy has made me a lavender bag, which helps me to breathe deeply if nothing else. I wish I was in bed right now, no matter how jovial our meetings may be. Deer peer down at me from the walls of the pub, full of insightful knowledge that I shouldn't really be here – not tonight, not when it's Jemima's birthday and she's feeling unwell. But she must be asleep by now, and all she wanted was to go to bed.

Ben produces a 'badger cage' for us from the boot of his car and it rattles all the way home. I wonder when I'll hear it next, on the way to some poor badger somewhere that needs help. Hopefully not a dead one.

I can't sleep again, I'm caught up in a scene outside the school earlier today. I could see Alex coming across the green and I wondered how to make conversation. Then there was shouting outside the pub, just beyond the school gates – a Carlsberg lorry was trying to reverse into the car park, but it was too big for the manoeuvre, and cars parked on the corner of the green were making a difficult task seem a ludicrous one. As we watched I asked if she had family coming. They had all been to the hospital, she said, though her dad was still with them and helped tidy and hoover when the head teacher and deputy were on their way – 'It was a mess. Bunches of flowers everywhere, letters, forms…'

I find some sherry at 1.30am – I can hear Jemima relaying it to me in my head – half-past one, see? – and soon after I'm asleep. The night is too short and I start the day with stinging eyes, but Jemima is more of a worry; the tummy ache is still there and worsening. Is she just stressed? The weekend arrives and her birthday treat to the wildlife park is all booked, but she's resting on the sofa, her knees tucked up to her chest. We debate whether it should go ahead, but it's just a few friends, it will take her mind off it, it's probably what she needs.

'Can we go home yet?' she asks soon after we arrive. She's holding my hand and letting her friends run ahead. 'Don't you want to see the penguins? We won't stop long, but we need to catch up with the others, come on.'

It rains and we find the soft play centre and she forgets herself for a while. But as soon as we're home she lies down on the sofa and refuses her birthday tea. I lower the cake so that she can see the chocolate bird's nest from where she's lying. She's really not bothered. I should have listened to her earlier, it will be a birthday she remembers for all the wrong reasons.

Her friends leap down from the table and drag her upstairs in their sugar-rush. They'll distract her, I think to myself. There is a quiet lull and all is well.

'Mum, Jem's gone to sleep upstairs while her friends are playing all around her,' says Maddy. I take a look and feel her forehead – she has a temperature, which is no surprise. The dads have all come to collect and are enjoying a drink downstairs, but concerned to hear Jem is unwell. Everyone's a bit nervy with what happened to Harry, and happy to take their children away.

The next morning her pain is worse than ever and we dial 111. We're called into hospital and I encourage her to get dressed. 'But that's tight on my tummy,' she says, 'and that.' The doctor prods and she winces and a letter is written to another hospital, 'suspected acute appendicitis' written on the envelope. I phone Annie from the car: 'We're being sent on to QEQM, can you feed the others some lunch? We'll be gone a while.'

The journey is making me feel queasy, but then I have been awake since two. Jemima is seen quickly: 'nil by mouth' instructions are given, she's weighed, measured, and her arm creamed, cling-filmed and bandaged in readiness for blood tests.

'Can she wee in this pot?'

Not likely, it seems. She's not eating or drinking and doesn't plan to any time soon. A grey Lego construction is sitting on top of the paper towel dispenser – it looks like some surgical device with small tubes, and I suspect it's been here for weeks. I doubt anyone dare throw it away in case it really is some medical implement.

We watch Shrek back on the ward and wait around all afternoon for the results. A doctor comes to visit and asks her to hop onto a bed. That's a joke. She prods where everyone else has prodded and reaps the wincing expression we've been watching throughout the day. 'The tests are clear of infection markers and appendicitis,' we're told. 'You're free to go.'

'Well, what's the matter with her?' asks Rupert.

'She may be constipated, or that may be contributing.'

Constipated? Really? That doesn't explain the high temperature and loss of appetite. They are not disputing she's in genuine pain, but for them it's case closed.

'Give her some laxative medication. Come back if you're worried. And give her something to eat now.'

Jemima is surprised she's allowed to go and all at once I'm aware of my hunger. We buy junk food from the hospital shop – we couldn't have eaten in front of her – but she's still not hungry. Perhaps this is an anxiety thing. 'You should get her to open up,' Mum says later on the phone, 'Tell her she's okay, that it won't happen to her.' I don't like to think that it's 'all in the mind' – that sounds so dismissive, as if it's not real but some attention seeking episode. What child wants to by-pass their own birthday? We're too scornful of fears, too keen for everyone to be chipper and not raise those searching questions. But I can't attempt to answer them if she won't ask.

What's to say the pain is any less real if it's caused by upset and fears? I don't know how exactly I'm going to help her – new stresses are going to come along and she'll need a coping mechanism. I remember that heart-sinking, first-time awareness as a small child when I understood that my parents would die one day – that we all would. The shock didn't last forever, and even then I believed in life beyond. I quickly processed the horror through finding nice pictures in my children's Bible, flicking past the lurid red devil, not daring to look at him, wishing that page wasn't there at all. She must be beyond that initial panic now, but something has changed in her: she's dropped from her hand that fairy-tale notion of a perfect life.

I reach for the nature cam when all is quiet, texts already sent to concerned family and friends – *It's okay, she's home. Not appendicitis, nothing to worry about.* The nervy vixen is back, I watch her scarper and now here's Wilbur, she must have heard him coming. His ear is healing nicely, with just a few scabs now where the gash had been; only recently there was a section hanging and ready to fall. A child would have picked at it – or rather been given anaesthetic and surgery. I didn't want to look too closely but forced myself. Badgers seem to heal far quicker than we do. I shouldn't ponder this too loudly or there'll be investigative experiments before I know it, the quest for a wonder 'badger salve' to speed scab formation.

A jay rounds off the night's footage and collects surplus peanuts in his beak, swallowing them whole. I wonder where he will stash them and if he'll ever feel the need to return.

Jemima is back at school the next day and I hope we're getting back to normal. I walk the woods again, and am noticing changes already. Lords and ladies are pushing through the soil, just furled twists of deep green leaves for now, succulent looking, like over-fertilised salad greens. Badger footprints abound, evidence of feet pressed purposefully on their path between camps, going about their business though my own routine had stalled. There are sticky buds on the sycamore and horse chestnut trees, and red-wood growth on branches, yet to be identified; most trees are still bare right now, and not always surrounded by leaf-fall. In some low-lying places beech leaves still cling on, now the same faded gold as the clusters on the resistant oak. The woodland path cuts through a lawn of lesser celandine, its yellow flowers lighting the woods like stars on the darkest night, nestling amongst the deep-green heart-shaped leaves.

Primary school's out, and in the car Jemima is now just plain difficult. I found her green coat in her room earlier, though I had put it in the garage for recycling. She had stuffed it under her bed where she thought I wouldn't find it. I confront her and drown out the ensuing tantrum with the radio. The next morning I remind her she has P.E and suggest she wears the school shirt with fewer buttons. 'But I don't want to do P.E, my tummy hurts.'

'Tell the teacher if it feels bad when the time comes. But they all saw you charge around the playground yesterday and not come back when you were called, like some out-of-control girl.'

'I can't tell her, she won't listen.'

'Then put your head on your arms, like this,' and I demonstrate. 'That's what we used to do when we were at school.'

'We're not allowed to.'

She loses it again, and I mean completely loses it. I'm not catching all the words she's shouting, just the odd 'you never...not fair...anyway, so there.' Her hair has flopped over her face and swings as she shakes her head. Cave girls would have more manners, and the look is all there.

'Go and sit on your bed. I'm not sure about the Brownies sleepover tonight, you're really not yourself. And if you're not up to P.E...' My voice trails off.

'I am. We won't be running around.'

'You will. And it's a late night.'

'It won't be.'

'Stop answering back. *Go* and sit on your bed.'

She's in tears and stomps off. I've handled it badly – so has she, but I should know better. I catch a radio programme later; it's half-way through but it speaks to me straight away. 'It's about building trust in life again,' says a subdued voice, calm and tinged with sadness. I have no idea who the speaker is, but it doesn't matter – she is the voice of universal wisdom. She has been bereaved herself and is now helping others learn to cope, especially families who have lost children. She explains the irrational fears she's experienced over her own children: 'Every time they had a headache I thought they had meningitis.'

I choose to let Jemima go to the sleepover. She needs stability and a sense that good things are in place for her. As I drop her off at the village hall I see that Jessica has come, too.

The weekend away gives her time to think, and most of the girls from her class are there. 'Mummy,' she says as she clicks in her seatbelt on the way home.

'Yes, Jemima?'

'If you were God, would life have the bad stuff?'

'I know, life doesn't make sense sometimes.'

'It doesn't.'

'We have to give the pain back to him and ask him to fill the holes it leaves inside.'

Eliott has a place at Dover Boys. Well, he's passed the test and so this should only be a matter of course. Already I'm sensing some regrouping at school though, perhaps a little resentment from some of those who didn't make it through, some ousting from friendship groups, some friends-one-day-but-not-the-next. I'm encouraging Eliott to take it in his stride – 'it's character-forming,' my mum tells me, and she's probably right.

The badgers are continuing to come, and whilst eating alone one night Robin looks up and sniffs the air, pausing between peanuts as Wilbur arrives. These two fossick around within sight of each other, but in minutes are eating side by side, their faces touching, coats brushing, contented in one another's presence. There is an obvious age gap between them and I had always assumed they were father and son, especially when both appeared with injuries recently. This must sound bizarre, but the ousting of last year's male cubs is often done with aggression so they understand they are no longer welcome. I can only assume that any power struggles have been abandoned. If Robin had got the message perhaps normal relations could be resumed.

A few nights later Dora is back. She's looking more pregnant than ever, I never knew a badger could expand that much. Hers will be a late litter. Wilbur is very comfortable around her – I'd assumed he was father to Georgie's cubs, but it's feasible that he is father to both. They bury their noses into the same hollow, like children bobbing apples. A moment later she all but lands her heavy weight on his head, though a quick shuffle from him ensures her bottom falls to the side.

SPRING

9: Badger wars

A Saturday morning early in March and wood pigeons are making out on the playhouse roof. They lock beaks – it looks aggressive but I understand it's a display of affection. 'Billing' is the correct term, and the hen will be reaching into the cock's throat for a food. He hops onto her, fluffs up his feathers and then loses his balance, stretching out his wings in a futile attempt to right himself. I wonder if that's all it takes for a pigeon anyway. Now he's recovered his poise and dignity, but she's hopped to the end of the roof. They both preen themselves and take a moment to recover before she hops back towards him.

Maddy and I head off for the woods with an eager dog, who's tugging me along like we really should get out more. 'Look out for the squirrels this time,' I say as we walk through the village. Seven o'clock is the time when they'll be moving between the woods on one side of the path to the back gardens on the other, the bird-feeders recently refilled. We take the narrow passage from the street now. 'There's dog poo in the middle of the path,' I say, turning back to her.

'Mum, watch out!' A tree shakes in front of us as a squirrel enters the wood, and I duck as another lands on the fence-top level with my head. This squirrel wobbles before running alongside me at eye-level. In a moment it leaps in front of my face and struggles over the opposite fence. Now it's chattering its teeth in the oak tree like some deranged chipmunk. Well, that's woken me up.

'I thought it was going to land on your head and get caught in your hair,' says Maddy.

We both pull up our hoods, there is a cold wind this morning – we're not afraid of squirrels, though it may look that way. I still can't help wondering whether it really would attack: teeth-chattering is meant to be a sign of pending aggression, and this squirrel was definitely het up about something. Mugged by a squirrel – no one would believe me. A doe squirrel will have her first litter of the year between February and March, so perhaps this was a somewhat defensive, jittery mother. If so, she will have chosen to parent alone, having sent the male away after mating. With as many as five young to contend with, I'm sure she'd rather not be disturbed.

'We've got a day off timetable next week,' says Maddy. 'The French class is coming.'

'That will be fun.'

'Not if I've still got Louis. I was meant to have Aliya last time,' she says. A bad French accent ensues, '*Would you considyer me as your fwriend?*'

'What did you say?'

'Well, what can you say? "*Oowi,*" I said. It's so embarrassing. He picked his nose and flicked it across the room. He made us sit at the back, at a desk away from everyone else. And he took off his wristband and tried to give it to me with the finger that'd been up his nose. I said no thanks – well, "Non, merci."'

Snowdrops and dog violets are mixed in together in the wood, as the seasons get acquainted for a short while, like strangers on a platform or in a waiting room. These most common violets have no scent about them, and cluster in heart-shaped leaves close to the ground. 'Are they called that cos the dogs can pee on them?' Jemima asked recently. Further in, a thick layer of dry oak leaves has blown against the fence that surrounds the sett. 'Look at all these new snuffle holes,' I say. 'Ow!' I've landed my foot into one disguised by the leaves – it's deep and it feels like I've taken the skin off my heel.

'That looks different,' I say and step over the fence into the enclosure. There's now a helter-skelter slope leading into the hole, sculpted during the rains and dried into permanence by the wind. The badgers may be hard to see this time of year, but at least we know they are still active here. In just a few weeks the cubs will come above ground and the watching season will begin again, though it doesn't feel possible – it's as cold as November, despite the occasional clump of primrose along the path, and deluded singing bird.

We check on the guinea pigs when we are home. Peppa is waiting by her bowl for food, but isn't squeaking. We've reached the conclusion she's lonely, as nothing else seems to be wrong with her. I can't provide her with company, despite my best efforts; the local pet shops and breeders are all out of females, and Rupert doesn't want another abandoned rabbit brought home. There's only one thing for it: Eliott selects one of his males and the two are introduced.

'Bilbo was *raping* Peppa,' blurts Maddy minutes later, cradling the wronged guinea pig in her arms. I'm not sure if her cheeks are flushed with shock or cold.

'What do you mean?' I say.

'He was on top of her and vibrating.'

'That's okay,' I tell her. 'It's how it's done.' Have they taught her anything in those science lessons? She doesn't look convinced. 'There's nothing to worry about – *really*.'

'No, but she really didn't like it.'

'Put her back. Get his sperm in there,' says Annie, looking up from her bowl of cereal. Maddy chooses not to argue with her sister and takes the guinea pig back outside.

'I don't think Maddy knows how animals mate,' continues Annie. 'With Katie's quails…' – she pauses for effect – 'they had, like, bare patches on the back of their necks.'

'Course she knows,' I say. 'She's just never seen it in glorious technicolour.'

The children still aren't convinced this is going to work and take it as an opportunity to research what livestock is to be had in the local area. 'There's a tortoise rescue centre in Deal,' says Maddy during the afternoon.

'Why do you need a tortoise?' I say.

'They're free.' Like that's an argument for anything. 'And they don't die. Not for ages anyway.' She has a point there. I always thought that was part of my attraction to wildlife – the enduring badger that always looks the same. A reliable English staple that's around for evermore, like Marmite, grey skies and drizzle. And yet now the badger is knowable I'm drawn all the more.

'The Stubbings family have one,' adds Annie – always one keen to acquire animals but not so keen to help look after them; not since Nigel the homeless bunny whom she doted on until his demise. Perhaps if he'd been a long-lived rabbit the story would be different.

'They don't have any other pets,' I tell them. 'You have.'

'And I told my friends,' says Maddy, 'and they're all really excited.'

I expect them to drop it, but a new Greville obsession has taken hold. 'I've written to the tortoise people like an adult,' Maddy explains later. 'I think I'm going to have to dress up in my heels and wear lots of make-up.'

'Yeah, that'll do it,' says Eliott.

Almost on cue, Annie glides into the room in the long chiffon dress she bought for the school leavers' prom. Her dark knickers are showing through and it's gaping under the arms – it's going to have to be altered or the boys will see her bust from behind. Perhaps she'll think of something, she can be resourceful. When I suggested that she iron the t-shirt she needed the other day, she reminded me she'd not used it before, but admitted she had used her hair-straighteners for the same purpose.

Maddy pops down to the village shop to buy some chocolate for Louis – the French children have been very generous towards her class and politeness demands that she reciprocate. We light the wood-burner and settle down with books, laptops and homework. I receive an email. It's from Eliott. 'Please can I put the telly on?' – the request of children up and down the land as winter holds on with its fingertips and digs its nails in deep.

In the evening I head down the garden before it's dark to set the cam for another night, and open up the hole under the fence. Something looks different and I take a closer look. A concrete block has been dug into the ground from Malcolm's side at the rear. He had been using sandbags recently, but this obviously wasn't working. I scratch a burn on my hand without thinking. So starts a new round of badgers doing battle for their stomping ground, though I fear our neighbour has a fixation to match my own. What exactly is it that drives him? He has no dog that might escape – why do the badgers worry him so much?

The badgers continue to find a way in, and I almost wonder if they are enjoying the challenge. Days later, a new hole has been dug alongside another breezeblock. I watch the footage I have of old Wilbur that night. Still in digging mode once he makes it through, he deepens the 'peanut pit' – a small hollow that we have watched them forage in, and now add extra peanuts to for good measure. We cover them up with leaves, as you might hide children's Easter eggs. I think they like to work for their food – perhaps the abundance feels more natural – even credible somehow – if they have grubbed it up for themselves. Wilbur lies down to eat and a mouse flits by, but he's not bothered. A scuffling at the hole and he rushes to see who it is, then resumes his eating. Dora comes to join him and finds her way to the remaining peanuts. She settles next to him, their heads together. 'Ah, how sweet,' said Jemima. 'Are they kissing?'

But soon there is no footage. A thorough job is made of blocking their entrance – now a row of slabs is dug in deep and covered with soil. It won't last. It can't.

A blackbird with a white tail feather flies a circuit of the garden and lands in the willow tree as I come back up the garden. At least he can't be chased out. I have seen him a lot lately and I think our garden is now forming part of his territory. A blackbird only claims a quarter of an acre, unlike the song thrush that requires ten acres, or a robin a mere one-and-a-half. Of course, a bird will find its own margins and won't follow our hedges and fences, but it's clear we are squarely in his patch.

Austen, whose garden runs parallel with our own, is out digging a vegetable garden. It's level with our chicken house and he strikes up a conversation as I stop to collect the eggs. 'Are they laying well?' he asks me.

'We probably have one from each of them a day,' I say. 'The teenage girls do like to bake.'

I admire his gardening efforts. 'This is such hard work, it's such a big space,' he says.

'It'll be worth it in the end.'

'If I can beat the slugs, that's about the only thing I have to look out for.' He doesn't know, then. Perhaps that's the end of it anyway. I feel a sharp metallic pain in my forehead and take myself inside.

If the neighbours succeed in keeping the badgers out I'll start watching them in the pocket of woodland near the church – even set up my cam there. But that feels risky as the area is said to be private, though, as I mentioned before, it's not fenced off. I recently saw a photo of some cams that were seized, having been set up 'illegally' on 'private woodland'. The police wanted to know if anyone from the badger group was involved – were they our cams? If it was an innocent mistake they would consider returning them. There was evidence of peanut shells on the ground, and concern they may have been baited. I very much doubt it. I suspect it was more about teaching trespassers a lesson. I think that's why badgers are so unpopular with many – Richard Mabey writes about the widespread 'revulsion against trespass' in the context of sparrowhawks in his book *A Brush with Nature*.

There is a broader application for this, as landowners and gardeners sometimes appear to feel wildlife needs permission to enter their space. An immunisation programme could tackle the TB issue at minimal cost – around £700 per badger, rather than nearer £7000 for each badger culled in 2014 – instead the proven 'ineffective and inhumane' cull is rolled out further against all scientific and moral sense. Bovine TB is, at least in part, an excuse to begin ridding the countryside of what's seen by many as a menace. A kind of ethnic cleansing of unwanted wildlife. I saw a picture last night of a trapping cage, modified to allow for a 12 bore shotgun to shoot a badger cub in the head. This has been sanctioned by our government. The badger could so easily be immunised once caught in this cage. It disturbs me to think of it. I moved away from the picture fast – Maddy had just brought her laptop over to show me her own Twitter feed, with a depressed wombat cuddling a toy for comfort. I will try hard to keep such details from her for as long as I can.

Out on the school run the next day, I see a sign has been banged into a beech tree close to the side of the road. 'We'll pull up near to the 50p house and take a look,' I say.

'What sign? Is the house for sale? Is that what it would cost to buy it?' says Jem.

'No silly,' says Eliott. 'It's the shape. Dur.'

'That cottage was a gatehouse once,' I tell her as I clamber up the bank to the beech tree. It's a 'Private' sign, and there is a second one on the footpath twenty metres along. I step underneath it to read the detail: 'PRIVATE LAND NO PUBLIC RIGHT OF WAY.' This is Long Lane, a well-used local road lined by some enormous beech trees that meet overhead, forming a dark tunnel through the summer months. It has the appearance of an old holloway as the road is lower than the banks, though not significantly. They are not wanting to close the lane itself, but the footpath that runs parallel with it, and routes into the woods. People will put themselves in danger if they adhere to this, walking instead along the road, and in dark clothing as they are bound to do. It's a popular route as it leads to other footpaths that form old ways in and out of the village.

I tell Rupert about it at supper. 'It's illegal,' he says. 'I studied footpath law on my MSc. You can't close a footpath that's been in use for twenty years.'

'They just did,' I reply.

'Can we go there?' says Eliott.

'I think it's our duty to,' says Rupert. 'Someone should write in the community magazine about it.'

'Go on then,' I reply. 'You know more about it than most.'

The badgers are absent for a while, the blocked hole has deterred them, and yet my spirits are lifted by the real arrival of spring. In the garden sparrows are sitting with soft, small chicken feathers in their beaks, like a new breed of ludicrously moustached bird. They take to the air, nest bound. There's a sudden urgency as nature liberates and many undertake what they have never done before.

Daffodils are out and colour is everywhere – nature's first clumsy brushstroke of spring, before the more refined and intricate detail of summer appears. Catkins are on the willow tree in that most optimistic of green: fresh, vibrant and innocent all at once. I'm waiting for the trees to burst at the bottom, the fear of being spotted by the badger-wary neighbours hasn't left me completely. I continue to set the cam and litter the ground with peanuts. Old habits die hard.

Out in the woods, new bramble growth is trailing from the trees. I spot a nuthatch on the trunk of an old oak, its long beak placed against it like a small woodpecker. A second appears and they chase each other in a circuit only they understand. It seems unnecessarily labyrinthine to me, involving the dodging of too many branches. Perhaps there is some point to it. There is bird activity everywhere; even on my route home a starling drops his bedding on the road below.

I open the front gate and click the latch behind me, pushing aside the old fuchsia bush that needs pruning, and the hollyhocks that have chosen to seed themselves in front of the gate. I take myself into the back garden to see what needs doing there, too. The hedges are getting heavy. I wonder if it's already too late to trim them – I suspect any nesting birds will have already taken up residence. I think the parts of the garden left to themselves are perhaps more beautiful than the areas of concerted effort. Hellebores have spread near the badgers' area and a new cherry blossom has self-seeded there, too, visible now its white flowers have appeared. Violets are advancing between paving stones around the playhouse, and towards the bottom of the garden. But something isn't right, and as I look into the guinea-pig run I realize what the problem is – Frodo has stopped squeaking. His brother Bilbo looked lethargic on Saturday and the children had him indoors in a tub in front of the radiator. I said it felt unnatural for him, that he wanted his brother. Eventually they put him in his hutch again, but he'd died by the evening. I knew what had happened when Jemima came up the stairs sobbing. Maddy stomped off in tears, and Eliott was crying too. These small creatures have brought so much grief into our household that I wonder about the wisdom of keeping them, but it's a slippery slope. A guinea pig shouldn't really be left alone – in Sweden it's illegal, such is their need for companionship.

Inside the house Eliott and Jemima are working on an Easter garden for a school competition. Jemima started on a paper-mache mound last year, but missed the deadline and it's been stored carefully ever since. This competition encourages family entries, and Eliott is taking charge. 'We really want to win this, Jemima. You must listen to what I say.' Some entries will be lavish and colourful, with painted eggs, bunnies and spring flowers. Jemima has chosen a garden of Gethsemane theme, and so far it's looking decidedly drab. They have made a hole for Jesus' tomb, and three crosses from twigs, tied together with loom bands. Their fingers are sticky and green with PVA glue and moss.

'How's Frodo?' asks Eliott, when he realizes I'm standing in the doorway watching them.

'A little sad,' I say without engaging my brain. 'Put him in with Peppa, they'll be company for each other.'

'Like a sleepover?' says Jemima.

'Kind of, but for longer.'

She leaps down from the table and runs through to find her pink wellies. 'I didn't mean you have to do it now.'

'We want to,' says Eliott following on behind.

They are back inside moments later, the kitchen door left wide open as they come to tell me the news.

'They started sniffing each other's bums and now they're onto piggy backs,' says Jemima.

'That sounds promising,' I say. 'You might get some babies out of it, but that's not the point. It didn't happen last time. But at least they've got each other.'

Morris, the now-named blackbird with the white tail feathers, is starting a fight outside the window, seeing another male blackbird off his territory.

'That wasn't very friendly,' says Jem, getting back to the gluing of moss and stones onto their creation.

'You should be pleased, he's claiming this as home.'

Two weeks pass and there is still no badger footage, though the resident birds soften the blow. Sparrow chicks line up in the gutter with their mother this morning, perfectly rounded balls of fluff and feathers, perhaps a little put off by the sheer drop below. They may wonder just why exactly their nest has to be so high off the ground. In Maddy and Jem's room a supposedly damp-proofed section of wall is still showing signs of moisture, and its only way in now is under the eaves. It'll have to wait until our summer visitors have finished nesting and moved back into the forsythia bush for their winter roost. There may be two or three more clutches to run this year yet. It's depressing to look at but there's little point painting over it at this stage. The sparrows do at least provide us with plenty of entertainment, and may well be loyal to this nesting site for life.

I learnt of the house sparrow's decline recently: I was shocked that it's now on the conservation red list, having decreased in number by 71% in the UK since the late 1970s. There is a danger that we overlook the vulnerability of the familiar sparrow, its song and plumage nothing to speak of, and yet how bereft our lives would be without it. I have always been envious of my parents' array of garden birds and I know my dad is proud of their diversity, but despite my different mixes of seeds and grains, I can never compete. Every year he tells me of the numerous varieties he's spotted for the RSPB Big Garden Bird Watch. I wouldn't want to attempt it; it would be just my luck that nothing much showed up that day. We attract the unpopular jackdaws and wood pigeons, and these days the robins and blue tits rarely come up to the house. Our predictable daily visitors consist mainly of a huge party of sparrows and collared doves. One reason for the sparrow's decline is the design of modern buildings, with no nooks, crannies or even eaves for them to nest in, plastic fascias often taking the place of the old style boards with no gaps behind. This house was built in the 1890s and it would be a near impossible job to block every conceivable space into the roof from the outside. By contrast, my parents' immaculate Scandinavian style bungalow can only host those birds that have no need for their rafters. I'm more than happy with my sparrows.

We take a late Sunday afternoon walk, feeling the need to get out before the week starts again: a grey sky has been building over the church and if we don't get out soon we'll miss our chance. We've gained an hour today with the clocks changing, but the weather isn't fooled by the pronouncement of British Summer Time – the wind is having one last lash, as if its time is running out. Metal doors shake at the village garage, and hanging decorative balls knock into windows along the road. The rain really starts once we reach the woods. We're feeling drenched and cheated of our escape; I could have spent the time reading – or more usefully, cleaning the house in preparation for the next onslaught. Instead there is weekend clutter everywhere – in the kitchen, a stack of muddy footwear by the backdoor, laundry and evidence of teenage cooking. On the family room dresser lie paintings and a tray covered in moss, feathers, stones and home-made sugar flowers.

I try to forget about it, but the walk is cut short anyway as Eliott and Maddy are moaning. Annie and Jem had the sense to stay at home. Soon we're contributing more muddy footwear to the pile in the kitchen and settle down to mugs of tea and some of Annie's lemon drizzle cake. As I sink into the sofa the back door blows open. 'The boiler's gone out,' says Rupert from the boot room. Then we hear a crash upstairs – '*Mum, help!*' comes a voice. What's Jemima done now? For once it's not her fault, we realize, as we gaze up into the attic space, the loft hatch having been blown up inside by a freak gust of wind. She's sitting on her bed below and has pulled her duvet over herself.

Outside, my new fairy lights don't come on, knocked out by the wind as they were blown against the garage. Rupert hated them anyway.

The next morning I head down the garden as usual. The chickens have gathered in their run and are looking at me with stunned expressions, as if I should offer them some explanation for the night they've just had. There's no obvious damage from the storm, and I retrieve the cam once more.

And the badgers are back. I really can't believe it. As I flick on from empty frames I see two sets of eyes appear in the darkness; the next picture shows Dora and Wilbur arriving together. She's playful, her fast, excited movements suggesting she's trying to catch something. She is enormous now, and her teats hang so low she's recognizable from the tail end. I'm surprised she's still pregnant, it is the start of April today, but it's clear that she is. Wilbur walks up and down the path for a time, pacing like a man outside a shop, before coming in to join her. Of all the nights to choose, they pick the wildest one in months. We have to be very local for them, one of the easiest options for a quick bite to eat, despite the blocked hole. I think it was the thought of someone disturbing their ground that was the problem, for the obstruction could have been shifted soon enough.

Later Robin arrives on his own. He hears a noise behind and is still for a while, then hides out in the area of undergrowth. Wind often keeps the badgers away as I guess it's harder for them to work out if they are in danger, the usual noises being obscured.

Later still the nervy vixen is out briefly, agitated by every gust. She can't handle it for long, and takes herself home. The male fox hangs around for longer, but he too is unsettled by the weather, jerking his head like a sufferer of Tourette's. His jaw is beginning to heal, it's not the first thing you notice about him now, though he'll always be distinctive after this. It's strange we had no visits for a while and then so many on one night. The blocked entrances had something to do with it, but I think those garden lights might be partly to blame. I know they've been glowing on the nights the badgers have been away. It should have occurred to me, but they are a long way from the house and above a badger's range of vision. Perhaps their sight is better than we are led to believe. They are good at detecting movement – hence the usual advice about standing very still when watching a badger sett – so this is a likely explanation.

A robin is out before dawn, followed by a jay that rounds off the footage in daylight, and even seems to pose for the camera. This is really bizarre, but he's peering in and tilting his head at strange angles. I don't think it's just curiosity, there's an element of pride in his demeanour, like he knows he's beautiful and wants his glory noticed. 'Can you see my blue wing-feathers? They're set off rather nicely by my terracotta pink, don't you think?' Corvids are meant to be clever, and I wouldn't put it past him. Now he crams a couple of nuts into his mouth and looks into the camera again, like a child caught eating in class, eyes staring, neck bulging as the supplies jostle through closed beak. I have seen jays this spring like never before, and even witnessed one just outside the window recently, taking his turn at the bird table. I was surprised by the size of him up close, and the strength and length of his confident hops. I'm sure they're drawn by the abundance of peanuts at the bottom of the garden.

Maddy joins me and we decide on some 'aiding a guinea pig give birth' research. This is where it gets scary. Just how likely is it that anyone else will be around when it happens? I can imagine the kids coming home from school to a depressed Peppa without her pups, it all going disastrously wrong as I attempt to help. Maddy starts to read out what to do if one of the babies isn't breathing: "Carefully lift it up and hold it at arm's length. Its head should be away from you. Spin around once." Jemima walks into the snug while she's speaking and is looking horrified. "The force should free any blockages from its throat and help it to start breathing. If this does not work –"

"What *are* you talking about?"

"What to do if the baby pigs can't breathe," says Maddy. "It will be fine, I know just what to do."

Eliott and Jemima win the Easter garden competition and share a giant Maltesers egg. 'I've never won anything,' says Maddy. 'At least I didn't come last in that egg-parachute competition' – that would have been gutting, for she'd sewn it herself. The badgers continue to visit – Dora is the most regular for a time, eating happily with whoever's around – last night it was Robin, who pushed her out of the way with his bum, that real family behaviour that's familiar and comfortable. 'Do you think she's had her cubs?' says Maddy. 'No, she's still just as fat as ever,' says Jem. 'I think she has,' I tell them, but there are no cubs with her yet. They will be kept safely underground for a few weeks. And the guinea pig is showing signs of pregnancy at last. 'What, have they been having *sex*?' asks Eliott. Well, what was he expecting? I think he just wanted an excuse to say the word. The 'pigs' have both found their squeak again – that didn't take long. 'She has got way chubbier,' he says.

'Is she really preggers?' asks Jem.

Maddy is admiring at arm's length two square lavender bags she's made on her machine.

Annie looks up from her revision. 'Why don't you make something useful, Maddy?'

'I have – I've made a fabric organiser and some Sylvanian clothes for Jem.'

'And how is that useful?' she says.

10: Difficult days

I've been struggling to juggle family commitments, writing and teaching for a while. I get the work done, that's not the problem, but it's the invasion of my personal space that's the real issue – the kids don't think of my 'work' as work at all, and it's just so hard to concentrate with them at large. The early morning writing was productive for a stretch, but now Jemima seems to get up earlier and earlier, so even that isn't a reliable slot. For a long time I've been pondering the acquisition of my own little writing hut, where I can watch the badgers in the evenings. It sounds a tad clichéd, but I really do need quiet to write, and it would bless the family if I'm less stressed out. Holiday time is always dangerous for pipe dreams. I have now found a shepherd hut company based in the West Country – it feels apt when you consider my Dorset yearnings; I've wanted to live there for as long as I can remember, what with those childhood badgers, and then an abiding Thomas Hardy obsession that took hold in my teens. With a Dorset hut I've come full circle, a writing and badger-watching base built where my badger habit and love of literature have their roots. It's the obvious choice. A timber framing company in the south west could supply and deliver a hut to me in a couple of months, and at half the price of the average company. The reviews are all good, and I think it's a decision made. By the summer holidays I'll be well ensconced, and my writing time will be ring fenced. I can feel the tension leave me with every interruption, every nuisance phone call, every time I'm called away to sort out a petty squabble. It's not that I'll leave the children free-range, but they're old enough now to give me an hour here and there undisturbed.

The night-time badger walks get going again in earnest, and through the holidays the children take turns to come. I'm out with Eliott tonight, but he just looks so bored. It was a mistake to bring him, but we're here now so he'll have to sit it out for a bit. I don't want them to come under any sense of obligation – I've never tried to persuade them to come anyway, but tonight he's making me feel like a bad mother. I'm reminded of sitting in a cold stone church as a small child. My mum is by my side and saying, 'Sit still, don't fidget,' in a loud whisper. I'm leaving Eliott to rustle and fidget away to his heart's content, and next time I'll leave him at home. I can hear a blackbird's crescendo in the distance, and now a robin in a near tree, always the last to stop singing. Beech leaves on a stranded branch brighten as if thrown onto a fire, then begin to fade. 'I've got earache,' he says. That's just great, they could be out in a matter of minutes. He has no sign of a cold or any other symptoms. A cub starts to mew in the field behind the enclosure.

'Do you want to go home?' I say.

'Yes.'

He comes to say goodnight later. I'm on my laptop, listening to a robin singing. 'This is the sound we were hearing,' I tell him. 'It would help if you could recognize some bird song, just one or two more would make all the difference.'

He looks at the time left to run. 'What, three minutes of *that*?'

He at least remains enthusiastic about the badgers on the nature cam, but I'm the only one to still study the footage every day. Dora comes almost every night and by mid-April she's definitely had her cubs, for her abdomen is deflating fast. In the latest footage she eats here for one whole hour, barely stopping at all. She reminds me of Jemima and her Easter egg consumption, going at it as fast as she can, just in case somebody comes along to stop the proceedings. I'm helping her cubs indirectly. Perhaps we'll see them soon. I think she's filling up with milk while she's here, her undercarriage seems larger and heavier in no time, the odd swollen vein protruding by the time she's finished. I remember that breast-feeding appetite from when mine were small, and that uncomfortable feeling when they were due a feed but I couldn't respond – we'd be on a long journey with nowhere to stop, or dealing with some other obstacle.

A local farm has opened up for children to come and pet the lambs, and I take Maddy, Eliott and Jemima along. 'Christmas trees here,' reads the slogan on the underside of the sign as it flaps in the breeze. This 200-acre farm maximizes on all the money-making opportunities throughout the year, with lamb for sale in September, and Pick Your Own strawberries in June.

We park up and follow the trail of families making their way down to the barns at the bottom of the hill. 'These lambs were born at 1pm today,' reads a label. 'Oh look, Mum,' says Maddy. 'He's trying to stand up. He's like me in these heels.' She's wearing some heeled boots, a present from one of my friends, and a burgundy jumper with a sheep on the front – quite by accident. 'Eugh, I've got sheep poo on my bag, it's orange!'

The children sit on bales and wait as lambs are passed to them. 'That's Naomi,' says Maddy, pointing to a girl who's lifting the lambs out of a pen. 'She leads CU at school, she's doing her A' levels.'

'How does she manage to work and revise?'

'She does get stressed but she's very bright.'

A lamb is handed to Eliott and the girls come in close, Jemima resting her face on the back of its head it while Maddy lifts and strokes its foot. It's a male, a misfortune that thankfully this creature is oblivious to. He has several creases along the width of his neck and across his back, a new fleece that needs to be grown into, and will hopefully be well-worn before the time comes for his dispatch.

A radio has been placed in a neighbouring pen and is playing to the ewes waiting to give birth. Or perhaps it's to give the teenage helpers a bit of light relief. One sheep starts to rock in time with the music. I suggest to the children that she could be going into labour. Two other ewes start to join in with the swaying motion and now I'm not so sure. I have in my head a picture of a group of heavily pregnant ladies exercising together, practising comfortable positions for labour.

To our left is an isolated sheep in a headlock device. 'Do not pat this sheep,' says the sign. She hasn't accepted her lamb yet, but apparently this should persuade her. Another ewe is being restrained by an assistant while a lamb is attached to her teat and held there.

When we are home, Patricia the chicken is sitting on the doorstep waiting for food, her eyes closing from the bottom upwards as she dozes in the sun. I put down some water and watch her through the kitchen door. She doesn't seem well. We decide to put her in isolation in case her illness is catching, and find an old unused guinea-pig hutch in a patch of sunshine behind the garage. Later Maddy brings inside part of the swivel latch from the hutch door – 'Do you think she'll be okay in there?' she says.

I come outside and take a look. The door shuts firmly and I tell her she'll be fine.

The next day I phone the breeder, who suggests I puree some raw red peppers, a natural antibiotic he was told of by a vet. 'It's not a magic cure but I've seen a chicken recover on it,' he says. Maddy has a teacher training day and takes charge, buying peppers from the village shop and blending them as required. The chicken is cautious to start with, but soon takes it from the spoon, then feeds itself from the bowl. Maddy spends a long time out there, and revisits her throughout the day. 'I think she's a bit better,' Maddy tells me at bedtime. 'She's happily eating it now.'

Early in the morning I head outside to check on her, opening the back door quietly so that Maddy doesn't hear me. The chicken is nowhere to be seen. And then I notice – a fox has ripped off the apparently rotten roof and taken his prize. A few stray white feathers litter the lawn, tumbling in a gentle breeze.

I wake up Rupert to tell him. 'Do you want to dispose of that hutch?' I say. 'Should we tell Maddy what happened, or let her think it was natural causes?'

'Tell her the truth, she'll find out soon enough.'

I study the footage in sombre silence, hoping for a little evidence. Sure enough, just after midnight a fox wanders from the wooded area and into the garden. She has a row of swollen, obvious teats. Perhaps she has cubs to feed, too.

Spring is unfurling with more certainty now, and a drive to a badger committee meeting takes me through Yockletts Bank, where primroses spill down the sides and bluebells and wood anemones light the woodland floor. We meet in a local pub and I chat to the landlord before the rest of the group arrive. 'I'm not sure whose side I'm on now,' he tells me. 'I hear both sides standing here. There's a house in Brighton, had to be pulled down, tunnelled underneath it they did.'

I've heard stories like this before but give him time to raise his concerns. It's good of him to allow us to meet here, after all. Very rarely do badgers begin to dig under a house, but if it happens they're relocated before things get too out of hand. The Daily Mail ran a story in 2012 of 'giant badgers' creating holes under houses, inferring there's some new super-breed that we should all be fearing. On close reading a garden wall was collapsing, and they'd made inroads under a carpark and community centre, but no one was in danger of losing their home. The story hasn't been updated – presumably because the problem has been resolved.

Towards the end of our meeting an elderly lady wearing a neat red jacket and matching lipstick comes over to chat to us. 'I think you're doing an amazing job,' she tells us, putting down her basket. At least someone does, then. 'Keep up the good work. It's very important you know.' I didn't realize our conversation was that loud, we're sitting down the far end of the pub as it is. She takes detail of membership and promises to come to the AGM in a few weeks' time.

The AGM takes me out to the village of Elham to collect keys from the village stores before closing time. My first 'gig' as secretary, I've arranged for Dominic Dyer, CEO of the Badger Trust to come and speak. The children are excited, and Rupert has told Jemima she can come, though I'm a little concerned his talk will be upsetting for her.

I pass a sign on the roadside, 'Ducks for sale.' That's a foregone conclusion, then – Maddy will see it later and our menagerie will grow a little larger. For a while it was the blind sheep she kept going on about. 'But she'd be no trouble, and I promise I'd look after her. *Please.*'

Who am I kidding? I've always wanted ducks. Just a couple would do. Eliott's pit at the bottom of the garden could easily be transformed into a pond, and Rupert does like a challenge. I wonder how much water they need. Will they trash the lawn? I'll do some research, I won't say anything just yet.

The meeting that evening is overshadowed in my mind by a major earthquake in Nepal. I can't seem to get beyond it. We lived in Kathmandu as a family when Annie and Maddy were small, and though we knew earthquakes were always possible, we put the prospect to the back of our minds. I'm fixated by the news coverage, and am now watching live rescues on my laptop, the crowd applauding and whooping every time someone is pulled free. They are talking of a child, a little girl, a *putali,* and now here she is, lifted out from the rubble. Where are her family? Does she even know who she is, what's happening all around her? I'm just numbed by it all. Laughter on the radio before the news annoys me, they just don't get it, they really don't get it.

Rupert wants to get me out of the house and suggests we go out to Elham, 'to have a little look… though we may as well do it in a day, if we're going that way.' He's no better than the rest of us, and I do manage a smile.

The females have all been sold and we decide on a couple of males to bring home. These are 'call ducks' and apparently only spend about 10% of their time in water, and a washing up tub would do. I think we can do better than that. Soon the girls have them in a cardboard box in the back of the car. Eliott is out on 'paramedic duty', assisting at an old people's event and probably giving out the bingo prizes again. He'll be sorry to have missed out on all the fun.

'Do you want the box, Maddy?' asks Annie. 'It's wetting itself.'

'Tip the corner towards the floor,' says Rupert. 'I don't want wee on the seats.'

'Shall I make the hole bigger? I want to see their faces,' says Maddy, the box now on her lap.

'Go on, don't worry about what Mum says,' Annie tells her. 'You know, we've got the ducks because of the badgers, if it wasn't for them she wouldn't have come down this road.'

I'm glad the badgers are good for something. Dora has been a nightly visitor of late, always full of milk, walking awkwardly. But today there has been a strong smell of fox again, and of course there is one in the footage, behaving like she's guilty, looking over her shoulder and around with an air of 'I shouldn't be doing this'. Her eyes are like green glass and she wobbles on her skinny catwalk legs. Dora has stayed away, though perhaps it's good for her survival skills to have a night off fending completely for herself.

We place the ducks in the chicken enclosure and shut them inside while the usual residents continue to peck around the garden, glancing up with the occasional look of misgiving. In a couple of days the ducks will be free to roam with the others. I wonder if they will retain a distinct identity or will think of themselves as chickens, too. Morris the blackbird is out and flies from the playhouse roof and into the trees, shrieking an alarm call as he goes. I follow him down and find a broken blackbird egg on the ground where the badgers forage. The yolk is still inside, this is not the evidence of hatchlings. I wonder if he's the father, he does hang around this corner after all.

A new term starts and the older ladies in my Folkestone writing class brighten my mood. They don't seem to allow themselves to get depressed – perhaps it's something to do with having lived through the war, but they are never defeated. This morning Gillian and Marion are talking about their medication at the end of class – they now have the same prescription. 'Well, it is making my hair fall out. Can you see?' asks Marion, lowering her head for Gillian to take a look. 'I can't see it myself,' she continues. 'But I'm up and walking, that's the amazing thing. That's all that matters.'

I brave a prayer meeting at a church a short drive from home – I'm one of those people who needs to go somewhere physically with the purpose of laying an issue down. Nepal is written on their prayer board as I walk in and sit amongst strangers. They don't feel like strangers for long, and a few people I know from the village walk in and sit with me. Sometimes problems seem too big to be kept in my own thought-life, and even between ourselves at home.

Soon a whip-round in this little Christian community has raised over a thousand pounds to help provide temporary accommodation, blankets and food. I try to imagine coming here regularly. Perhaps I will. But I have to admit, taking myself into the woods provides its own solace. I appreciate being with other believers, yet this alone isn't enough. The outdoors always feels like a spiritual place to me, and more specifically woodland and open countryside. It's my go-to place where I can pray and encounter God. I can't get away from the thought that birdsong is at times heartfelt praise and I suspect heaven will be an even better version of this.

If ever I was homeless I would want to try living in the woods first, with what seems like a larder of free food and of course ample timber to build a shelter. I'm sure it's not that simple. But I think it's partly the abundant provision of nature that gets me, and the peace and stillness that are so often present this time of year. It all points to something bigger, and reminds me of my part in a wider scene. To me it's like being invited into a divine workshop, and I'm in awe of what I see. It is calming and restorative and affects me no matter what troubles or stresses I take with me. There is a verse I like that says 'In him we live and move and have our being,' (Acts 17:28), and no man's faith should be confined to a building or specific location. I read recently of Bunyan's dell, a wooded valley that forms a part of Wain Wood, near Preston, Herefordshire. Bunyan would have preached there until he was arrested in 1660. Believers met there out of necessity, but this would be my preferred setting for any church service. I think I would have gone there even if I wasn't a Christian: a gathering of up to a thousand people, lit only by the moon, defiant yet covert with the reckless air of the early church. Perhaps that's how some teens rebelled in the woods back then.

Out in our woods beech leaves are loosening themselves from pale orange leaf buds, and bundles of horse chestnut leaves hang down like half-open umbrellas, heavy with rain. Soon they will unfold as they start to grow, stretching to the size of dinner-plates. Rabbits appear from many places at once before running for cover, and I spot a blackcap, perhaps a new arrival now that England's considered warm enough again. It's chattering at speed with its hidden companions, as a school child reacquaints himself with the familiar playground and old friends.

Bluebells are out in the teenage wood, and Herb Robert lights up dark patches of green in the far-flung shady corners. Garlic mustard, or Jack-by-the-Hedge, stands guard where the path meets the field edge. It was once used to treat gangrene and ulcers, its leaves now sought merely for the basis of a homemade pesto.

Jemima is after leaves she can eat raw. She gathers handfuls of wild garlic, but drops it all when her bike chain comes off. 'The dogs have probably weed on it all anyway,' Maddy tells her. 'Here, have these. They're from higher up.'

Grannies bonnets and violets line the path as we draw close to the village again, with echoes of back gardens rather than the wild woods. In our own garden the apple trees are foaming with full-on blossom, like magic crystal tree kits that mutate in shades of pink and blue and white. Willow catkins nod in the breeze, and a thrush tries out our garden for size.

It seems to be the time for new arrivals. As I check the night cam I see a hedgehog put in an appearance. I wonder if it has just come out of hibernation – I've only been filming since Christmas, and have no idea if this patch is his. These small creatures can travel a mile in one night, and he is most likely just passing through. A major reason for their decline is the increase in fences up and down the land, and fortunately for him our garden is mainly edged with hedges. He's welcome, though if he sticks around he may encounter a badger, which might not go too well for him. Soon Dora arrives but he's already made his exit. Georgie comes too, and I wonder if these nursing females are given preference by the others, an easy foraging ground for them when they have cubs to feed. Dora visits again at the end of the night. Perhaps she is still hungry. She skirts round the wooded area at speed, a blur of flying fur as she sniffs the ground. There is nothing left and she returns home to her cubs. I'm looking forward to them showing up one night; it'll be interesting to see how they're managed (or not).

A few days later there's a call from Martin. He has an orphaned badger cub with him that needs to be taken to Folly's Wildlife Rescue, and as soon as possible. Could we do it? The badger must be there by 8 p.m. It's supper time and we've not yet finished our meal. But I don't want to turn this one down, things have been very quiet lately on the badger front.

Rupert comes through with his laptop and I hold the phone to his ear whilst he follows Martin's route. I'm glad he's coming, and without me needing to persuade him.

'Is it Martin?' says Maddy in a loud whisper, joining us in the kitchen. I nod a reply. 'I'll come,' she says. She doesn't even know what she's agreeing to. 'And me,' says Eliott, appearing behind me. 'Me, too,' says Jem, and they crowd out the kitchen with their excited pacing.

I round them all up and take them back to the family room so Rupert can hear.

'Just Maddy,' I say. 'It's too late for the rest of you. You've all got school tomorrow.'

'What is it?' she asks.

'Oh, just a cub to relocate,' I say, trying to sound disinterested.

'That's not fair!' 'Please let us come.' 'We're hardly going to get injured this time!'

'It'll be a really late night. You won't cope with tomorrow. The rescue centre is out near Tunbridge Wells.'

'Don't you think that's a little bit irresponsible?' says Annie.

'I don't see why. I'll get Jem ready for bed, all you need to do is read her a quick story. You've always got Lisa across the road and my phone will be on. We'll get back as soon as we can.'

The so far unused badger crate rattles in the boot as Rupert drives at his 'on mission' speed, his reactions fast, his eyes focused on the road ahead. We've brought the small car, easier to handle on the country lanes, and Maddy is sitting in the back with the seat down beside her, her arm on the crate already. 'I'm going to have a badger next to me!'

Drifts of knee-deep bluebells stretch off into the distance, and accompany us for much of our journey. They seem to glow from within in the evening light, their brightness increasing as the woodland deepens. I'm reminded of children's nightlights that give off a dim but reassuring glow. Maddy and I are feeling queasy by the time we reach Martin's. We've been looking over our shoulders for too long, whilst bouncing along at an inappropriate speed. Martin and Gilli are waiting on the road above their property and wave us in.

'We're just worried you're not going to get there on time,' he says.

Martin takes us into his garage as soon as we're out of the car. I'm standing on bubble plastic that's used to insulate the floor. He lifts the towel on the cage and we all peer in. 'It's a he. Willow. He is a little lively, feisty even. Is he not going to come up and say hello?'

The badger really isn't going to oblige, though we stand watching for a minute. We take the crate and leave them ours. 'We need it back,' says Gilli. 'It's the only one I can carry.'

Maddy climbs back into the car and we slide the container in beside her.

'I thought you'd probably have him on your lap,' says Martin to me. 'But decided no, not with this one. Before I forget –'. He goes back into the garage and returns with a huge log for Rupert. 'It's seasoned cherry, I put it aside for you.'

And we're off again. I keep turning back to look at Maddy and the cage, but Willow has buried himself in the shredded paper.

'How did Martin end up with him?' asks Maddy. 'What's the story?'

'I think he was handed on to him. Martin's known by all the animal welfare people locally. It's Willow's story from here that matters.'

There's a very strong smell in the air; it takes a while, but then I realize what it is: puppy. Perhaps it's the smell of wee on newspaper, but there is something very distinctive about it, something young and new and covered in fur. It is partly sweet but in no way floral. Think newly cut hay on a hot dry day and you nearly have it, with a shake of talcum powder thrown in. Maddy and I are soon feeling queasy again, it's hard to look where you're going at times like this.

I catch her with her hand right inside the crate. 'Watch your fingers,' I say. 'He might bite you. He wouldn't mean to, but it's really not a good idea.'

'But I did get to stroke a badger,' she says, her cheekiest grin ever on her new brace-free smile.

'I've worked out how to undo the cage now.'

'Well don't.'

I'm feeling hot and sick. I'm not sure we're going to get there before they have to close. Apparently they are always very punctual. There's a cold parcel on my lap of food and injections, with a yellow post-it note detailing Willow, 2 months, male, no TB test, time last fed: 4 p.m.

'We're going to need more petrol,' says Rupert after a little while. 'It's further than I thought.'

'We should have taken the other car,' I say.

'I don't mind if we don't make it tonight,' says Maddy. 'We'll have to bring him home with us, keep him for a bit.'

'He's a fragile little thing,' I tell her. He'd need feeding in the night and we've no idea what we're doing. Not really.'

'We'd manage,' she says. 'I could have the day off tomorrow to help out.'

'Nice try,' Rupert tells her. 'We'll get there in time, I'll make sure of it.'

We soon stop for petrol and Maddy and I get out and open the boot, shifting his bedding with a pen. 'Look, we can see his face!' she says. 'Aw. He's so small.'

He *is* tiny, A4 sized with a shock of electrocuted looking fur. I head inside to pay for the fuel and tell the guy at the till we have a badger cub in the boot. I realise it must sound dodgy, so go on to explain we're from a badger group, and where we're heading. I think we've made this young lad's evening, and I get the feeling no one says anything much to him.

Back on the road again, I make several attempts to phone Folly's, and finally get through. 'We will be a little after eight. It's taken longer than we thought.'

'That's okay. I'm still here.'

I'm feeling relieved and start to enjoy the journey again. It's been bluebell woodland or pasture most of the way, with a complete absence of dual carriageway. We decide Martin doesn't come up for air very often, sticking to country roads as much as his commitments allow.

We stop the car after a few minutes to check the map. Willow starts to move whenever the engine stops. 'It's a womb thing,' says Rupert. After a couple of wrong turns we find the track we need that will take us to Folly's. The Broadwater Forest Wildlife Hospital, reads the sign; they are changing the name from Folly's, but the folly of accepting all manner of jaws, claws and venom will continue just the same. I glance back at Maddy – her face says exactly what I'm feeling but would never say – all this racing to get here, and then we have to hand him over. I'm starting to think her plan of badger-sitting for the night was a good one after all.

I open the boot and take out the cage, heading over to the entrance. A girl called Jenny leads us down to a clinical reception room, its walls lined with cages. She plunges her hands inside, lifting him out as if it's really no bother. And then he's in his new cage, and dives for the back, nosing his way under the torn newspaper. That's that then.

'You can phone in a few days, have an update on how he's doing.'

I take a couple of photos on my phone before she shuts the door.

'He's not going to stay in that cage?' says Maddy as we leave.

'No, they'll check him over and test him for T.B. Then he'll be in the play area with some other cubs. It's really okay,' I tell her.

The journey home is on smooth, straight roads, with a garage pit-stop for late night munchies. 'I don't know what Martin was thinking of, sending us round that way,' says Rupert as he drives, ginger biscuit in hand. We travel through Tunbridge alongside a river, and pass a goose and her goslings on the grass verge, a metre from the car. Soon Maddy is asleep, but wakes when I phone Annie: 'What, what? What did you say?'

'I'm talking to Annie, go back to sleep.'

Annie is still up, which doesn't surprise me – 'I'm doing my art. I'm not going to bed yet. Yeah, they went to bed fine, you put me in charge, didn't you? *Okay.* I need to get on. Love you too.'

Maddy crashes again, head on window. We're home by 10.30 and I phone Martin before putting out the cam. I hear something squeak down there, probably a mouse. In the morning I see a new hole has been dug – I'd forgotten to unblock their usual entrance into the garden before going out, but that wasn't going to stop them. The footage shows a now thin-faced Dora to be the culprit. Was she desperate to eat, determined to find a way in despite the obvious route being closed to her? We've got ourselves a dependent, at least while she has young to feed. She's still leaving them at home, dashing out on her own for a few precious minutes to nourish herself in order to nourish them. I mustn't feel sorry for her, she knows what she's doing and no doubt her hunger times will pass.

Morris the blackbird was singing from the highest tree when I went outside this morning, directly above the badger territory. I'm surprised to find him landing himself meaningfully on the back of a female blackbird in the concluding footage. She looks stunned. He flies off and she remains motionless, as if wondering if that really did just happen or she had in fact imagined it. She stays there for what seems an age.

It's May now and the garden take over has begun. A group of ten young starlings are out enjoying our lawn, the long grass giving them a sense of protection. The chickens look on from a distance, tolerant of these temporary squatters. A blue tit is searching our garage eaves for a place to nest. She will build her home with very little help from her other half over the course of a week or two, but apparently we haven't been selected, as I don't see her again. She'll have to be quick. She should be laying her eggs early this month, one a day for up to sixteen days. That's a hard task.

There seems to be a general feeling of unsettledness out there, and a need to explore; driving home from work today, I saw a group of three goats that had escaped from a paddock. They were eating someone's hedge on a steep slope, just beside a front door.

Our badger-wary neighbour has been sampling the fresh air again, too. The badgers had been left to get on with it for a while – I think he hadn't noticed – but now he's filled in their hole once more. The fool. Now instead of digging behind his ornamental grasses as they were they can select any entry point they choose. Nothing short of an electric fence will keep them out. Evening comes and I empty the bag of badger nuts down there and throw in a few custard creams for good measure.

But soon my confidence in their ability to overcome is waning. I'm tired, and yes, dare I say it, starting to feel a little glum about his efforts. What's more, my Twitter feed is filling my head with news of the cull. It's time to see some badgers unhindered. Only Rupert comes with me as the children are feeling bound by school deadlines – 8.30 p.m. but it's still light. We reach our usual watching spot in the woods and in less than a minute I can hear badger cubs keckering below ground. We're standing downwind of a strong breeze and I'm watching the barley in the field behind me, a delicate green layer like gossamer blowing on top of the crop. I turn back to the sett and one large cub appears – he's much bigger than Willow, our recent passenger for the night. He runs onto an old abandoned blue tarpaulin sheet in the wooded area, before entering the field via the tunnel. We watch at least four cubs in total, and the parents are nowhere to be seen. They roll together, holding on tight with their jaws, then breaking apart. They are travelling by bouncing and with a sideways skip. Soon one walks towards us and we look into each other's eyes, the mutual fascination unhindered by his mum or my children. No one has taught him it's rude to stare, though it won't be long before he knows.

Our own badgers are kept away for a couple of days, but soon appear from beneath the fence of the other property at the bottom. My nature cam records all the goings-on, as usual. Wilbur enters at speed, perhaps hassled by the obstruction and feeling there's something of a risk involved. A fox eats in the background, untroubled by his presence. But he glances up as his hunger subsides. He is hesitant, respectful, like a small child who stands back to observe the behaviour of the older ones. Dora emerges from the new hole she'd made during our night at Folly's, and later Robin, also apparently agitated. He attempts his usual route first and unearths a breezeblock, before accepting defeat and finding the new circuit adopted by the others. That didn't take them long and I feel encouraged.

'Maddy, you don't need to tuck that top in,' comes a voice from the other room.

'It's fine,' she replies. 'Look, I even plucked my eyebrows today.'

'Well it doesn't show,' says Annie.

'What, just because I haven't filled them in with a crayon?'

I need my shepherd's hut. It will be here in a couple of weeks, during the May half-term if all goes to plan. I think we'll be able to camp down there till late some nights, and watch the badgers in relative comfort. Jem is in the playroom this morning, clapping out of time to some pre-recorded tunes on the keyboard, the volume up high. I envy the badgers' quiet existence. Just a few minutes each day would be nice, but the thought of my hut under construction offers me some hope. Annie starts her GCSEs today with an R.S exam, and they're set to drag on for six weeks or more. Eliott and Jemima have their SATS this week too. The intensity of school means they need a little rage time at home.

Somehow we reach Friday with tempers intact and Jemima has

earned herself her first ever night of badger watching. Straight after school she appears wearing a green long-sleeved t-shirt and Brownie leggings. 'I'm dressed like a tree.'

'I can see that. I said you'll have to *stand* like one, but you're okay, it's a good look. You'll need a coat though, and a fleece.'

Out in the woods, her anticipation level equals a small child's who thinks they're about to see the *real* Father Christmas. The expectation goes back at least a year now, and she's so proud that she's a member of the East Kent Badger Group, though most people have never heard of it. We've been standing still for little more than a minute, when she announces, 'I saw one.' She's way too early. This is going to be challenging, she has no idea how much patience is involved. Maddy looks Jemima up and down and smiles at me. But soon I spot a badger at the very back of the sett, and then various heads coming and going in the distance. Perhaps she did see one, but this is pretty fluky, I have to say. We watch as a wren hops along a rusty fence rail, trailing an alarm call as it goes; these short bursts are not its usual song, though it's not so bothered by us that it feels the need to fly away.

The badgers aren't coming close tonight and I crouch down low. Maddy and Jem copy me, and in no time at all a cub makes its way forward, then through the tunnel and out into the field. Another appears beside it and they sniff the air before entering the cover of the crop together. There is a proud grin on Jemima's face, tight-lipped like she's trying to suppress a smile, but she really can't – it's broad and her eyes are shining. We watch one of the cubs make its way back. It stops to wait for its sibling, but after a minute or two gives up and takes the tunnel on its own. The cub pauses when out the other side, waiting as a distant car passes, its music up loud. There's so much for them to make sense of, to categorize as dangerous or harmless, and our presence here doesn't make that any easier.

Jemima, however, is made up and she floats home on a cloud of excitement. It's like this was some rite of passage for her, a significant life-shaping moment to be remembered forever. I'm keen not to impose my own interests on the children, but this one is catching for sure.

'I can't sleep,' she calls out later.

I head upstairs and poke my head around Maddy and Jem's bedroom door.

'She's not trying,' says Maddy. 'She's been talking to that stuffed badger of hers.'

'Badgey wanted to hear all about it,' she says, stroking its head as she holds it up to her face. 'I'm too excited to sleep, anyway.'

I hear her again at ten o'clock. 'Jem, it's really *really* late,' I tell her. 'I'm getting ready for bed myself. You could have been asleep ages ago. You *must* get to sleep now or I'll never want to take you badger watching ever again.'

That did it, there's not another peep until six in the morning.

SUMMER

11: Moving on

Spring is passing into summer all too quickly. The weather has turned wild again and the blossom has fallen from the apple trees, lingering on the grass like old confetti. Twenty starlings are out on the back lawn, digging away, but there are none next door. What's going on? The ducks are burrowing into the lawn with their beaks too, side by side like nervous twins, their matching upturned tails curling into an elaborate 'e'. You'd struggle to get a pencil between them at times. They walk past the pond that Rupert has dug for them, oblivious for now.

Before long the barley grows tall in the fields and it becomes harder to spot the badgers – wheat is a far more accommodating crop. I can't see the back of the enclosure, the nettles have grown up and the elderflower is drooping down, heavy with leaf and flower – there is only a small gap in the middle, like the viewing slit of a bird hide. The cow parsley is at head-height and the whole scene is an adventure playground for the children, as they hide behind lanky plants and scramble down steep banks, the roots like steps or the rungs of a ladder.

Sally tells me they now have two badgers visiting their garden. She is sure the original badger is no longer around, and thankfully has no suspicions that the current visitors could be responsible for the loss of the first. Or perhaps she just has the maturity to accept whoever comes. I imagine this is an adult badger with a young one.

'They are quite disruptive though,' she says.

I start to tell her of ways of deterring them, but she stops me in my tracks. 'No, we love seeing them, and besides, we've invited them in, we can't go back on it now.'

Half-term arrives and Maddy returns home from the park one day with a baby bird in her cupped hands. At first we're not sure what it is, and we both fire up our laptops. I suspect it's a blackbird, but it looks as if it could be a starling or something else. 'Young blackbirds leave the nest when they are fully feathered but not yet able to fly. They will remain flightless for a couple of days,' I read to her. 'I thought so. We should take it back.'

'But a cat would get it. It was just on the side of the path, it will never survive there, Mum.' She's holding it all the more protectively now, her other hand sheltering the bird from my view.

'We'll look into it a little bit more, but I think we should return it.'

'Not unless we're sure what it is.'

'What are we supposed to feed it?' I say, wandering through to the boot room and opening the fridge door. 'I suppose we could tear up some little strips of this ham. It looks a bit worm like. Well, vaguely.'

Maddy tries to drop it into an open beak while I continue my research. I'm not totally sure it's a blackbird – though looking at the pictures I think it's too big for a starling nestling. It still has fluff on its head. 'Nestlings do not yet have their eyes open.' Ours does – this is so confusing. One hour in and it starts to flap its wings. Maddy is holding it in her hands like some precious orb, a big inane grin on her face. Now it sits patiently and shuts its eyes, no resistance whatsoever. Its beak seems too large for its head and is wrinkled at one end, reminding me of a newborn baby that is yet to grow into its skin. Why would this little creature be likely to fare better here with us? We've no idea what we should be doing for it. Finally I hit on some useful advice: 'Colour in the poop indicates the parents are feeding the baby and the bird should be put back where found.'

'You can't be sure, Mum.'

'Just look at its poo in that box! We really should return it. Imagine how its mum is feeling right now.'

We wait for the others to come back from the park and Rupert agrees with me. Jemima and her friend are at eye level with the bird. 'Awww, it's so cute. Why can't we keep it? We'll look after it,' she says. 'It will follow me around outside, like a tame bird.'

'We can't,' I say.

Maddy is in negotiating mood. 'Okay, but if it's still there at 8 o'clock tonight we'll bring it back, it might get hurt.'

'If it's still there,' I say.

Soon we're wandering back along the road, bird in hand. I hear a blackbird when we arrive and then spot a male just metres away. I can see a dead baby one on the other side of the path, the same size as ours. I don't tell Maddy.

'There, I'll tuck it in just here,' and it edges its way out of her hand. 'It has some leaves hanging down to protect it.'

By 7 o'clock she is getting agitated. 'Mum, would it be alright if I go and check on the little bird now?'

I let her go and she's back in no time. 'It was there and calling out. Its parent was really close. He was really happy and he hopped onto my hand and I moved him into the side again. I'm going to the park tomorrow.' She pauses. 'I'm going to the park every day.'

I read up on the subject later on, and discover the dads are usually the ones tending to the fledglings while the mums are already gearing up for the next brood. I flick through photos of Maddy and her 'rescued' bird on my phone. She's there with her mascaraed 'on-fleek' eyes, holding this creature in a way she always dreamt of as a young child – 'Want to hold it,' she'd say of birds in the park back then. 'Want to cuddle it.' I hope her joy in the small things can live on through her teenage years.

The two of us head off to the park at 7.30 the next morning. It has gone, which I hope is a good sign. At least she didn't find it dead. There is a bird around with a tradesman's whistle, a swaggering confidence in summer as the landlash of recent days is all forgotten.

I'm feeling excited today – the shepherd hut will be on its way at last, having been delayed earlier in the week by a breakdown. Rupert is home and will help with the logistics of getting it in place. Then the nesting will begin, and the girls will be at home to help. I have told Annie and Maddy they can use the hut as a bolt-hole too, perhaps revise in there sometimes or sleep in it with friends. That's as long as I'm not using it.

Annie needs a focus, her existence of late has started to worry me. She's not surfacing of her own accord – she knows that I'll be waking her up by 9.30 each morning – but that's not the issue. My real concern is that the life-lustre has gone. I think perspective is an issue and it's hard for her to imagine her existence beyond exams.

'Annie, are you going to get up some time today?' I call out.

'I am up,' she says.

But by nine o'clock there's no sign of her, so I take her a cup of tea. I knock gently and enter before she's had a chance to tell me not to. She's still in bed, one leg hanging out over the floor and the curtains are shut.

'The hut's coming today,' I say.

'Urgh. What? Oh yeah, I know.'

'Do you want to come out for a coffee this morning, break the revision?'

'Where?'

'We could go to The Railway Café.'

'No, you're okay.'

'Can you get up now though?'

'I am, you just need to give me some space. The phone's ringing, you'd better go.'

Rupert calls me down and I take the receiver from him. It's Jon, my shepherd hut man. The cheque hasn't arrived and could I arrange a transfer instead? It's all ready but they can't send it on its way until they have received the remaining funds. I talk to the bank and stop the cheque and phone him back when it's all sorted. It's being loaded now and they will call when they are half-an-hour away.

'You should get out with the kids,' Rupert tells me at lunch time. 'Why don't you meet up with a friend or something, I'll be here. There's no point us all waiting in all day.'

Maddy, Jem and I walk down to the old railway line. The later hour hasn't made Annie change her mind. The café is shut and we head on to my friend Anita's, who invites us in and makes us drinks. I tell Anita what's going on at home, but the children are getting fidgety. It wasn't the best day to come out, I'm very distracted, too, but it's good of Rupert to take the strain. I'm wondering what I'll do first. We can take cushions down there and a rug I have ready. Annie has painted me pictures that I'll have to put somewhere – a watercolour of the ducks, and another of a badger. She has some bunting, too. I will hang that up and keep it there, at least while it's new.

We head home when I know it will be in place. It's not. I'm standing in the back garden where it's meant to go and it's just a bare patch of grass. I run up to the house with the three children following me and burst in the door.

'Ru,' I shout. 'Where's the hut?'

'There was a call when you were out,' he says, coming through to the kitchen. 'It's been damaged on its journey.'

'What? When?'

'They hadn't gone very far. It got caught up on a high branch and it wasn't worth pressing on.'

'That's ridiculous,' I say. 'He's not coming at all. It's just some scam. The man's –'

'It's just unlucky. I'm sure it will be here soon.'

Does he really believe that? I'm starting to feel just a little bit sick. I phone and Jon doesn't pick up, so I leave a message asking him to send pictures of the damage. Soon there's a text from him:

Hi Caroline, the hut arrived has arrived back at the workshop a while ago. The structure of the hut appears sound and undamaged but the flue and the woodburner itself have taken quite a knock! And will certainly need replacing. Tomorrow morning I will action the following: order a replacement stove and flue kit, book our heatas engineer to reinstall, email pictures to you and call with a revised delivery date.

I fully understand your anxiety and will deal with it as swiftly as I possibly can.

I will be in touch prior to 10:00 tomorrow morning.

Regards, Jon (26.05 17:56)

I visit their webpage again – the reviews have been positive, or at least they were until today, but now I find a message from someone else asking him to get in touch about their delivery. I think it's a case of a good company turning bad. There's nothing I can do about it, but I want to scream, or at least punch the guy. I read the text again – how can a cast iron wood-burner 'have taken quite a knock' from an external blow? Rupert still thinks I'm overreacting, that I should wait and see.

I have to get out in the evening and we witness a small cub in the usual place, though it's hard to see very much. There's not much ground visible in there now, it reminds me of Annie's bedroom floor. And in the field the barley is up to my waist in places – we watch it move, but that's all we are likely to see, for it's too high for their heads emerge over the top as they did last year. I can recall seeing them playing and hunting in the wheat and I so want to be back there. I return home feeling glum. 'Some folks want their luck buttered,' I think to myself, recalling a phrase of Mrs Cuxcom's from *The Mayor of Casterbridge*. They are still there, why should it matter to me whether I get to see them or not?

We wake in the night to birds going crazy in the roof, and I feel like I'm swaying slightly, though I'm lying down. 'It's a tremor,' says Rupert. We're all up before Jemima the next morning, and Eliott meets her outside his room when she surfaces, the girls and I sitting on the high steps into two of the bedrooms. 'Jemima, it's okay,' he says. 'You mustn't cry, but we've had an earthquake.' Her eyes widen and she steps closer to him for reassurance. 'All the other houses on Sandwich Road are destroyed. Ours is the only one left standing.'

She squeezes in beside me. 'I know the worst that could happen here is a broken flower pot,' she says with the unusual assurance that belongs to her siblings. I assumed she'd be a little frightened after scenes of Kathmandu, but the age of gullibility must be passing.

'I thought it was the woman in black, creeping round my room at first,' says Maddy. 'I put my light on and realized it was my shirt making a strange outline where I'd left it, but it *was* moving. That story has really freaked me out. We screamed in the lesson when Ofstead were next door. The teacher told us to stop or they'd make them take it off the syllabus.'

Annie's maths paper goes viral just minutes after they sit the exam, with outraged teens asserting it was 'too difficult'. I'm glad I didn't have to sit it. The revision has stopped as Annie takes time to read all the comments on Facebook and Twitter.

I reach for her curtains behind her and start to open them – 'Oh, Mum–'

I'm looking down on a mother and daughter sparrow out on the patio together. The fledgling is crouched on the stones, shivering. The mother comes and goes in her quest food, then administers it to her young, beak to beak. They venture onto the lawn and peck through the long grass together, like some mother and daughter outing.

'You're not going to do any work today are you?'

'Do you blame me after that?'

'Course not. Do you want to go somewhere?'

'Canterbury. Can you take me shopping?'

And so I trail round her favourite haunts, feigning an interest in identical looking garments. I should be at home, I have students' work to read before term ends, and encouraging and constructive comments needed for each one. But this is relaxation for her, a mid-exam reward. It's how she wants to spend her time with me, so I should just go with it.

'How about these?'

'You'll never walk in them.'

'You mean you couldn't.'

She needs shoes for her school leavers' prom that's just a few weeks away. But those have to be five inches of heel. Champagne sling-backs with pointed heel and toe.

'You'll wear them once and they'll sit at the back of your wardrobe for evermore.'

'But I've always wanted some like this.'

She tries them on and looks me in the eye, then wobbles a little.

'Well, perhaps not these ones.'

I encourage her to keep looking and she comes away empty-handed. 'I'll find some when I'm with Katie,' she says.

We've been dodging showers and a thunderstorm has been rolling in the distance. 'That sky looks like a badly painted watercolour,' I say on the way home, looking at the streaks of grey with harsh unblended edges.

'I know, like wet on dry.'

The next day I'm home from work at 1.30 p.m. and go upstairs to greet her. It's a sunny day but her curtains are shut again. She's on her beanbag, laptop in front of her. I brave the suggestion that she hasn't done much. 'I have done my hair in a plait and I have got dressed. And I've done a few minutes on BBC Bitesize.'

She looks pale, tired and far from healthy. 'Come out for a walk with me,' I say. 'It'll do you some good.'

'Okay then.'

'What, really?'

'Just let me put some make-up on. I'm not going out like this.'

We take a country lane off the roundabout, I won't risk taking her on a long circuit but just a twenty minute stroll. 'Eugh, flies are going to stick to this,' she says, looking at her lollipop as the occasional insect hangs in the air.

'Well keep it in your mouth then,' I say. 'Come on.'

'I really don't see what you get from this.'

I have to admit, I'm not getting much from it either with her reluctant presence, but we've started now. Tyn runs ahead with unashamed enthusiasm, cocking his leg on almost every available blade of grass. We take a steep narrow footpath that leads up behind the Baptist church and find a white-grey horse in a meadow that comes to greet us. 'I'm getting away from here,' she says, speeding up. Was I wrong to encourage her out? Could I have instilled in her a love of nature if I'd tried harder? It's meant to flounder in the teenage years, but should resurface if cultivated early on. At least we have cooking as common ground. Perhaps next time I'll bake with her, but thinking about it, she prefers to do that on her own. Jemima is so dissimilar, and I don't think we've raised her differently. She practically begged me to take her to Tom's hole in the holidays, a dell in the wood that started out as a manmade pit, dug for trench training during the war. Kids love to ride bikes down it and swing across on a rope – Jemima likened it to jumping off the high bales in *Charlotte's Web*. 'It is, it's just the same,' she said.

My garden badgers continue to come. Robin, the adolescent badger, is in pristine condition and faring well on his own. His face has broadened considerably, and his head is sleek, almost otter-like. This is badger perfection: he's fit and on the brink of his adult life, though perhaps a little more wary than most since his injury. I have seen him eating with Dora lately who I suspect is his mother, a new balance of family relations now established.

The most recent stormy weather that chased us from town that day brought out only the die-hards: a night of the patriarchs, Wilbur came, unperturbed by the wind and rain. The mature dog fox with the thick neck was out, too. His mouth has now healed, though he looks a little strange with giant fangs on permanent display. He has an unfortunate looking tail, strangulated in one place and full elsewhere, as if a string has been tied around it and pulled tight. Perhaps he risked losing it at one time, and the prospect of being unable to balance and catch his prey. All is well for him, for now.

Further afield, Willow the rescued cub is reported TB free and is becoming part of a group of orphaned cubs that will be released together. 'We know we have him,' was the comment made on the phone to me. 'He's a naughty little thing.'

Summer has settled in and made herself very much at home. Peppa the guinea pig has her babies, and fresh blood is still on her nose when Maddy finds her, no doubt from cleaning her young. We are just leaving for a party, and perhaps it's for the best, as mother and young can get acquainted in peace. The pups are huddled in close to her, the size of adult hamsters.

'Please don't name them,' I say to the children. 'They're very small, they might not all survive.' I can hear them whispering amongst themselves. 'Toffee, Fudge, Caramel.' Oh, please. 'Stella, Becks,' says Rupert. Jemima starts to sing 'We have some baby guinea pigs' to the tune of 'It was on a Starry Night'. 'We're never ever going to sell these piggies,' says Eliott. Bang goes his entrepreneurial plan then. But they are so small and so perfect – hours later the umbilical cord still hangs from one, though they are up and running as if they've been on the planet for weeks.

I take the dog for his walk, and out near the badger sett a myriad of tiny voices is coming from a sessile oak tree. I stop to watch for a while and see a great tit fly from the nest and back, quick and purposeful. The barley below is now white and looks soft to the touch, like the plush of an antique teddy bear. The cow parsley is over, turning to green and brown while elderflower plugs any gaps in the hedgerows with that same splash of cream. I watch a badger here a few days later – she is a small female who is unfazed by my presence, and sits just above the hole, smelling the air. There is a warm sweet scent out here tonight, dry and with echoes of fresh bread; I wonder if it smells like that to her, too. Wood pigeons in the trees behind her are making loud, startling noises, but she doesn't seem to notice. She is like a dog on the beach, sitting for a moment to enjoy the breeze, just quietly contemplative and at one with her surroundings. Her black eyelids are half-closed as she continues to rest, and I'm lulled by her serenity. She has the marks of an old injury on her chest, but it is long forgotten. I'm reminded of that German word, *Waldeinsamkeit* that we English don't have an equivalent for, more than simply forest (wald) and solitude (einsamkeit), but that other-worldly peace that can be found in nature, a profound sense of well-being, and she and I are both feeling it here.

These moments can feed you for weeks, a few seconds that transform your existence, and soon I'm back into the busyness of life. Everywhere dog roses are scrambling high into the trees this year, rampant with new growth. As I take country lanes to work I hear them scrape the side of the car, thinking to dodge them only when it's too late. There's an abundance of horse poo on the roads, too, as riders make the most of the fine weather. An elderly local is out driving his mobility scooter again, as fast as it will go, his overweight brown Labrador running ahead on its lead with a sideways lollop, tongue hanging out. I wind down my window: 'Good afternoon,' I shout. 'Your dog's enjoying that you know.'

The primary school are keen for the children to enjoy the outdoors, and I'm enlisted to help Jemima's class on a farm visit in the village. The sun is shining again, but the children are moaning on the twenty-minute walk from their form room as they struggle with the heat.

'Can I have some of your drink, Caroline? You've got two. I can't reach mine,' says Jemima's friend Sorrell.

'If you can get to the top of the hill.'

We arrive with thirty weary children, all desperate for the toilet and something to eat, and once needs are met they are taken into a pen to visit the sheep. 'What do you know about farming?' asks the farmer.

They smile at him and then look back at the sheep.

'How many of you live on farms then?'

About twelve hands go up. Well that's hardly right.

'Ooh, it's pooing!' says one.

'Did you see what that sheep just did?'

'Eeugh. I don't want my lunch now.'

The farmer prepares to show them how he shears the sheep, launching himself at one and holding onto her like his life depends on it. He grabs her front legs in one hand as he shears with the other. Now she submits and stiffens for the few seconds it takes to demonstrate. The children gather fleece from the ground and pull it between their fingers.

'Lewis, that's too much,' says the teacher. 'Put it back and come and stand over here.'

That seems a little harsh.

I ask the farmer how much he's paid per fleece, at the back of my mind considering how viable it would be to keep sheep for the wool alone. 'It's gone up to about £5 a fleece,' he says. 'It used to be a pound, pound-fifty – it barely covered the cost of sheering.'

*

A Monday morning and Annie is sixteen. She'll have to go into school today, she has a history revision session, though she'll be finished by lunchtime. Jem can hardly contain her excitement and we go in together to wake her up. 'Happy birthday,' we shout. 'How long do you want before opening your presents?'

'Just leave me alone, I'll try to get up.'

She surfaces without much bother and is soon dressed for school, new iPhone in hand. This is what she's wanted for months, a phone on a contract with internet access, a Snapchat account and Facebook wherever she goes – you never know when you may need it, after all. She objects to her June birthday every year, feeling the injustice of exams when she should be free to celebrate. Yet today she heads off to school without moaning and I'm impressed with her maturity. I mustn't doubt her. I guess she may well have been working hard these last few months – exactly how much revision *is* going on when it's done with a laptop, and freedom's just a tab away?

A few days later the exams are all over and she spends the afternoon preparing herself for the prom. She looks effortlessly glamorous and not so different to a normal day, though the hair has bridal waves and the eyebrows are pimped to perfection. Then she appears in the dress – pale champagne floor-skimming chiffon – high heels and a clutch. I take photos in the garden and move her so the trampoline and green plastic slide are no longer in the background. It's all come much too soon. Perhaps the fact that it's our wedding anniversary is making it worse. We'll have to celebrate that another night, our chief babysitter will be out, and besides, she'll need us to collect her when her night is done.

I drive her down to Russell Gardens on the outskirts of Dover, the meeting point for friends to gather before taking taxis to the town hall. Some have arrived already and I watch from the car as they totter on unsteady heels. A tiaraed bunch walk off without her and I'm starting to see why she'll be so glad to move on – she doesn't really fit in, well, not with that crowd anyway.

As I drive away I can see her in the mirror. I hope she'll quickly find her friends. I wish I'd stopped but there was nowhere to park. I wince with pain and catch sight of my heavy eyes in the rear-view mirror. My head is pounding, the pain roving like thunder – I think it's passing and then comes a crash, louder and closer than before.

Should I find a space nearby, then seek her out? But I'll only embarrass her. She'll be fine. I start to run through the list of known shepherd hut dupees as I drive. I found the names and numbers on the company's Facebook page, they had all posted bad reviews in recent weeks. There are at least seven of us now, and I spent much of the afternoon talking to them. 'I can't believe I fell for it.' 'I hope they've got a cell ready.' 'That was for our retirement.' 'Have you seen what he looks like? He's a complete thug. Wouldn't let him near your granny – but he sounds so *nice.*' 'There's a picture on his own Facebook page of his woman wearing a diamond ring. The day he received our funds.'

I dose myself up on tablets when I'm home and head out to the woods with Maddy. '*Teenagers,*' she says to me as we approach our usual spot, 'Mum, get down!' I crouch for a moment, but wonder why I'm bothering – we shouldn't be intimidated, they don't own the place and they should know that other people come this way. My head throbs again, just to remind me it's still here. 'Come on,' I say. 'Let's walk round the loop, the badgers won't surface if they're around anyway.'

She looks a bit unsure but realizes she has no choice. We walk beyond the sett and up to the far corner where the badger latrines line the base of the fence. 'That's maize,' I tell her, looking into the field. 'Lucky badgers, they're in for an easy few months with this growing here.'

'It's getting late, Mum. Do you think we should have come?'

'There's nothing to worry about. I guess we didn't set out very early but we're here now.'

We follow the path round the back of the sett and soon reach the teenage wood. 'They've made a bonfire, Mum!'

'They must've done it earlier in the day, they couldn't have put it together that quickly,' I say, taking my first branch and walking with it to the edge of the wooded enclosure. Maddy is joining in. 'What if they come back?'

'Well they'll have no bonfire, and they wouldn't dream of trying anything on with you here. Don't worry. And dump the branches as far away as you can. We don't want it too easy for them to put back together again.'

It's dissembled soon enough, anger is fuelling my limbs and I'm glad to be able to channel it somehow. The bonfire was positioned right near a badger hole, though I suppose it's an improvement on setting fire to them.

A red glow is spreading through the sky over the village and we stop to watch. Just when you think it's as vibrant as it can possibly be, the colour intensifies and deepens, reaching out a little further, like a lingering embrace that you never want to end. I feel in my pockets but they're empty. 'Come on Maddy, we should be getting back.'

'Can't we stay a bit longer?'

'It may be dark before we're home, and I don't have a torch tonight.'

A Saturday morning and the phone goes early. 'Can someone get it? It could be badgers.'

'They're clever these days,' says Eliott through the bathroom door.

'Get the *phone.*'

'Oh, hi Gilli,' I say, taking the receiver from him seconds later and shutting myself in the kitchen. 'Injured you say? In broad daylight? Thanks, I'll take their number. Yes, we can go now.' I hang up and call from the bottom of the stairs. 'Who's coming? There's a poorly badger in a field a few miles away!'

Maddy and Jemima arrive in the kitchen while I pull out high vis tabards from a cupboard in the boot room. 'We'll need Dad, too,' I tell them. 'I don't know exactly what we'll find. It might be in a very bad way. You seriously up for that?'

Jem reaches for a tabard. 'I'm coming.'

'That'll drown you.'

'No it won't. You need me, and it'll keep me safe.'

'I'm definitely coming,' says Maddy. 'I've got my phone, I want to get some good pictures of this one.'

'They might not be very pretty.'

Rupert knows the location – we are looking for a field just outside the village of Capel le Ferne, and we follow a very busy road into the village. 'Chapel in the Ferns' is its meaning, but this quaint picture must hark back several generations, as now the road that runs through it is built for speed, easily accommodating two buses side by side. The badgers that once only had to negotiate low-slung plant life are still determined to follow their old routes, hence the need for our visit.

We pull up in a side road and head towards the traffic on foot. I phone the dog walkers who notified the badger group as we walk. We're on the main road now, looking conspicuous in our yellow high vis. They tell me we are in the right place and soon join us at the field edge.

'He's in there somewhere,' says the lady, pointing at an area of thick scrub. 'He was just sitting in the field in broad daylight, but I think all the traffic has frightened him.'

I'm not surprised, vans and lorries are thundering past at way more than the forty-mile-per-hour limit, and this is a Saturday. I guess it's no quieter at night when the badgers are out.

We all climb down into the field and take a look.

'He must feel poorly if he's happy to hang out here,' I say.

'I can see him,' says Rupert. 'He's stuck in the middle of those bushes. I'm going to go round the other side. Can you pass me a towel, I'll cover him with it if he's feisty.'

'I'll go with Dad,' says Maddy.

'Keep your hands out of it,' I say to her.

I have been told how to catch a badger before now, but I'm glad Rupert is taking charge. The committee keep talking about obtaining dog graspers but we haven't got beyond finding prices, and here we are. 'Martin says the best way is to wear the glove low down on your hand, so if the badger bites it finds empty fingers,' I tell him.

Jemima kneels in the field and peers in. 'Ooh, I can see it. It's sooo sweet. *Look* at it, it's a cub I think. He's coming towards me.'

The badger spots Jemima at close range and turns, wedging himself in a dense and inaccessible patch of shrubbery.

'I can almost reach it,' she says.

'I wouldn't,' I tell her. 'He's not comforted by your presence as you are by his. Just look.'

The dogwalkers are watching too. 'He's heading to the other side,' says the man.

'Coming your way,' we call.

'Can we have the cage round here?'

'I'll bring it,' I say. 'Just wait here Jemima.'

Rupert is in his shorts and his arms are also bare. 'Okay, open the lid,' he says. 'I'm going to reach for him. I can hear his leg clicking every time he moves. That's got to hurt.'

The badger turns and limps back into the thicket. He must feel so frightened and I wish we could make this easier for him.

'Perhaps we should leave it, Mum,' says Maddy. 'It doesn't want to be caught.'

'It has to be in a lot of pain. I don't think it'll survive long in the wild like this anyway,' I say. 'We have to see this through.'

I return to Jemima. 'He's coming our way!' she says. I crouch down and lean in, talking to the badger as you might a small child that has lost its way. 'It's okay, it's okay. We're here to help you. Take it easy, little fella.'

The badger settles in, prepared to sit this thing out and we wait. He has a couple of grazes on his face that have rubbed away his fur: one on the wide white band between his eyes and the other, larger raw patch is in the black stripe above his left eye. He's pretty alert, but perhaps that's just fear. Has anyone ever failed on a badger mission, I wonder. Could I be the first? Relegated to making tea and producing minutes, but never let loose with a badger. Some people would be happy with that, but it's not why I got involved, and quite frankly, badger groups will take all the manpower they can get – once the volunteers are judged to be harmless, of course. This is one determined badger, we've been waiting like this for a good ten minutes.

A lorry rumbles past just metres from us and the badger hops in Rupert's direction again, clicking as he goes.

'I've got him,' says Rupert. 'Can you all get round here? Caroline, bring the cage nearer, that's it.'

And he's in. Or should I say, she. This is definitely a female, now that I can see her properly. She has the fan tail of the females and is quite delicate. A cub of about five months, but still very small. There's not much of her and I wonder just how long she's been surviving with this injury.

'Look, Mum, her nose is really grazed underneath too,' says Jem. 'What's wrong with her?'

'She's been knocked by a vehicle, but the driver didn't stop. It would've been better if we could have got to her when this happened.'

We thank the couple who say they are just relieved she's safe now. Back to the car and the girls pose for photos with their badger while we phone the local badger-friendly vets in the area. One has an answer machine running – this is a Saturday after all – and another is engaged.

'Let's head towards Dover anyway,' I say. 'Jeremy is usually pretty good at accepting wildlife. You ready girls?'

'Take a photo on your phone, too, Mum,' says Jemima.

The cage is in the boot now and she is posing with her widest grin, arms outstretched in front of it while Maddy perches on the edge of the open boot, embarrassed but grin equally wide. The badger is lying down, resting her little head on the gardening glove that I lost as we tousled her into the cage. She's taken to it like it's the best feather pillow. I wonder if she's feeling secure now or just exhausted. I place the towel over the top of the cage to give her the darkness she is probably missing.

'They might need to put it down,' says Rupert as we drive.

'I've stroked her,' says Maddy. 'With my bare hand. She didn't mind.'

'She's pretty perky,' I say. 'There's not much else wrong with her. We might be lucky.'

The road we want to take is closed so we pull up to rethink. 'I'll just phone the vets again,' I say. 'If we've got to take the long way round we should make sure it's worth it.'

'We could just drive off with her, keep her for ourselves,' comes the conversation from the back seat. 'Pretend we never found her.'

'That'd be really helpful,' I tell them.

'She needs a name,' Jemima says.

'What was the last one called that we rescued?' says Maddy.

'That was Willow,' I reply.

'Something naturey,' she says.

'Fern,' says Jemima. 'She's from that Fern place. What's it called?'

'Capel le-Fer-' I cover the receiver and look back at them. 'Hang on, I'm through to the vet. It's an injured badger. We're from the local badger group,' I explain. 'Yes, please, if you could. We have her with us now. Please call us as soon as you can.'

'That sounds hopeful,' says Rupert.

'Can we open the boot and look at her while we wait?' ask the girls.

'Leave her be,' I tell them. 'She needs quiet and rest.'

The vets agree to take her in, and soon we're walking along a Dover street with a badger in a cage, as most people would their pet cat or rabbit. We turn a few heads. 'Ooh, I've never seen one before,' says a young man to his girlfriend.

'*I* want to carry her,' says Jemima. 'She's my badger.'

'It's too heavy,' I tell her.

'She's injured,' I say to a lady who raises an eyebrow at me. 'Just going to the vets.' As you do.

I enjoy the feeling of sitting in the vets with a badger on my lap – in the cage of course – but then I realize she is pretty smelly. A spaniel growls at her and I lower the cage to the floor and tuck her underneath my legs, as far as the bench will allow.

We are not kept waiting long, and a veterinary nurse comes to speak to us. 'The badger?' she says, looking at me. I hand her the cage like it contains the most precious cargo, which, as far as my family is concerned, it does.

'We think her leg is broken,' I say. 'That's all. We know where to return her to when she's sorted.'

'We won't be able to operate today,' she tells me. 'It'll probably be Monday. We don't have the staff.'

'You can give her something to keep her comfortable?' I say.

'Of course.'

We stop at the supermarket on the way home in our wellies and muddied knees. Rupert has scratches on his arms and I'm sure we all have twigs in our hair.

'I didn't think it would take that long,' I say. 'I'll see if Martin will let you come to the release,' I tell the girls. 'It will be pretty amazing.'

Well, it would have been. During lunch Rupert takes a call and it doesn't sound good. 'I see,' he says. 'I understand. Yes, I know. Okay, thanks for everything.'

'Fern?' says Jemima. 'Has she died?'

Rupert sits down again at the table to explain. 'They've had to put her to sleep. The leg was broken at the elbow, that wasn't something they could fix.'

Plates are pushed away and for a moment there is a stunned

silence.

'That's rubbish,' says Maddy. 'It was only a broken leg, for goodness sake.'

'They say they couldn't help it. At least it's no longer in pain.'

'Not *it*. She,' says Jemima. '*Fern.*'

'Should've left it where it was,' says Annie.

I talk to Rupert about it when I get the chance. I'm really not happy about what they did, I feel so glum about it. I guess it's nothing new for them and they make these decisions all the time.

'It *was* a bit hasty,' says Rupert. 'It's quite disempowering. If it was a pet they would have consulted us, but this was just an inconvenience. We should have spoken to Martin at least, they should have given us time to do that.'

'It was cheap and convenient for them,' I say.

'A quick dispatch. You know, that badger could've been part of our menagerie. Just think, a resident badger hopping around the garden on three legs.'

I feel a pang of regret before rationality kicks in. 'But it didn't belong to us either. And they are nocturnal creatures anyway.'

'I know, but so what?'

This experience has the reverse effect of what I expect from nature, of what it usually does in me. It creates a sense of loss, not of healing or mental balance. I won't forget her eyes: they were more than round, as if she was trying to open them even wider in a quest to understand. Those black eyelids formed an outer ring that exaggerated the look, like a made-up Pierrot clown's. I can't recall her eyelashes at all; there was no barrier, and that steady gaze had such a vulnerable innocence. I feel like I have betrayed her trust. Yet I suppose we saved her from a lingering death. She probably felt really lovely as she drifted off to sleep: no pain, only warmth and peace.

I need to think less about what nature can do for me, and more about what I can do for it, anyway. Why am I concerned about what it can give *me* in the first place? The reality is that it so often does touch me, but perhaps our expectations of the wild are unfair. We should let that amazing feeling of connection surprise us, rather than seek it out. Be grateful for the moments it gives us, not feel entitled to more.

I return to collect the cage a few days later, when I can face it. There is a newspaper cutting of a seal on the wall by the reception desk. 'So ours isn't the only unusual animal?' I ask.

'Oh no. We had a piglet in here the other day, too.'

She phones for someone to come up with the basket. A vet arrives in scrubs, she's a girl in her thirties.

I pluck up courage to talk about what happened, trying to make it sound completely natural. 'Oh, I just wanted to say, if it happens again, do you think you could phone us first, before putting a badger down? We might have been able to organize something for her. We have links with Wildwood, they have lots of our orph-'

'We help Wildwood too. We made a decision that was best for

the animal. We always put the animal's interest first.'

'I do appreciate that, but we felt out of the loop. We'd have liked a phone call *before* it happened.'

'We can't do that with wildlife,' she says.

I thank her and take the cage from her. It feels very light now. In the bottom lies a lone glove and I turn and run.

Eliott is preparing to go to France today on a one-week residential trip with school. The port of Dover is just minutes away and the primary leavers do the trip every year. He's been up since six, his bags all ready and is in hyper mode. He and Jem have a near-tearful parting in the car when I drop her. I send him to the village shop for sweets when we're home.

'You were quick,' I say when he returns. 'Did you run back?'

'I might of.'

'You've got until ten,' I say. 'Why don't you find something to do?'

'I'm okay.' He's unzipping and zipping sections of his holdall, then his hand luggage.

'What's the matter?'

'Just checking.'

Now he's straightening the tea-towels on the cooker handrail. 'Since when did you start tidying my kitchen?' I say. 'Do you want to go early? Nathan's in already, his dad dropped him with his sister. And I saw Harry go in.'

'You're going to miss me, aren't you? It'll be ages before you see me again.'

'I'm sure it'll pass quickly. Come on, let's get those bags in the car.'

The headmistress and a teaching assistant are waiting in the reception area where kids' travel bags are stacked around the edges. 'Medication?' says the assistant, and I hand her some emergency Calpol. 'Right, give him a kiss and off you go, Eliott.' She's done this before.

I discover late in the afternoon that their ferry hasn't yet made it in – friends have phoned me full of anxiety, though I was blissfully ignorant. 'Our services are currently suspended,' says the P & O website. School text messages filter through during the evening, informing us that they are still on the boat but fed, watered and all fine. It has something to do with French blockades. Hopefully the children are finding some sense of adventure in it all. Then, at ten o'clock, a final message for the night: 'Just spoken to Mrs Bird. They are in Calais and will be at the chateau in about an hour.' That's 11 o'clock French time then. I wonder how easily they will get home – I imagine it won't even have occurred to the children, though the staff will be worried.

We hit the hottest July day on record…Eliott and friends will be wearing long sleeves and trousers for all of their activities, and I try not to think of his past fainting episodes as he climbs towers and abseils. Back home Annie and Katie spend the day painting for a local exhibition, to be held in the neighbouring hamlet of Barfrestone.

'What do you think, Mum?'

'Well, it needs a bit more work if you expect to sell it. It's not your usual standard.'

'What do you mean?'

'You're not working from a photo for a start. Where is this beach? What are its features? What time of day do you think it is there?'

That didn't go down well, and I try to lighten their mood with lunch at the pub. 'It's too hot to sit outside, Mum, we'll sit in that corner over there.'

They settle underneath a speaker, phones at the ready. 'We could go to the beach, it'll be inspiration for me. We should go back to yours, Katie.'

'I can't take you anywhere yet. I'm looking after Amber this afternoon,' I tell them. 'You just need to press on, you'll get it done.'

Baby Amber screams to the best of her ability, which is pretty top notch. 'Does Lisa know she's a nightmare, Mum?'

'I doubt it. Amber screams when she's out of earshot. She thinks it's a learning curve for her anyway. You know how laid back she is.'

'Can't you shut her up somehow? How are we supposed to work with *that* going on?'

'I'll take her into the snug. Put your music on or something.'

Towards the end of the afternoon I check the internet for details of where to take their work. I can't believe it. They've missed the deadline, the exhibition opens next week but work had to be in a couple of days ago. It would have been good for them. There couldn't be a more beautiful setting than that old Victorian threshing barn, with the swallows flying in through the open doors and up to their nests in the high rafters. There is always a good local turnout; last year a call was put out to the locals to provide more cake for the event.

I think the girls will learn from it. Next year I'm sure they'll be ready and can build towards it gradually. This was just a rushed attempt to earn a bit of cash, a moody post-exam frenzy, with anxieties over grades already kicking in.

The badgers are feeling the heat, too. I watch Robin arrive at 11.30 p.m. and stretch out on the ground – it's the first time I've ever seen him do this. I thought it was the behaviour of the old or pregnant badgers, but perhaps the ground feels cold in amongst the trees. He looks decidedly lethargic, and I resolve to put water down the following night. Badgers can die through lack of water during a hot summer, and it starts to play on my mind, even as I'm teaching my last class of term. *They'll be okay*, I tell myself. *You can't do anything about it now – and besides, they're sleeping.*

I'm given chocolates and a beautiful orchid that I fear won't survive long with me – 'neglect it', I'm told in the office, 'it's an air breathing plant, just leave it alone' – and as I wend my way home and the euphoria subsides my thoughts turn again to the badgers. I'll fill some empty bottles, put them in a large rucksack and take them out into the woods. I hope no one will stop me and ask perfectly innocent questions, make quips about my Duke of Edinburgh award coming a bit late in the day. Still, it has to be done.

Just a chat with the window-cleaner who makes no comment on my appendage and I'm into the woods again. Bramble flowers, yellow meadow vetchling and lilac scabious are attracting the bees today, and a large skipper butterfly, moth-like and furry while dense as a bee itself, flutters by on its double layer of wings. The barley heads are drooping and a spider has slung its sack between grasses on either side of the path, like a kid's impromptu effort at making a tent, with a sheet thrown over a couple of chairs – it won't last long here. I wonder how long it needs. The babies are crawling around inside the sack and there is a small hole on one side.

A profusion of grass heads meets us and the dog tunnels his way through overrun sections of path. I'm surprised by the variety of shape and colour in the grass seeds. They create their own fabric that I run my hands through, soft and with the delicacy of fine lace. There are suggestions of old-fashioned haberdashery shops everywhere, an array of superfluous trimmings with subtle variations in texture and shade. Pink yarrow is dotted along the edges, and purple thistles are growing high. I trample through the nettles now and attach the dog's lead to a fence post as I climb into the enclosure. It's thick with nettles here, too, and I'm stung a few times as I tread a path for myself. Where can I pour the water now that I'm in here? I had imagined tipping it into the plate-like bracket fungi on the old beech tree, but it would run straight off. I could never fill the gaps at the base of the tree as I had hoped, to be trough-like and brim full as they were in autumn.

I make an existing dip in the ground deeper with the sole of my boot and fill it up – it's holding water for now, though I doubt it will remain until the badgers begin to surface.

I check on the teenage wood before heading home, and see sawdust at the base of another old beech. I stand and watch a couple of carpenter bees fly in and out, then crouch down to take a closer look. There's one dead on the ground – it has more than likely been brought out by the others, a common bee tactic that prevents any disease taking hold in the group.

I can hear the maize leaves flapping like sails just the other side of the trees; these plants dominate the horizon now, concealing the old clock tower and chimneys of the Waldershare estate just beyond the fields. I take an empty bag from the rucksack and help myself to the abundance of elderflowers, to supplement what's left in the garden. I'll make some cordial while Eliott is on his boat this afternoon and have it ready for his return. I had a text from the head-teacher again this morning – 'We are going straight to Calais after breakfast as advised. The children will have a packed lunch. Coach has fridge, aircon and toilet.'

They make it back sooner than expected, having boarded an early ferry. They've caught the sun and look a little weary, even bewildered, but excitement to be home soon takes over. 'It was such a cool trip, Mum,' he says as I throw his bags in the boot.

'The best holiday I've ever had.'

Oh really? I like to think he's forgotten a few.

'Why's that bag so heavy?'

'It'll be all the wet stuff. I think it smells a bit, some of it's been in there all week.'

'I've got some sweets left,' he says as he sits beside me in the car. 'Do you want a blue bon-bon?'

'Go on then, thanks.'

'Down with the kids, Mum. Did you know, there was a crocodile in the lake, where we did all our activities.'

'I don't think so, the leaders were having a laugh.'

'There was! I knew no one would believe me. Nathan felt it on his legs.'

I raise an eyebrow as I turn to look at him. 'It was safe,' he says, 'they'd taken all of its teeth out.'

The photos from the school trip are available to download now they're home, and Annie is the first to access them on her phone. She makes us all feel like Luddites, but it doesn't always pay to be adept at something.

'Annie's photos from her phone were put on the white board,' Eliott tells me after his first day back. 'They were all up there, selfies where she's posing, her prom, 'n' everything. Scrolling for the whole class to see. She's going to kill me.'

'Well, it wasn't your fault.'

He tells her at the first opportunity. 'So they were all up there?'

'You should've signed out,' he says to her. 'You were probably still logged into Facebook when you downloaded them, connected with the school system.'

'I didn't know. Mr Lamb owes me a present. That's the last time I do anything like that for you.'

'Eliott's little friends are going to be even more in love with you,' I tell her.

'I do deserve a cash reward, I completely do.'

Eliott confides in me a few days later when he's up in his bedroom. 'Don't tell her, Mum, but I made that bit up, that bit about the whole class watching it. Only Ivan saw. But Mrs Restall did take half an hour deleting them.'

'Ivan loves her anyway, he won't be put off by the odd embarrassing pout. You're probably best off not telling her. Just leave it now, hope she forgets.'

Annie has not lost her confidence and refuses to live in fear of something like this happening again. The following evening Rupert suggests she's been on her phone a little too long.

'It's cos I've got to check my Facebook page – I've changed my profile picture – I need to see how many likes I've got. I'm doing well, twenty-eight and I only changed it yesterday.'

'Has Ivan liked it?' says Eliott. 'I bet he would if he saw it.'

'Shut up, you little git.'

Family tensions are always exacerbated this time of year, be it down to the heat or some other reason, and our birds are no different. The next day ducks Bingley and Darcy are getting into a fight over their washing up bowl. They are still oblivious to their pond that's been there for weeks now. Mr Darcy is back in the water, always the dominant one, and Mr Bingley paces round the bowl on his orange legs that look like they're made of rubber, the stuff of children's buoyancy aids. I plan to move that bowl closer and closer to the pond until they finally realize it's there.

Amy the chicken is cross with new chicken Daisy for taking her patch under the sweet peas, and is clucking for England. Sufficiently intimidated, the youngster hops out. Amy takes up her favourite place and Daisy confronts her, and so the cycle continues.

A smell of clover rises from the grass as I sit back in my deckchair. 'Watch your feet,' I tell Jemima as she runs over to me, 'The bees are everywhere.' I point out a fledgling blue tit to her with dull, dirty looking plumage. Deep-throated pigeon refrains are coming from the trees at the bottom, and more of the same from the far distance. I'm trying not to look at the planned site of my shepherd hut – I hate seeing that patch of ground where it was due to go, yet the ducks are swaggering their way through it now, treading their slapstick into the very soil of my disappointment. While the badgers carry with them a certain awe-inspiring dignity, the ducks simply make me laugh with their endearing ways. I like to think of them all filling this place, knowing the badgers come here, that it's still their territory, that creatures burrow under it, roll through it and claim it as their own.

Jemima's class are going on another outing and I've been asked to come along. Rippledown Environmental Centre is a short drive away, and they're kept busy from the moment they arrive. 'Now children, listen up, we want you to build a den for a wild animal or insect of your choosing. Make its own special hideout. You can put a feather on the top for a flag, or a leaf. Let your imaginations run wild. What would you want if you were a small creature?'

Jemima and best friend Isabella begin creating a hedgehog home with a well-disguised tunnel, its purpose neatly written out in sticks, just so the local hogs can be sure. One small girl adds her own room to her group's insect den. 'It's for the mummies to smoke in when they want some space.' The teaching assistant thinks it's really funny. 'Did you hear that?' she says, telling everyone as she goes. 'A smoking room. Young Amy wants a smoking room.' It's a little unfair, she thought it a perfectly sensible addition.

The children spend time at the pond, taking turns to dip a net into the water while their 'buddy' hangs onto their ankles. Then after lunch they make 'smelly cocktails' with the most pungent smelling leaves and debris they can find. 'Eugh, how did you make that?'

'I'm not saying. She said there's a prize for the best one.'

'Mine's grosser than yours.'

'No, mine's more gross.'

'Now children, gather round. This is a very special woodland,

and here you are going to find your own special tree. You have the map already.'

The children exchange glances with each other.

'You all have lines on your hand,' the instructor continues. 'Can you see them?'

They stretch out their palms and take a close look, then compare them with friends.

'Quieten down class,' says the teacher.

'Come up one at a time and I'll draw over those lines for you. This will be your map. Let it guide you to your very own special tree in the woodland. Look for that shape in the roots, or in the fork of the branches.'

Soon it's Eliott's last day at primary school and I'm up earlier than usual. It's Dad's last day of radiotherapy too, a day of moving on for them both. I sit in the family room overlooking the bird table, and watch as a jay comes in to land, heavy on its feet. This supposedly shy bird is nothing but, seeing off first a blackbird and then a jackdaw. He isn't being rushed by anyone and takes what he needs, king of the table for now. Soon he's gone, and a young jackdaw is fed by its parent on the roof. A collared dove comes to sit at the other end of the table – the jackdaw parent stops and looks into her – just that one glare from those pale blue eyes and the dove bails out. She must be waiting nearby, watching, because the moment the jackdaws leave she's back, and begins to feed her own. Now a sparrow comes to interrupt and she gives him the same treatment she's just received. Finally the sparrows take their turn, arriving en masse from the forsythia bush just metres from the table. A fledgling begins to feed itself, its competence only seen after its dad flies out through the willow tree and away.

The sun blazes in the most perfect blue sky today, as if somehow endorsing these kids as they reach the finale of their time at primary school. Mid-morning I take a call from Eliott: 'Can you bring my cornet in please?'

'When do you need it?'

'Now,' he says.

I pull up beside the green just in time to witness his class filing from the school gates and into the church across the road. They will be rehearsing for their leavers' service that we parents will attend this afternoon. 'Looks like you're in luck, Eliott,' says Mr Lamb, and Eliott shoots me a bashful expression as he takes the case from me. Did he think I'd kiss him in front of his friends? Of course I wouldn't. What should he care now what his classmates think of him anyway? There are some overly confident, irritating ones he won't miss, but surely he can let down his guard today. The class are wearing signatures on their white t-shirts, good wishes to each other in bright green and yellow pen. Already arms are slung around each other's necks and an air of nostalgia is creeping in.

Before long I'm back for the service with Annie alongside me, keen to support her little brother in a transition she knows all about. The children sing 'One more step along the world I go,' an assembly favourite since they started as four- and five-year-olds, and the tears are flowing, as much from them as from the parents. Eliott plays a blues tune that we've heard plenty of at home. Soon they take turns to come up to the mic and share their significant memories. During the final song they group themselves on the stage, and turn placards round that show their secondary school destination. Eliott looks content – he's going where he wanted to and with a strong group of friends around him. I call that a happy closure, and I can see he feels the same.

The next morning I'm awake early as usual and head outside to collect the cam. I can't quite believe it, but there on the screen is a badger cub, visiting our garden for the very first time. He's with his dad, the venerable Wilbur, and the two stick close together for several frames. I just love these moments when they come along, and probably take more assurance from them than most would, but then I'm fine with mild insanity if it can bring a smile to my face. I have to see these images on the TV, I don't want to miss any detail, and take myself through to the TV room. Eliott's school leavers' order of service is on the sofa and I push it aside and sit down. I click on 'my content' and begin to play. The pair's arrival time is a quarter to eleven. The cub has an elongated face that reminds me of Georgie's – in fact, it's too early for Dora's cubs to be this size, her pregnancy went on so long. After half-an-hour Wilbur makes his own way home, leaving the cub on his own. As I watch I see a fox appear and wonder what the cub will do – a fox usually takes second rung when in a badger's company, but I doubt this will be the case here. The badger cub hides behind a tree, though the fox can of course smell him and may have seen him already. Uninterested, the fox takes his turn with the peanuts and lingers a while, but as soon as he's gone the cub reappears. He shows no sign of feeling ruffled, leaving finally at half-past midnight.

I guess the parent badgers are happy for the cubs to have a few adventures of their own and feel sure they will make it home. Though protective at first, they cannot contain them forever, after all. This one leaves via a different exit than the one he came by, and yet I know this is unexplored ground for him; I haven't missed a night since I had the cam back in December. I know how that must sound. So I'm a little addicted, but it doesn't take much effort – it's just routine, like locking the back door and putting the milk bottles out at night.

Rupert and Maddy find me downstairs and I unload the dishwasher as if nothing has happened, enjoying my discovery before I have to start answering questions. But they surface soon enough.

'Who came last night, then?' asks Rupert as we're sitting down to breakfast.

'Wilbur and a cub,' I say, trying not to let the excitement sound in my voice. 'Dora came later, but without any cubs, I think hers are still underground. Don't laugh, but I think the cub is Georgie's.'

'She's got Wilbur's eyebrows,' says Maddy.

They are already laughing uncontrollably and the conversation hasn't gone very far. 'No, seriously,' I say, pausing so they will actually hear me. 'It's too big to be Dora's, she had a late birth – don't you remember when she started to deflate?'

Now they are trying not to laugh, biting lips that are still inclined to spread into broad smiles. Do I dare say it? 'And she looks like Georgie. She has a long face.'

Well, that did it.

'They're *badgers*,' says Rupert, sharing eye-contact with Maddy that suggests I've really lost it. 'They all have long faces,' he says once his laughter's subsided.

It's lucky it's the holidays and Annie is sleeping in.

And yet despite the playful mocking, the badgers are truly fascinating right now and I suppose I am firmly in the grip of an obsession, if I wasn't before. When Wilbur is out he has a renewed energy, leaping to attack and defend, though for no particular reason – he's just skittish, and with that extra spring in his step that comes with new parenthood. He frequently comes with a cub in tow, though occasionally I've seen him go to the entrance hole, perhaps to check one is coming, and sure enough, they appear. I am beginning to wonder whether he's bringing them or they simply tag along until they feel they know what to do. One particular cub is very regular in his visits and I worry he may become dependent on us – he arrives on his own one wet night after a week or two of coming accompanied, and now there is nothing left for him to eat. He looks so small, so vulnerable, with his pot belly that needs filling and wet fur that sticks to him, making him appear all the more undersized. This little guy needs to learn to forage, and I determine to put out less for the time being. He eats a large piece of chalk and when I wander down there again I find the remnants on the ground.

There is a young fox around too – this one looks adolescent and struggles with the brushwood in amongst the trees, getting her feet caught and seeming unsure of herself. She has a ludicrous air about her, with enormous ears that dominate her slim, discerning face.

It's the very end of July and at last Georgie arrives with a cub – I have wondered why she's stayed away, but now she's here, and with the cub that I thought was hers all along. She is still a heavy looking badger, and appears not to have suffered for her cub-bearing. It is Dora's appearance that surprises me the most. Her tail looks thin and mothy and has a new kink at the end, but the most noticeable thing about her is her stretched abdomen: it is sinewy and veined, bearing the worst stretch marks imaginable. The ridges run lengthways and her teats are still swollen. She is literally half the badger she was, it seems she's has little in the way of reserves left for herself. I watch as she backs down the hole as if pulled on a string, but it's only a cub coming from the garden direction. I hope her nerves aren't frayed too.

I know that Dora and Georgie have had at least three cubs between them, as one night the youngsters are all out together.

That makes for seven badgers in total, including the adolescent Robin who still puts in an appearance from time to time, though now only ever on his own. I suppose he's decided to give the clan some space, as no doubt Wilbur will be defensive with the cubs around. Do badgers ever long for company? I think they do. In his book *A Lifetime of Badgers* Peter Hardy suggests a rarely heard shrill cry is an expression of sadness when a badger, and most likely a young one, finds itself alone. I think this is what I've sometimes heard in the woods. I hope Robin starts a grouping of his own before the next season comes round. He may have reached maturity – some claim it takes them two years, while others think it happens when they are just over a year old. The likelihood is that by now, at fifteen months, he will be ready. Perhaps he's off claiming territory, and a mate to go with it. Nothing stands still long for any of us it seems.

I make the most of having the children home and we're out in the woods day and night. The heads of barley that hung bowed and ready for execution have met their fate already and the field has been disc harrowed. The badger hole into the field has been demolished by all the activity, but I'm not worried for them – I have Kipling's poem 'The Way Through the Woods' running through my mind, thanks to Eliott's summer memorization project from his new school. '*Weather and rain have undone it again*' Kipling says of the road in his poem. I can't help thinking that the badgers will still have their way here, will still 'roll at ease'. No farmer can really be assured of remaining in charge, no matter how hard he tries.

Jemima's always appreciative of the subtle changes, and reaches for a thistle head that is now soft and downy. 'It's not rabbit fur,' she says, picking some out with her fingers, 'it just looks like it.' Around the other side of the sett the maize towers above us and looks tropical, alien, like it really shouldn't be growing here. Hogweed reaches the same proportions, and can no longer be confused with cow parsley as it was a few weeks ago. This imposter was introduced as a decorative plant to gardeners in the nineteenth century, and little was understood then of its dangers – it can cause burns with close contact, and blindness with an accidental rub of the eyes.

It's early August and I can't help feeling that summer is racing to a close, as if it wants to be done with all this exhausting growth and move on – one final surge of energy before stepping aside once more. The elderflowers have fruited into green berries and blackberries are turning varying shades of red and purple. Apple boughs are hanging low as fruit grows heavy, stooping with welcoming arms, as if burdened with the weight and requesting the fruit be picked. Stay inside for a week and you might feel you've missed summer altogether, that autumn has seized the baton while you were distracted, with a resentful trip of the ankle as she takes hold.

And yet the obvious contentment of the birds and animals around is so satisfying to watch, and I want this stage to go on and on. It's not just the badger cubs that make me feel this way. There is a nest of wood pigeons in the forest yard, and the mother is making the most wonderful noise at times – it is almost a purr, a restful and serene utterance of oohs, as if she cannot contain her happiness. I challenge any pigeon-hater to hear that and still consider them a nuisance. I haven't heard this sound at any other time of year and I associate it with her motherly delight, a declaration that all is well with the world. It settles me. I think it would work well on a meditation CD, or a recording to play mothers in labour: *relax, you're not alone, this is a way of life shared by many*, the utterances say if you listen hard enough.

In the evenings the pipistrelle bats come out and fly low circles in front of the trees. It's as if we back on to a happy community of wildlife, each doing their own thing, unaware that they are appreciated, but loving life every bit as much as we do.

It is with some reluctance then that I leave all this behind for our summer holiday, as I know things will have moved on by the time we're back. I don't want to miss any cub appearances, and set the cam as we leave – it won't run for the entire holiday, but most of the week will be covered. As we drive along the wood-side road that leads out of the village we spot a dead cub lying on the side. The harvest has affected their behaviour and we haven't seen them emerge into the field lately – I suspect their foraging routes have been altered, and they have felt the need to cross the road into a wheat crop that's still standing. There will be at least three cubs left in the clan we watch up there, but it saddens me all the same.

We're holidaying in France this year and find Rupert has chosen well, with a cottage inside a walled estate and an outdoor pool. Our nearest town is Laon, just three-and-a-half hours from the Kent coast. We are soon immersed in a heatwave, and all excursions give way to demands for a swim. The location is beautiful – tranquil and slow, with the ubiquitous locals who could be paid to stand and stare at the occasional tourist – but something seems to be missing. Yes, I know the badgers are miles away and that unsettles me slightly, but there's something else that I struggle to locate for a while. It's not the Wi-Fi that's a problem this year, or the remoteness. It's the dearth of my preferred background noise – birdsong. I've spotted some long-tailed tits in the cedar tree beyond the pool and one great tit, but on the whole birds seem strangely absent here. I try to put it to the back of my mind, but the silent soundtrack begins to niggle …I decide to look into it, and the results make for uncomfortable reading: sixty-four varieties of wild bird can be hunted in France. Thrushes can legally be caught on lime sticks in the south-east, and, in the Ardennes region, in noose traps. Clap netting of lapwings, wood pigeons and skylarks is permitted throughout the north-east and south-west. There are limits and permits have to be sought, but of course illegal hunting is prevalent. The ortolan song bird is facing a new threat as chefs campaign to have the 2007 ban lifted, arguing there is an unfair black market operating. The traditional way to eat them is with a cloth over your head, so your offensive act can be concealed from the sight of God.

We can perhaps forgive the French for their more earthy way of eating – good bread, cheese, wine, it's all very simple really, and appealing when the weather is hot. They don't dress up their food to appeal to vegetarian sympathies – vege-what? Maddy was horrified by the sight that met her in a butcher's shop window – a skinned rabbit with its head still on, and those innocent, searching eyes looking out. The duck complete with beak was what did it for me, and we learnt to walk past them quickly, our eyes averted, heads down. I suppose you could say their way is better than ours, where chicken is mashed and minced and coated in breadcrumbs so children consume it without question. But the willingness to eat birds whose survival is under threat for me takes it to a different level – should they even need laws about these things? Shouldn't a distaste for them be completely natural? We do at least feel confirmed in our vegetarian ways – we are nothing if not consistent, and won't be found eating a bird or animal because its kind is unattractive or plentiful.

'I want to go vegan,' says Maddy soon after we're home. 'I don't want leather shoes next time, either.'

'It's going to make life difficult,' I tell her. I know she is in many ways a more extreme version of myself, but I'm not sure we're quite ready for this yet. It was a shock to Rupert when we found enough evidence to support the nutritional value of a vegetarian diet, and she is at least clearing her plate now. 'You can't get much kinder eggs than the ones you bring in,' I say, 'and can you imagine a life without chocolate and cake?' I know there must be alternatives, but this is a regime change I could really do without.

It's always good to be home, no matter how enjoyable a holiday has been, and the next day I'm out in the woods before the others are up. Cobweb strands link the trees, visible as they catch the early morning sun. There is a delicacy and lightness about them that contrasts with the dense, expansive tree trunks – they look as if they could be here for mere decoration, strings of white fairy lights of the smallest proportions. I must be the first walker through, for I feel them on my chin and across my face as I walk into the ones I cannot see. In fact, the cobwebs are everywhere, like cat's cradle between tufts of grass, and in the fields between clods of earth.

I am watching some small white butterflies with a lazy, almost drunken flight and hope they are Wood Whites, as opposed to the Small (Cabbage) Whites. Wood Whites are rarer and in decline, and I'm keen to spot one. I follow them into the overgrown areas, pushing aside the Rosebay Willowherb and thistles while the dog tugs at the lead and glances up at me as if I'm in need of his instruction. I can't see the tell-tale spot markings that give away the Small White's identity, and these are hovering around the tall grasses and pink Common Vetch flowers as the Wood Whites would. But I can't see the smudges and curved edges of the Wood White's upper wing either. I think I'm willing them to be something they may not, and it's really too difficult to call.

Annie is up when I'm home – unheard of at this hour – and I wonder if exam result nerves are kicking in, though she'd never say. She makes out she's unconcerned, but at times her guard has been down; she's confided in me that she wants to prove to herself that she's able, and this sixth form of her choice has been the real drive. 'What if I get in and Katie doesn't? Or the other way round?' she asks me now. She's lining up some euro coins that have been left by the phone.

'Your friendship would survive that. You've been at separate schools for the last few years anyway, it wouldn't be any different.'

'I think we'd go to the same one,' she says, making a final adjustment to her row of coins. 'We still could. We've both had offers from the same two schools, anyway.'

'If you get into Manwood's you should take it. Don't worry about Katie.'

'Yeah, it's easy for you to say.'

'You mustn't be defined by whatever you get. It's about how well you've performed on a given day, and there's always some subjectivity involved with the art and dance. Just treat them as a stepping stone. It'll all be fine, I think you'll both do well anyway.'

Annie lies low for much of the day and we give her the space she needs. I decide not to head for the woods tonight, but take the night vision scope into the garden instead. I'm only half-way down, but can see a badger looking through the trees from behind the pond. I go closer but the battery gives up, and it somehow triggers the cam at the bottom to start flashing, crazy paparazzi style. It's not going well. I head inside and find the small infra-red torch – this enables me to see a badger head coming and going at tantalisingly close range. I can hear it eating, if it can sense me it's really not bothered. My curiosity gets the better of me and I shine the torch – the badger scarpers. But now there's the sound of a helicopter flying close by over the trees, *our* trees. It hovers, very loud and low. I've probably taught this badger to fear – perhaps not a bad thing – though he must associate all this noise with *me,* which is grossly unfair.

I don't think that thing is moving, don't they know how loud it is? I wait a while, then head up the garden. 'It's the police,' calls a voice from a neighbour's upstairs window. 'You'd better go in or they'll think it's you.' They have a point – I suppose I would have shown up on their thermal imaging equipment just loitering in the shadows, and I run inside.

I can't wait to examine the footage the next morning, and creep downstairs before it's light, collecting the cam and settling on the sofa with the lights off. The first badger I saw last night was Georgie, who'd arrived soon after nine. She'd enjoyed some garden plums, with a neighbourhood cat looking on. It's a bumper damson year, and I'm glad she likes them. I see her glance over her shoulder at me, the moment our eyes met as I wandered down the garden.

The badger that I'd frightened away with the red torch and accompanying helicopter noises was Wilbur. I watch as he hot foots it towards the hole, legs flying under him like a hare's.

These are blurry images, but he's running low, ducking his head as I sometimes do under car height-restriction signs. Then, the same minute, he's statue-like, taking it all in. He returns, nose to the ground for peanuts, then changes his mind, turns and runs. He's back again just after midnight and comes via a different entry point. He doesn't stay long but that doesn't matter. He's not put off, that's all I care about.

And so it's results day, and I drive Annie down to her school. 'I don't know why we have to go in for them,' she says. 'Why don't they just post them? Public humiliation or something.' We arrive a little early and she has a text from Katie as she waits in the car. 'Her results are brilliant, Mum. She's got into Manwood's. Mine won't be nearly so good. Do you want to hear what she got?'

The students and accompanying parents gather outside the school, and when a teacher emerges they begin to surge towards the door. 'You're not allowed in until 10 a.m.,' he tells them, and explains the proceedings with his hands on his hips, his stance wide. He's enjoying this and smiles at them. It is his last moment of power over this particular group of students, but they're oblivious as they huddle now in small groups, and hands are nervously flapped in front of faces – 'Oh my God, oh my God, I can't believe this is happening.'

Oh my God, I'm sounding like a teenager, too, but I'm genuinely thanking him. She's got her results and she's done it. I'm so proud, and now she's choosing between her A' level options as more subjects are open to her than she expected. 'Well, I could do French, I'd never even thought of that. I didn't believe him when he said I was that good.'

Not everyone is looking so happy, but she talks discreetly until she's in the car, and the relief if palpable. 'I got the same as Katie! I've got to tell her.'

'What now?'

'We need to take my results over to Manwood's and show them, then I can sign up for my courses. I don't know what to do. Shall I do French? I'm not sure about R.S now. What would you do if you were me?'

Her siblings look on a little bemused, but the magnitude of Annie's achievement is understood by the tray of carrot cake, jam tarts, muffins and smoothies they are allowed to assemble once the school visit is done. The older three Snapchat and Instagram pictures of their treat, novelty that it is.

'Can we go to the library, Mum?' says Jemima. 'I want to do the reading medal and then I can be like Annie and you'll buy us all cakes again, won't you?'

The Sandwich library is closed, as it has been for weeks already. A note on the door explains that nesting seagulls have delayed the building work: 'We are waiting for the babies to leave the nest.' They are in no hurry, this incubation period has been far longer than the usual twenty-six days. I suspect there's something intentional here on their part; they are known to be intelligent birds, 'worm charming' with a dance that imitates rainfall. They throw molluscs from a height to open them, too, suggesting more reason than we like to suppose.

Back home, our second litter of guinea pig pups need their nest-leaving enforced upon them, now their three weeks with Mum are up. We are sure Peppa has one daughter this time – the desired result – and remove the three boys whilst trying not to feel cruel. 'She'll get over it,' I tell Jemima. 'Do you know what the alternative is? It'd be irresponsible,' I tell her.

Frodo quickly adopts one of the pups as if he was waiting for him all along, and accepts the others without a second glance. The children monitor their behaviour. Peppa is pronounced grief-stricken. But another pregnancy would be unfair on her and I feel we're lucky she survived two so close together.

A walk with the dog helps me process events of the day further. Blackberries are very ripe now, warm, soft and half-baked in the sun. A Little Blue butterfly rests on the bush and slides its wings together as we would dust sand from our hands. Autumn is feeling close, having battled with summer for weeks: empty hazelnut shells litter the path, and the variety of birdsong is already declining as many depart for warmer climes. I stop to listen to some garden warblers by the cows' gate alongside Churchill's field – they sound like reunited schoolgirls after a summer apart, gossiping at Disney-pitch, their voices on fast-forward. Yet they will be leaving soon, and the sense that they are celebrating something is deceptive; perhaps they are excited about the pending journey, and communicating their expectations and fears. I wonder if they are assembling so that they can fly together. Their departure is most likely to happen at night and my chances of seeing it are minimal.

Later on, Maddy, Eliott and Jemima are drawn out by the promise of blackberries. They cart empty Tupperware with them as we revisit the locations I earmarked earlier in the day. The plums we find are much larger than the ones at home, and we gather these, along with our first blackberry haul. An elderly lady passes us and looks a little surprised: 'You will save some won't you, my husband likes a good crumble.'

'Oh, we will. There's plenty here, and more coming, too.'

The badgers have a taste for them and their latrines are full of purple, seed-rich dung. We are sure to leave them lower down the bushes, and only take from where a badger cannot reach.

The children are satiated with blackberries, fresh air and sunshine, and school is beckoning. Once again Annie's is the first school back. I don't need to wake her and she even sits with me at the table before she leaves.

'I can't eat this,' she says, pushing her cereal bowl away.

'I thought you'd eat anything with chocolate in.'

'It's not that. I'm just too nervous. I may as well leave now.'

She looks like the model sixth former, with her immaculate blonde hair, black jacket and fitted skirt. 'Is this too short?' she says, pulling at it as she stands up.

'It's not like you to worry. It looks fine.'

She kisses me and calls out to the others, 'I'm off.'

'So that's what the smell is,' shouts Eliott from the snug.

She ignores his comment as she walks out of the door.

'It smells gross out here,' she says.

'I know, Eliott and I have been outside already. They've been muckspreading on the fields.'

'I don't want to go to school smelling of this. Do you want to drive me in?'

I head to the snug to open the curtains and see Annie walk down the road to the bus stop.   Eliott is sitting in the dark with Rupert's laptop in front of him.

'Annie's just left.'

'I know,' he says, eyes still on the screen.

'It's a big day for her, I thought you might've said goodbye.'

'I did. Ha. I've got two more days, she broke up way earlier than me. Can I play with Nathan online?'

'No. Find something useful to do. You still haven't memorized all those poems.'

'I will. Nathan *is* up and we're going to be at the same school together.'

'No.'

'You know, I don't know anybody in my new form and the rest of the boys from my primary have all been put together.'

'It'll be fine,' I say. 'But you're not playing with Nathan now.'

'It's okay, I'll just play with someone I don't know.'

'Please don't.'

'It's alright. I don't talk to them, we just race cars.'

I'm relieved when he's back at school, but Jemima misses him when he is gone. 'Will Eliott be home soon?' she says at eleven o'clock.

'He won't be back for ages,' I say. 'Why don't you draw him a picture or something?'

She returns minutes later with a picture of the two of them wearing their primary school red fleeces.

'You've got him in his old uniform,' I say. 'You have to let him move on. You wouldn't want to be at that school forever.'

'If Eliott could still be there I'd do year two again,' she says. 'He could stay in year six.'

'You'll love year three, just wait and see.'

Sure enough, her term starts and she's perfectly happy without him. 'I really liked it,' she says after her first day back, having almost forgotten what it was all about. 'I want to go again.' Well, that's just as well.

The badgers are coming very early now, winter is already detected on their bristles, the need to eat at every opportunity understood as the lean months come into view. Apples sit on the kitchen window sills like it's Harvest Festival, dropping black debris and turning brown when I don't sort them quickly enough. They litter the lawn too, the inedible ones left out for the birds and badgers, though more fulfilling grub is hoped for. Wilbur is the last to arrive each night, and scoots round at speed in a desperate attempt to find any peanuts the others have missed. But the younger ones are respectful of him, and there is one offering they always leave for him: eggs. We put out for them any laid by our chickens and ducks that are too grimy to bother with.

Tonight I'm out waiting for them at 9:30 p.m. I stand very still and in minutes a couple of badgers arrive and come very close to me, my scent familiar enough so as not to threaten them. Perhaps they are checking me out, making sure no one else is lurking round the side of the hut, but soon they resume the feast that they have come for. Wilbur isn't with them and I have to catch up with him on the badger cam, his hours really don't suit me. Sure enough, they have left him his egg, that understanding is set to continue.

Think how long it takes to actually boil an egg. Four minutes, five or so if you eat them firm. Wilbur is taking this long to break into the large duck egg I have given him. The time on the cam records six minutes before the shell gives way to his aging teeth. He has the egg between his paws and is bearing down on it like a dog with a bone, intense concentration needed. No sooner is he in than Dora arrives and settles down beside him. She really has to be his next of kin, the behaviour is just so familiar – she lands a claw on his face, in his eye even, but he doesn't flinch. This isn't a fight, just natural interaction, as siblings would behave together on the back seat of a car, or muscling in on a bag of chips. They must be so used to sharing space, sleeping on top of each other, jostling elbows in close quarters for many an hour that conduct above ground is really no different, at least, not when the badgers consider themselves as equals.

'You know, we haven't used any of those poems I memorized yet, Mum,' says Eliott when he's home. 'Most of the class don't know what I'm talking about.'

'Perhaps he was just some random old guy from Dover and not a teacher at all,' I say. 'I bet he went to your school when he was a lad and thinks you ought to be receiving a 'proper education'.

'But he was roaming around at that new year seven evening, looking all official.'

'Stranger things have happened,' I say.

AUTUMN

12: Missing badgers

Autumn is kind to us and allows the outdoor lifestyle to continue. I walk with Jemima the most, and we find conker shells that are opening, or can be, aided with the heel of my boot. Inside they are waxy and new, like furniture that's been polished to a high shine and ready to be sold. Honeysuckle berries glow with an opaque lustre, like understated jewels worthy of greater recognition, draping themselves over the front garden fence, and lighting dark corners out in the woods. An extended blackberry season gives another reason to visit the sett, for here they are prize-winning. 'It's as big as a gobstopper,' says Eliott as he examines one, before putting it in his mouth. 'You know, I'd have come more often if you'd told me there was food involved.'

We've seen a further dead cub from here on the road in recent days, its life prematurely taken; there are around 50,000 badger deaths on UK roads each year, and I'm sure at least some of these could be avoided by more careful night-driving. Experts believe the actual figure is much higher, as many injured badgers crawl away to die in a peaceful spot. There is a peak in badger road deaths in September as many badgers are on the move for another round of mating in October. I hope that'll be all we lose from the sett for now, though it deters me from coming up here to watch – what if their numbers are really depleted? I know of two cubs that haven't made it from this group because of the road here, but of course there could be more. This particular clan wasn't coming out very early after the harvest anyway, preferring the darker, quieter hours to go about their business, and it seems the badger year has moved on again. I'll be back watching them in the spring, when perhaps there will be another litter of cubs. Till then, I will walk this way in daylight hours, and focus more on our garden badgers.

Only once have I seen all three of 'our' cubs together, and I'm trying to tell them apart, but one is quite distinctive. I'm studying the cam later in the day for once, with Jem beside me on the sofa. 'It's Wilbur and a cub,' I tell her. 'Look at how broad his face is getting, it has to be a boy.'

'Tommy,' she says, with an authority that's hard to dispute.

'That was easy,' says Rupert.

'If I'm wrong it'll be Thomasin, or Tamsin, courtesy of Hardy. Is that okay with everyone?'

The badgers really help my mental well-being, as the stresses of life press in on me. Rupert comes home from work complaining about rumours of closure, and the shepherd hut has not materialized, though soon after the excuses started I knew it never would. Jon's complaints got worse and worse – his wife had 'had a miscarriage' and he was too upset to go into work (other customers were told that excuse – and had we heard the one about his dying child?) The company is being investigated by the police, and quite unexpectedly a generous benefactor is arranging for a replacement – I make them sound like some character from a Dickens' novel, but I know they would not wish to be named. I have found a local cabin company and am staying well clear of shepherd huts for now; they have lost their rural charm for me and the associations will be there for a long time to come. All the same, I couldn't help feeling satisfied recently when learning of the discovery of Gabriel Oak's shepherd's hut, or to put it more correctly, Hardy's inspiration for it, abandoned in a field. A museum curator by the name of David Morris spotted the derelict hut whilst out walking through Waterston Manor, the basis for Weatherbury Farm. It was enveloped by a bramble thicket, and the owners were glad to see it go. He took it home and restored it himself, and it now sits in his garden looking very much as it would have in Hardy's day. 'We have a small antique settee and a couple of milking stools, a cider barrel and some shepherd tools. We use it and enjoy it. It is a superb store for fruit and veg in the garden and a great place to just have a cup of tea and a bit of cake in,' Morris said.

I'm out walking again and hear a gathering of long-tailed tits at the bottom of Flax Court Lane, a short distance away – then I see them, masses of chanting, bobbing birds that fly in and out of the bushes. I've admired these little fellows for a long time, more for their behaviour than their cutesy looks, though they are of course endearing, with their badger-striped head and ball-like appearance, a puff of feathers and absence of neck. It's known that at times, certain members of a group will help bring up youngsters that are not their own – usually they belong to siblings (42%), or other close family members. This is most likely to happen when their own nest has failed. You could question the wisdom of building a nest close to the ground, often easily accessible to a determined cat or fox. And yet these birds are far from clueless, weaving complex, intricate structures of cobwebs and moss, then camouflaging them and lining them with feathers. Perhaps their vulnerability is part of their beauty, giving them the opportunity to demonstrate kindness, reassuring us that the world isn't really so bad. I have a picture of them in my mind's eye, huddled together in a row as they do during the winter-roosting months, each the weight of just three sugar cubes and dependent on each other for warmth.

Yet somehow it's night-time wanderings that bring me a profound, churning kind of satisfaction, the encounters that leave me feeling moved and sometimes changed. It's not only the badgers that do it for me either. I suppose it's like entering a different world after dark, we may feel as if we're out of our own territory, trespassing if you like.

Later I'm outside setting the badger cam for the night and have one such experience. As I wander back to the house I look up to see a tawny owl flying its silent path across the gardens. It's about the size of a pigeon, its round head large in proportion to its solid, powerful body. It looks weighty, perhaps all the more so because darkness is coming on, and its outline is visible in stark silhouette. It lands in the damson tree as it sees me and I bask in its presence while it ponders my own. My potential threat is dismissed and it takes to the air again, flying over our neighbour's house and beyond. I stand watching where it has flown, as if there's something still to be gained by the looking, willing it to come back but knowing it probably won't.

Young owls will be making their own way at this time of year as they seek out territory, and it's a good time to hear them at the very least. An encounter with one hasn't always been viewed so positively; they were once considered a harbinger of doom, foreboding imminent death or misfortune. In 1612 John Webster wrote of the 'screeche-owle' commanding the dame to 'quickly don her shroud'. Half a century later Wordsworth, in his poem *The Waggoner*, displayed similar superstition: 'Yon owl! – pray that all will be well!/Tis worse than any funeral bell'. Life expectancy was of course far shorter, and folklore gave explanation for illness and misfortune. People lived in closer proximity with nature: houses rattled in the wind and double-glazing was yet to be invented. 'The wind of winter mooed and mouthed their chimney like a horn,' writes Hardy in his poem *The Homecoming*. 'Rattle rattle went the door; down flapped a cloud of smoke,' he continues, and although this 'lonesome' house was fictional, we understand that nature could not be kept at bay in the way that it is today.

Now that life is so comfortable, we feel we have lost something, though we're not sure what. We sense we're less in touch with ourselves than our ancestors ever were, and seek an encounter with nature, the wilder the better, to plug the deficit of experience. Perhaps we crave these brushes with nature all the more because the superstitions of the past increase their mystique – could an owl really carry with it some unseen power, something that points beyond our own experiences? In 2014 there were reports of an owl being burnt alive in Durango, Mexico, where villagers thought it was a shape-shifting witch. Its reputation is taking time to recover from centuries of accusations, and yet its awesome presence somehow compels us to create stories around it, to assume it carries an even greater significance on its outstretched wings other than it simply *is*.

From my brief moment of connection I'm not led to fear the future, or giving way to the dark corners of my brain, but left wanting more. I want to walk the woods again at night and simply wait there. I want my connection with badgers to go further, too. I read recently of Gareth Morgan, the Welsh badgerman who had wild badgers eating out of his hands. I immediately looked him up, thought I could make contact on the premise that I'm now researching a 'badger book', and would he mind if I came to visit, as Hugh Warwick did when planning *Beauty in the Beast*? I discovered that Morgan had died with his secret back in 2012. In an interview with a newspaper he'd said, "At first I watched from a distance and then I got close enough to whisper to them. People ask what I whisper but that's between me and them." Perhaps this is the new level of challenge, should I wish to take it up. The thought won't leave me alone and I find myself researching the idea further. Is the ultimate aim to be accepted by wildlife, is this how we should measure success? Have I finally got alongside badgers in the best possible way if I can ensure they have no fear of me, but approach me with boldness, as if this is perfectly natural? I've come across another character who seemed to have no problem with this – artist Eileen Soper, daughter of the more famous painter George Soper, developed a fascination with badgers back in the 1950s, and after years of following them was finally able to have them eat out of her hand. She wrote in her diaries of how she lured with syrup smeared over the base of a tree, then with honey in a coconut shell that she held out for them. A cub took the honey from her fingers, though seemed to prefer it from the roots of the tree. 'They came to the tree and began to take the syrup once more. They lapped fast and furiously, their little noses pressed hard against one another to get every drop.'[6] She persisted, and the next night they approached her. She explains 'The nearest cub started to take it at once, but it was not long before his nose came up against my thumb. This made him withdraw a few inches, as though not quite sure of the strange contact.' Her recognition of the 'strangeness' of this is reassuring. She writes of overcoming their 'mistrust', yet the more I have pondered the issue the more uneasy it makes me feel. I would question whose benefit this hand-feeding is for – surely it makes the badgers vulnerable and has the potential to damage their natural, self-preserving wariness. And they are drawing close to the syrup, not to her.

Eileen Soper's diary is now on Twitter, with daily posts from a modern-day devotee, and a recent post catches my eye:

May 19th 1957: 'The cubs came for syrup, twice licking my hand, all over thumb, fingers and knuckles.'

I had to respond. 'Questionable tactics for wildlife engagement. Beautiful illustrations though, artist for the Famous Five books.'

'Agreed!' came the reply, 'But history/science filled with questionable tactics (Darwin?!), from which we built today's greater understanding of nature.'

I remain unconvinced, and think physical contact a step too far.

---

[6] Soper, Eileen. 1992. [1995]. *1954, Badger Favours'* in *Eileen Soper's Book of Badgers,* Edited by Duff Hart-Davis. UK: Robinson Publishing.

I don't come away feeling uneasy, wondering if I have crossed a line, yet am warmed and encouraged, emboldened even by their endurance and ready to face another day.

The next night I find Dora outside when I head down the garden with a torch. She stares into the beam, then carries on. Another glance, but the peanuts mean too much to her to stop for me. I hope the badgers simply feel safe in our environment, that this is not an indication of how she will behave elsewhere. I wonder if I should feed them less than I do. I had thought my impact pretty minimal, and I'm sure it is. Enough perhaps to ensure survival during the lean times, a supplement to their diet only, and a healthy one at that. (I didn't get into giving them Sugar Puffs – they might like the taste, but can't be very good for them.) It's not like the badgers are all queueing up at nightfall, but a small part of me is now beginning to doubt myself. I like to think that if we were to move from here the badgers would fare equally well, being perfectly able to fend for themselves. I watch for a while, not venturing any closer. I can hear other badgers in the wings, probably less tolerant of me and wanting to join the feast. After another ten minutes I turn and leave, which spooks Dora, which spooks a duck in the pen who flaps as the badger makes her exit. Her fear is still there, which is good to see.

*

I thought this narrative would be over by now, but Rupert came home with news of his redundancy last week and I'm surprised at how badly I've taken it. There have been echoes of mourning in it for me. I know that may sound ludicrous and Rupert would think it very O.T.T, but it is how it feels. I've since found the comparison several times online, so I'm not totally losing it. He's taught at the immigration removal centre for the last twelve years while our brood have been growing up; a fulfilling role for him and security for all of us. This morning I helped him get an application together in the before-school-chaos, and now home from dropping Jem I'm facing a kitchen with bowls and plates everywhere, and clutter round the house. I really don't care though – I've had depression before, and this susceptibility to tears is a warning sign for me. The woods are beckoning, and I know I'm not responding to some stupid whim, but an instinct that protects my inner being, that settles me on the inside in a way not much else can. It's where I can pray without distraction and God can get my full attention, shouting through every twig and leaf, 'You're not alone, I'm with you. Can't you see? I made this place, I made you and I'm here.'

I've already looked over the badger cam this morning with Jemima by my side. We're always up before the others surface. 'They keep me sane, you might say,' I told her. 'Keep you insane,' she replied, with a look of provocation on her face, a wide grin, her eyes looking deep into mine, as if surprised at her own audacity but proud of it all the same. Well, whatever. It was badger central here last night, and all because of some abandoned maize Eliott and I found in the field and placed at the bottom of the garden.

'Look at that sky,' Annie had said at supper time, from her vantage point overlooking the sun as it sets over the fields. As we watched it redden, its warmth spreading and intensifying in every direction, I knew I had to get out. I hadn't had a decent walk in days, what with all the downpours and the teaching routine.

'I'm going on a walk, who's coming?' I said.

Eliott hopped down from the table and rushed through for his boots. Jemima begged me to let her come too, but she'd never keep up, and I knew it would be dark in no time.

We could hear them harvesting when we were in the woods, the heavy machinery growling through the fields around the sett. We reached a clearing and could see a tractor far off on the brow of the hill. Where they'd been, stray cobs lay in amongst the mud and stubble. They weren't coming back to collect them, and we gathered a few and carried them home.

And so this morning I'm feeling the pull once again. There's light drizzle falling, but it's bound to get worse later, so I grab a rucksack and the dog's lead and we're off. In the woods the ground is turning to orange as the beech leaves form a deep layer on the ground, the colour of copper pennies. The holly bushes are splashed with orange too, as rusting beech leaves lay impaled on their spikes. I can hear the farm machinery in the fields again. There's some therapy to be had in gleaning. It's not that we'll be without funds for the next little while, but there is a satisfying edge to being frugal. It feels like a positive outlet for all the anxieties jostling for my attention. Back in the summer when there were rumours of closure I had a wave of foraging, and concocted a 'mixed vegetable' soup containing nettles.

'Mum, what've you put in this?'

'That's taking nature too far.'

The leaves weren't young enough and the soup had a bitter after taste – I tried to explain, but the damage was done. 'Don't do that again, Mum,' was the general consensus. Since then they demand an ingredients list before a spoon is lifted. Last night the children wanted to try the maize and Maddy put some in a bowl with salt, but it wasn't that appetising. I'm really collecting it for our badgers, who can get through a four kilogram bag of peanuts in a couple of weeks. Badgers are going to eat the cobs, whether in the field or our back garden, and at least this way we have more chance of watching, being able to catch them on the cam. Maize is something of a treat for them. Martin has told me of the extra badger latrines that spring up at the edges of a maize field. These are usually exclusive to particular clans and mark territory, but in a maize field they can be communal, such is the carnival atmosphere and the urgent consequence of over indulgence. It makes me think of summer festivals: the party's on, the music is playing, and no one wants to go far.

Today there are half nibbled cobs here and there, at the field edge, in amongst the grass and further into the field. The corn is even more accessible now that it's at ground level, but it won't last. There is still half a crop to gather in, and then their abundant supply will have gone, stashed away in a barn to be used as fodder. For the next couple of weeks there won't be any shortage though, but then things get a little more interesting for them. My rucksack is feeling heavy and now the rain really starts, so we don't linger as we usually would. The dog pulls around the badger latrine, desperate to trump their scent with his own, but I tug him along and out through the field.

The ducks appear at the doorstep once we're back inside and peer in through the window. I fill a fist with their grain and let them take it from my open hands, feeling their smooth close feathers as my outstretched fingers touch their necks, their beaks burrowing deep into my palms. There is a slight suction as their enthusiasm for food takes away their fear of me. It doesn't hurt, their beaks are blunt and pretty harmless.

My mind turns to the badger cam, I think I need to study it properly now. I'd only flicked through when Jemima was with me earlier, a quick once-over to check they'd been and to gauge the activity of the night. I just need to set the kitchen straight, and then I'll settle down with it.

I ponder what I've seen so far as I rinse the breakfast bowls and sweep the floor. Wilbur hasn't been for several weeks. Jemima tells me he'll be back, but I'm not convinced. This dear old loveable patriarch was here almost every night, even when the weather kept most of the clan away, making his absence now all the more marked. Ours must have been a favourite haunt of his. I keep returning in my mind to his appearances with the cubs, introducing them to our ground as you might show friends into a new house. Perhaps he felt it was time to resign, to allow himself to fade, with so many more mouths to feed since spring. We shall miss him. To be honest, I already do.

Dora has been two days in a row now. I've often wondered if there is some kind of pecking order for foraging grounds, though on occasions I have seen these two eat side by side. Her face has broadened significantly, which made me question if it were really her, but that torn ear is unmistakable. The rest of her has broadened too, so much so that Eliott and I laughed when we saw her again. I know badgers are meant to fatten up for winter, but this is just ridiculous. If she were a person she'd be classed as morbidly obese, the extra weight hanging beneath her like sandbags. Jem thinks she looks as if someone has taken a straw and blown her up like a balloon. It's not elegant. She's recovered well; feeding her cubs had meant that for a time her frame was little broader than theirs.

I make myself a piece of toast and spread it with sweet-smelling blackberry jam, the product of our most recent haul, before heading through to the snug with the nature cam tucked under my arm. I plug it into the back of the TV and sit down. Last night a young cub made it to us first, and after a good twenty minutes of peanuts found one of the cobs. I watch now as he picks it up in his mouth and runs away with it. This badger will be distinctive for a floppy ear, which is useful – it's hard to tell them apart from some of the older ones now that they've grown. A second badger enters, and is joined by Dora, and they eat together for a few minutes. There are various comings and goings of badgers that all look very much alike; a few run-ins with each other and the occasional fox will see to that. The night footage ends with the neighbourhood cats stalking and pouncing on mice. I wonder if the one Maddy and I released down there is one of them. I bought a humane trap to catch the culprit that's been filling our boots and shoes with peanuts from the sack. 'What should I do with it?' I asked Rupert when the first mouse had been tempted in. 'Well, you know what I'd do with it,' he replied.

The next day my sadness is underlined by the absence of one of my ducks. Darcy fails to appear at the door with his brother, and reluctantly I search the garden, pushing under every bush and shrub with a long stick. He's nowhere to be seen, and Bingley is quacking inconsolably. It is, of course, possible that he's taken to the air on a big adventure. We clipped their wings when they were new, but haven't done it since. In recent weeks they've picked up some height when flying down the length of the garden for the pond, often crash landing with comic effect. 'Are you crying, Mum?' asks Annie.

'No, no I'm not. Not about that.'

'They were basically like a gay couple weren't they?' she says.

Bingley is not himself once he realizes his friend is not coming back. He stands down by the pond looking on, not swimming, just gazing for much of the day. I try to feed him his favourite corn from my hand, but he runs away, quacking. He just wants to be left alone. On a normal day they'd come and seek me out at the house, looking through the patio window or the back door and tapping it with their beaks. Then they would devour the corn from my hand. They went everywhere together and would move in unison, as if magnetized. Darcy was favourite with the girls, his noticeable white-bibbed chest giving him a distinctive edge; perhaps the fox chose him for this reason, too. Poor Darcy. We heard ducks when out for our walk yesterday – *Could it be him? It's not far away. Imagine if he's just relocated* – came the optimistic voices. Probably not.

I email my duck-keeping student for advice. I search the internet. Then I decide that Bingley's not likely to take on the identity of a chicken and try to find him a friend before his depression takes hold too deeply. I engage in some email communication with a nearby poultry keeper:

"No sorry, call ducks unavailable but they can mix with other ducks fine. To be honest he will mate with anything as long as not ornamental fowl they arnt fussy :) i have khaki girls or indian runners think he would just be greatful with someone of opposite sex x Im out all day tomorrow but give me a text/call if you want to view what we have."

Perhaps a female will be even better for him, and he'll feel more fulfilled than he did before. It's not what he'd have chosen, but it could work out for the best.

My parents keep up their weekly phone calls, and today have an invitation for us. 'We're wondering if you'd like to come for Christmas,' says Mum.

She hasn't mentioned the redundancy, but I think that's what's behind it. I thank them and tell them I'll just run it past the family. I manage to gauge opinion while the kids all take turns to have their chat.

'Can we go? Can we?' says Annie.

'I'd like to,' I say.

We haven't spent Christmas with my parents for years as the kids have wanted to wake up in their own beds, and I've enjoyed doing the catering. They have never wanted to come to us. Besides, we don't have enough beds and a Bed and Breakfast is never the same to wake up in.

'Let's do it,' says Rupert. 'But make sure your mum lets us help.'

'We'd love to come,' I tell them when the phone reaches me again. 'If you're sure it won't be too much for you both. I'm doing all the veg prep, and I'll bring–'

'We're so pleased,' she says before I can finish. 'Last year Dad was in and out of hospital, it was such a lonely time.'

I feel selfish for not having realized how Christmas day must have been for them then. The nosebleeds, the diagnosis with treatment yet to start, and all the time they were trying to appear cheerful. They did a good job, I never picked up on how hard it was for them. But I wish they hadn't, we could have changed our plans. But then a house full of grandchildren would have been noisy and tiring. I wish we didn't live so far away sometimes.

Dad has been clear of the cancer for a few months now, but he's still exhausted for much of the time. None of us realised just how much he would have to adapt. He's told his strength will return gradually, but not to expect things to be as they were before.

I'm amazed they feel able to have us, and I hope Mum won't think she has to put on a show. Cheese on toast would do, but I get the feeling it will be the usual gourmet extravaganza.

26th October.

Wilbur is back! This feels like a lost toy showing up when you are small, but better. I scroll back and look at the images a second time. It really is him, I'd recognize this old badger anywhere: the ear that's looked flattened for months now, the dented nose, but most strikingly, the way he carries his years with him in his broad head and silver fur. He has a presence that reassures, simply because he has lived through so much and is still here, calm and untouched by the trials life brings.

'Maddy, come and look at this,' I call. I hear her hurtle down the corridor, jump the kitchen steps and land heavily on the wooden floor.

'I'm in here, it's Wilbur, he's back.'

She climbs onto the dark red sofa beside me and peers in. I hand the cam to her. 'Aw, where's he been? Silly old badger. I thought we'd lost him. So he needs us after all.'

Quick steps on the stairs, and in seconds Jemima appears and lands herself between us.

'What is it?'

'Wilbur,' we say together.

'Let me see, let me see!' She pauses. 'Didn't I say he'd be back? I know as much as you about badgers. You know, they tell me things in my dreams. Do you get that?'

Soon Rupert and Eliott arrive together.

'What are you lot so excited about?' says Rupert, flicking on the kettle.

'They've got the badger cam,' says Eliott.

'Wilbur's back,' comes the cry from the sofa.

'Oh, Wilbur, I can't believe it, I thought you were dead!' says Rupert.

Eliott needs no more encouragement and they're away. Hands put over hearts, melodramatic poses, laughter as they congratulate each other for their mutual cheek. Yeah, yeah, all very funny guys, but actually there's a huge feeling of relief here. Sometimes it just feels like life is going wrong in every corner, as if you've had an unlucky throw of the dice and everything's cascading down on your head. I do have a natural pessimism about me that probably isn't helpful, always expecting the worst at every turn. Perhaps it won't be months before Rupert gets a job. I need to get over that everything-must-be-perfect-before-life-can-be-enjoyed thing, and learn to be happy in the muddle and confusion, trusting that all things work together for good –

eventually.

And so, in life-seizing mode, we head off to collect the love of Bingley's life. The children play with names in the car. 'Who did Mr Bingley marry?' 'Jane.' 'That's no good, it's boring. What was her surname? Miss Bennet then, it'll do.'

'No it won't. It's even worse,' says Jem. 'We're calling her Jane.'

I'm taken by how big all the ducks look when we arrive, but there's no going back now – his girl has been chosen for us in advance, and we stand and watch as she's chased round the pen and scooped up with two hands. The assistant brings her over. Well, she appears no smaller close up. I lift the lid on the wire badger cage that we pulled out of the garage and crouch down beside her. This khaki duck will look more like a mother for him than a girlfriend, but that can't be helped.

We shoo the chickens out of the run when we're home and leave the ducks to their introductions. Bingley, Jane. Jane, this is Bingley. If he had visible ears they would have pricked up by now – he cocks his head on one side as if to listen to the full-toned quacking she makes. It's somehow primeval and a privilege to watch, deep calling to deep. The moment doesn't last long – she chases him round the enclosure like some pent-up Benny Hill character, and he won't stop. Later on when we check on them things have calmed down. They are standing close, like kids told to get acquainted as they're family friends.

We round up the chickens and Honey launches herself at our

newcomer, who in response rises up and puffs out her chest. She's chased inside the coup, at which point Bingley also stands tall, arching his back and expanding his chest as if he's somehow been affronted too. *Calling my bird ugly? I don't think so...* Bingley, true to character, is the perfect gentleman and always knows how to behave.

The mice are on the increase. We're emptying my humane trap with great regularity. 'They're just coming straight back up the garden, Mum.'

'Well, Martin thinks they'll visit some of our friends at the bottom. It's nearer. They need some more wildlife to do battle with after all.'

'They're coming from somewhere,' says Rupert.

I make the mistake of telling him that one's just visited me while I was on the toilet downstairs, popping its little head under the door, peanut in its mouth.

Rupert wants to 'deal with it'.

'Give it two weeks,' I say. 'We'll release them further away and see if that helps.'

Maddy is making her breakfast, and catching the conversation starts to cry. 'You can't kill them, Dad. That's murdering them.'

'Dad has agreed to give us two weeks. We don't want an infestation.'

'We've already got an infestation,' he replies.

The badgers seem to be lying low and it's hard not to feel glum. Our near neighbour on Sandwich Road finished his garden workshop, and now it's not the banging that bothers me but the blue tardis lights, a row of five that illuminate not only his garden but the gardens all around. I think that may be deterring them. Besides that, it's too cold to see them in the woods and I'm struggling to feel excited by the time of year: dullness everywhere, damp leaves, penetrating grey skies that work their way inside you. We take a Sunday afternoon stroll, wanting to capture that traditional, ritualist feeling of walking off a big lunch, but it's just dismal. 'I'm missing sunshine and birdsong and flowers,' I tell them. Not to mention the badgers. My foot slips on a slimy stile, and as I slide off onto the ground I start to cry. How ridiculous. Rupert offers me a hand and pulls me to my feet. It's not rational, I'm fine really, we've been through far worse than this.

'What's that tree?' says Eliott.

'It's sweet chestnut. It's Churchill's tree.'

'Will there be any chestnuts?'

'I doubt it. Go and have a look.'

He, Maddy and Jem run ahead. 'There are lots! Hurry up,' they shout. We stand on the armoured cases, sharp all over like loaded pincushions. Our hands reach in amongst the nettles, thick and ankle deep, not hesitating for a moment, with the enthusiasm of Christmas morning. The cases open to reveal clusters inside, most with three nuts, one having thrived and the other two thin, empty shells. The children are all keen to find the biggest and to collect the most, filling their pockets and my bag, comparing each 'beauty' to my prize specimen. 'You could write in your journal about this one, Mum,' says Eliott laughing. 'And this one.' I think he saw me cry and is determined to cheer me up.

There is some colour to be had out here, though many trees have had the leaves blown from them ahead of time, their autumn glory unreached. There is a spindle tree on the footpath towards home, its orange berries hanging beneath brilliant pink casing, like small bulbous Japanese lanterns or something that should be bought from a florist, vibrant and exotic. As we reach home I'm struck that the silver birch is an interesting colour for once, its leaves glowing with an amber warmth like never before. Perhaps the weather has been good for the colour on this tree, while causing others to dwindle.

November is punctuated with a few rejections for Rupert, by email, by post, and some that don't bother to reply, but as the dates expire we get the message. And then a recorded message about a job he's told me he doesn't want any more. He tells me he's not going to take it. But he calls back and explains and starts to make assenting noises. It sounds like she's not giving in easily.

'She's allowing me some time to think,' he tells me as I come into the kitchen and loiter. 'I've got to call back at six.'

Soon he's out cutting the grass with more concentration than the task requires and I stay out of his way, knowing I'll struggle not to give him my opinion. They are five long hours, but he reaches a decision. 'I'm going to take it,' he says.

He'll be involved with a project for adults with learning disabilities, managing a garden with them and producing plants and crafts to sell. I hope it works out. I think he'll enjoy it once he gets started, and if it doesn't he'll have plenty of time to think.

There's another important call the next day, this time for Eliott.

'EJ, it's Amy from Cubs. Do you want to talk to her?'

'Can you?' he says, emerging from the snug.

'Okay. The vicar wants to know if you'll play the Last Post again.'

'Of course I will.'

'What, really?'

I cover the mouthpiece on the phone as he comes and sits beside me on the kitchen step. 'No, I really want to, Mum. I can do it this time. It doesn't frighten me like it did before.'

'Looks like you're sorted,' I tell Amy.

'Thank him for me, won't you,' she says.

'Don't look surprised,' he says to me as I put the phone down. 'Can you put the kettle on?'

'Hot chocolate?' I ask him. I know I'd need something a bit stronger if I'd just agreed to that, but I mustn't discourage him.

'No. I want a hot water bottle for my cornet. I'll put it in the case with it and leave it out in the cold for a bit. See if it keeps it warm. That was the problem before, you don't play an instrument from cold.'

'If you say so.'

'Just don't tell Dad, he'll think I'm weird.'

The day arrives and he's far quieter than usual. It feels like he's avoiding me and Jemima, walking out of any room that he finds us in. He practices his piece before his older sisters are out of bed, but no one grumbles. At a quarter to ten I find an empty hot water bottle beside the kettle and I take my cue and fill it for him. Minutes later it's gone, but I don't see him take it.

I knock on his door a few minutes later. 'You alright?' I say to him. 'We should be going soon.'

'I'm fine. I'm ready now. Can we go please?'

The church is full when we arrive, though we set out earlier than last year. Eliott still isn't giving much away, and takes a seat with the Cubs that's been reserved for him. This time he's wearing his school uniform as he left the Cubs a while ago. Before long we're out on the green again with the crowd assembling around him. The cornet is still in its case and I can see he won't pull it out until it's time. The vicar nods at him and smiles and he crouches down and unclips the case. As he stands up the vicar nods at him again.

He begins to play, it's smooth and steady with little evidence of nerves, which surely must be there. The crowd are quiet and still, the only movement coming from the flags that are flapping in the breeze. He's doing it, he's come back despite last year's struggles, and decided not to be beaten. Annie is filming it on her phone this time but he hasn't noticed, I don't think he's been aware of anyone else all morning.

He's stopped and we're waiting for the rouse now. I'm trying to pray, but I have to confess, my thoughts are more with Eliott than with the fallen. Another nod and he's off again and playing through to the end.

He's finished and looks across at me from under his blond fringe. That's the first eye-contact I've had from him all morning.

'Was that your boy playing?' says Graham afterwards. He's become a friendly face on the school run as I park outside his house every day.

'It was.'

'You must be proud, immensely proud.'

You could say that. I simply nod and smile though, and land a hand on Eliott's shoulder. It wouldn't do to have him think himself the hero of the moment. If we make this such a big deal it will be a hurdle for him every time, and I don't want him playing for the praise, but the enjoyment of it. He'll always receive quiet affirmation from us, regardless of his success.

'Well done, Eliott.'

'Hey, EJ, well done!'

'Congratulations, mate, you've done us proud.'

I'll say.

The badgers remain elusive. Our cub with the folded ear has been a couple of times in the last fortnight, but there is a definite change since Hallowe'en, when firework season began. I've checked the area I'd always thought they come from, and there's no evidence of holes being tampered with. I have found another issue, though –

the decking is up between Simon and Louise's house and shed and I fear some of them may have been living under there. Jemima's pink binoculars have been left lying around upstairs, and I think I have seen too much. Perhaps I've been wrong to encourage them in when they have to cross gardens to get here – but there was activity before I'd started to feed them. Our tally of seven badgers is at present down to one. I can't name him. I shouldn't get too attached. But I fear I will.

I understand from my research that badgers come out less in November. They sleep more. There is a theory of a 'semi-hibernation' and I'm hoping that this is what I'm encountering now, though it's a little early – late November is the usual time, when winter temperatures have set in. Badgers enter a deep winter sleep that can last for days. But this doesn't account for the dramatic absence we're experiencing – this hasn't been a 'gradual decline', but a sudden drop off. My serious garden monitoring didn't begin until late December last year, and so I'm still a novice in all these things, but my instinct tells me it isn't good. The neighbours are hardly likely to own up to badger crime. 'I notice from my snooping with binoculars that your decking is up – could it be that you've had trouble with badgers?' 'And what does that have to do with you?' I could get myself into a lot of trouble. We could always infiltrate – befriend them and hope to find something out – express enthusiasm for the cull, mention we haven't had any of those destructive little beasts digging around in our garden lately, but that would be wrong and I don't think I could bring myself to. And so I watch and wait, putting out the peanuts, studying a blank screen most mornings and doing my best to hope.

13: Heritage and belonging

Mrs Stephens is filling a basket with groceries in the village shop when I pop in for stamps.

'Hello,' I say, in a voice loud enough for her to hear and she turns around, startled.

'Oh, hello, Caroline. Haven't seen you in a while.'

Mr Patel the owner is on the phone at the till, but leaves us to it and heads out the back, continuing his conversation in Gujarati as he goes. He knows we won't be paying for anything any time soon.

'How have you been?' I ask her.

'Oh, I'm okay,' she says through her permanent smile. I wonder if it makes it easier to face the world when this is your default expression. 'I had a fall recently,' she continues.

'I'm sorry,' I say. 'Always ring me if you're in trouble. You have my number don't you? It's not just for the badger problems.'

'Oh, I know.'

'Where exactly is your house on the road?' she asks.

'It's the old detached white house, opposite where Dorothy used to live.'

'Oh, I know, I know.'

'And how are the geese?'

'Oh, the fox got the last two. I saw him, there was nothing I could do.'

I thought she kept three geese in her back garden, not two. Best not to ask, it'll only upset her. At least it wasn't the badgers as she'd feared. I can't help looking into her shopping basket while she talks. She has collected meals for the week – a chicken dinner for one that's ready to heat, scotch eggs, sausages and tinned carrots.

'I had a letter this morning,' she says. 'I'm having my eyes done in a couple of months. You know, if I were to crash before then they'd ban me from driving. But I have my little dog on my shoulder. I couldn't have asked for a better little dog. She's looking left and right for me, taking it all in. I should give her the wheel.'

I wish her well and as I leave I remind her to phone me if she's ever in trouble again. A supermarket delivery van is stopping outside a near neighbour's house and I wait for the driver to step out before I pass.

I often think of those I've been called on to visit. I'm surprised how much easier it is to give advice now, though it rarely happens this time of year. It's a restful season for the badgers, and I suppose I should be glad. My only case recently didn't even require a visit. A lady was phoning on behalf of her friend, who had a badger visiting at night. 'It's dug a hole,' she said. 'Could it be because it wants somewhere to curl up and die?'

'That's not very likely,' I told her. 'Badgers dig all the time.'

The lady in question phoned me herself a few days later. It had to be her, because she raised the same issue – 'Now, this may sound strange, but it's dug a hole in my garden. Could it have some sickness and need a hole to die in? They carry disease, don't they? And I have children playing in my garden all the time. They pick up balls –'

I had to interrupt. 'I think you're thinking of bovine TB. Badgers have been linked to its spread in cattle, though it's been a bit overplayed. People can't catch this strain, so you're okay. We drink pasteurised milk and we've all been vaccinated as children. But I can come and see your garden if you like.'

'No, you're okay. But what can I do to try and keep them away?'

I don't have to think about this one any more, though it still astonishes me that anyone would want to.

I'm nearly home. I'm going to see if the Finglesham house with the snared badger is still on the market when I get in. I wonder what happened with their nightmare neighbour, or if they've escaped to live in the town as they'd planned.

I settle on the sofa in the family room, where Annie and Maddy are busy at the table. Maddy is needle-felting 3D snowmen to sell as Christmas tree decorations. She takes a polystyrene ball and adds a layer of felt-wool by pulsing it with a needle. She joins it to a second felted ball, then ties on a tiny scarf and hat before finishing it with eyes and a smile. They look as good as anything for sale in the shops, and her sewing abilities now far exceed my own. She has a shoebox beside her full to the brim with the snowmen, baubles and bookmarks that she's made.

'Why are you making so many?' says Annie from the other end of the table, paintbrush in hand. 'It's a little obsessive, don't you think?'

'And your painting isn't? That one robin has taken you an hour already.'

'It's a picture for Grandma and Grandad. I've run out of cash so I thought I'd paint them a present. So why are you doing so many?'

'Me and Vivien are doing a sale next week. It's all for charity, we've chosen a homeless charity called Porchlight,' she says.

The sound of 'Jingle Bells' travels through from the playroom. Eliott is practising some Christmas tunes on his cornet, in preparation for the 'gigs' his band will be playing in pubs, churches and village fairs before Christmas.

My laptop is ready and I search for the Finglesham house I visited several months ago. It's sold, but a faded image of the property remains, to show the efficiency of the estate agents I presume. I wonder if Margery told the new owners about the badgers. Will they regret having moved? I never heard from them again so I can only assume things had settled down.

It's Monday again and the day of Maddy's sale. I receive a text from her at the end of her lunch break: 'Hi mum me and viv raised £44.55.'

I ask how it went when she's home.

'The teachers bought loads, though one said she would later but never came back.'

'What about the students?'

'Lots of them were quite rude. The little year sevens said they were too expensive, but they weren't.'

'I'll buy some from you,' I tell her. 'I could use them as presents for friends. Oh, we picked up your bus passes today.'

'I like the way you talk about bus passes when you're thinking about presents,' says Eliott, shutting the back door behind him and landing more eggs on the draining rack. 'My Christmas present better not be a Stagecoach pass, or you and Dad are in trouble.'

I know he's joking but I get the feeling he's somehow stressed by the prospect of the school bus. The next morning I hear him in his room way before the alarm and soon he throws up. I force myself out of bed and go and find him.

'Are you alright, mate?' I say, landing an arm across his shoulders as he dries his face with a towel.

'I probably am a bit worried,' he says.

'You don't need to be,' I tell him, ruffling his hair. 'It'll all be fine.'

I think it's the thought of being reunited with some of the

annoying kids from primary, but he won't admit it. 'We can't keep driving to Dover, it was fine when Dad worked there but you know that's all changed.'

Maddy sends me texts from the school bus – the roads are icy, she wants me to know, and I reply to her and send one to Eliott. I hear nothing from him, a good sign, of course.

I close the badger hole when the morning chaos has died down and see that all the peanuts have gone. I kick through the leaves, just to make sure, then run up the garden to look at the cam. *It's Wilbur!* I can't believe he's back yet again. Perhaps I just need to accept the fact he can disappear for weeks on end, but I'm still new to all this, and I had got used to him coming almost every night. I flick through the photos for an overview of the night. It looks like he stayed a while, the footage is all of him. There are close-ups of him devouring a chunk of apple that he holds with his front paws, head on one side as a dog might chew a bone. I can only see one tooth in there, I might need to find him some softer treats. I hardly think looking after one old badger and his son a crime. I'm reminded of that school of thought that says they should be left to their own devices, but there are plenty of badgers with an actively hostile reception, possibly even our own clan, it would seem. A little positive support at the other end of the spectrum might just balance things out. After battling with this, that's the conclusion I've reached, at least for now.

If he's still around then perhaps one of the females is, too, for they would be living together. So next door hasn't done away with them, and the blue lights on the nearby garden studio haven't kept them away for good. I am aware that my emotional well-being shouldn't depend on a few badgers, but it does, at least a little – perhaps more than I'd like to admit – but is that really a problem? Perhaps we all need our 'badgers' in some form or other.

I'm often asked just what it is about badgers that draws me – isn't it obvious? Apparently not. I know that when I watch them in the wild my breathing deepens and slows, whereas today my heart began to race when I realized that we're still part of their narrative – or our garden is at least. I think they bring a feeling of hallowed ground to an ordinary place, a feeling of well-being, of 'I'm okay now, life can go on.' That enthusiasm simply that they've bothered to grace us with their presence says something to me in spiritual terms: it reminds me of the Christian view of God brooding over mankind, just longing for each individual to communicate with him, but perhaps I'm over-internalizing here. Watching them feels like being let into a mysterious secret – they come out when it's dusk or dark and they think no one is looking. I guess I share their reserve. There is a sense of privilege when I see them, of being taken into something, and this of course extends back into my childhood when we first saw them from the holiday cottage window. I like the many things they represent, too – their freedom and wildness, for they are untameable and will do as they please, treading territory that has been theirs for hundreds of years; almost every favourable depiction of them in literature presents a figure of old England, waistcoated, often monocled and always ancient and distinguished. They are the embodiment of heritage and of belonging, going down into the very depths of the earth and dwelling there. It is their group dynamics and vulnerabilities that perhaps inspire me most, the ability they have to trivialize my anxieties and remind me that they are out there and their problems are not so different to ours, and they get by, and so will we all.

Bingley is sleeping outside the back door, his beak tucked in between his shoulder blades while he rocks rhythmically. He opens an eye and sees me and soon he's eating out of my hand. He's so warm underneath his beak where it's been tucked into his feathers. The cold that I'm letting into the house hasn't touched him at all.

Christmas passes again and I realize I've been watching my garden badgers for just over a year. I now feel sure only Wilbur and a couple of cubs are still visiting. I am convinced something has happened to the others, though I doubt I'll ever hear what. That's probably just as well. So I'm looking after the old guy who's on borrowed time, and the new ones who are yet to establish themselves. There is no female amongst them now, but at least they haven't been wiped out completely. They are my metaphor for endurance, and I trust that all will be well.

Postscript – Waiting up

I gave up on the idea of a shepherd's hut but the need remained, and I soon settled on a locally made log cabin. We have it now: the perfect retreat, painted willow green so as not to shock the wildlife, and situated at the bottom of the garden, just to the side of the badgers' entrance. It has leaded windows, electricity and a fire, comfy furniture and a desk. Perhaps this all sounds very self-indulgent, but I am so glad we have it. I never knew how important it would become to our routine, but it has. You see, this is now pretty much the only way Maddy gets to watch badgers. Over recent months she has developed a joint condition that means walking is very painful, and we have been told this will stay with her. In fact, in all probability it will be life-long. It has been hard to adjust to, for all of us. We have talked wheelchairs – off-road of course – and explored every kind of therapy that she will consider. I have suggested driving her the short distance to the woods and parking up, helping her across the field to our usual spot, but even this is too difficult right now. So the hut is her best hope, and my own badger walks are tinged with sadness.

Tonight Maddy wants to wait up for them and I am only too happy to oblige. We both change for bed early and head down the garden with sleeping bags – we're not spending the night out here but it adds to the excitement. We leave our wellies by the door and I hand her a hot water bottle for her knee pain as she gets comfy in the big swivel nest chair. I sit on the floor, leaning back against the sofa bed – I won't be in the direct range of vision for any wildlife here. It's a windy night and the old buddleia is banging against the side of the hut. In minutes the gloaming gives way to darkness and I take the cap off the night-vision, handing it to Maddy.

'I can see something,' she says.

Sure enough, a badger is there in front of us. I can see it without the night-vision. They look so much smaller in real life. We had scattered redskin peanuts in front of the hut before dusk and this badger is having a wonderful time.

'*Look,*' says Maddy. A badger is walking in front of the hut doors, just centimetres away from us. A third comes out of the trees and they eat together. 'It's a badger party,' whispers Maddy.

'I think that's Wilbur, there at the back,' l say. As he moves forward I feel sure that it is.

'Who are the others?'

'The cubs,' I say. 'They are much bigger now.'

One of the cubs will always remain small. This is the 'pot-bellied pig' who came on her own at times and seemed especially vulnerable. Jemima named her Slipper and she is a slip of a thing, perhaps the cub who would have been least likely to survive, but here she is. No old-style bicycle saddle-shaped face for her, rather the streamlined speed seat. I hope she'll go as many miles as old Wilbur. Tommy is from the same mould as his father, his face unquestionably male already. His ears are still floppy – it's not always the same one as I'd thought. I wonder if they are like a puppy's, yet to stay in the upright position.

We watch them in silence for a time, so pleased they've come. I'm unable to take my eyes off them, gorging myself on their company. It's good to see they are still a family group. There have been no more cubs so perhaps there was no need to send Tommy out from the sett. 'They're taking ages, Mum,' whispers Maddy. 'I'm going to be so tired tomorrow.'

'If we open the door we could frighten them, then they might not return.'

'A couple more minutes, then.'

'I tell you what, I'll put the light on,' I say. 'That'll make them head home.'

I stand up, so far they haven't noticed me. I flick the light switch and still nothing. 'Can you believe it,' I say. 'They're really not bothered.'

Now Maddy is sitting on the floor in front of the glass doors. 'That's amazing. Look at Wilbur, oh my goodness, he's just so adorable.'

I can pick out his features – dodgy ears, the old scars and saggy profile – it really is him. I'm completely mesmerized and follow his every move. 'And that's Dora,' I say. '*Dora*. The one who's just joined them. Four badgers, who'd have thought?'

And we settle in again, but leave the light on this time. Wilbur is up close to the hut door, his battered ears moving in time as he eats. His coat is very light, it would be impossible not to realize how very old he is. The two young badgers are eating together, their noses almost touching. Dora can't settle and is roaming in and out of view.

'They're such slow eaters,' says Maddy. 'We've been out here another hour.'

'I think they're nearly done now, there can't be much left.'

So my quest for badgers ends here, one hundred metres from my own back door. Life brings its unexpected challenges, for us and the badgers, but I have much to be thankful for. My faith is growing more important to me, and I think Maddy's is, too. If ever we needed God it's now, and he doesn't disappoint. On a human level, Maddy is a resilient girl and whatever happens, we muddle through. Hopefully her condition will improve, but we have each other. And there will always be badgers.

Bibliography

Bekoff, Marc. 2002. *Minding Animals: Awareness, Emotions and Heart.* New York: Oxford University Press Inc.

Corbett, Jim. 1947. *The Man Eating Leopard of Rudraprayag.* Oxford.

Dahl, Roald. 2001 [1970]. *Fantastic Mr. Fox.* London: Penguin.

Drayton, Michael. 2008. *The Complete Works of Michel Drayton.* London: John Russell Smith.

Hardy, Peter. 1975. *A Lifetime of Badgers.* Newton Abbot.: David Charles.

Hardy, Thomas. 1991. *The Complete Poems.* London: Macmillan.

Hardy, Thomas. *The Homecoming,* December 1901. A poem about a newly married couple returning from their wedding to the marital home. She is a young bride, and unhappy with the remoteness of her new environment. From *Time's Laughingstocks.*

Hardy, Thomas. 1985 [1886]. *The Mayor of Casterbridge.* London: Penguin.

Hardy, Thomas. 1974 [1887]. *The Woodlanders.* London: Macmillan. Chapter.

Harris, Cresswell and Jefferies. 1989. *Surveying Badgers, An Occasional Publication of the Mammal Society, no. 9.* London.

Hine, Reginald. 1927. *History of Hitchin, volume II.* George Allen and Unwin.

Long, William J. 2005 [1919]. *How Animals Talk: And Other Pleasant Studies of Birds and Beasts.* Vermont: Bear and Company

Mabey, Richard. 2014. *A Brush with Nature: Reflections on the Natural World.* BBC Books. Random House: London.

Monibot, George. *The Spectator.* 1 June, 2013. *Feral: Searching for Enchantment on the Frontiers of Rewilding.*

Neal, Ernest. 1948. *The Badger.* London: Collins.

Paiba, Helen. 1998. 'Scary Stories for Eight Year Olds' chosen by Helen Paiba. 1998. London: Macmillan.

Soper, Eileen. 1992 [1955]. *'1954, Badger Favours'* in *Eileen Soper's Book of Badgers,* Edited by Duff Hart-Davis. UK: Robinson Publishing.

Stocker, Bram. 2007 [1897]. *Dracula.* London: Vintage.

Thomas, Edward, 'The Combe': Thomas, Edward. 2011. *Selected Poems* edited by Matthew Hollis. London: Faber and Faber.

Warwick, Hugh. 2012. *The Beauty in the Beast.* London: Simon and Schuster

Webster, John. 2014 [1612-13]. *The Duchess of Malfi.* London: Bloomsbury.

Acknowledgements

This book grew out of the love and commitment of many people. Firstly, my wonderful family, who lived and breathed this project with me. You made it always a joy and never a chore. You will find yourselves cherished in these pages. Secondly, Professor Scarlett Thomas, who encouraged me to stay on at the University of Kent and write this as a PhD project – one insignificant essay on a Masters course led you to imagine this book, and I'm very grateful. You asked all the right questions, never telling me how it should be written, allowing me to reach my conclusions in the best possible manner. Thank you.

Thanks also to Dr. Alex Preston and Professor Sarah Moss, my examiners. It was a privilege to have input from such insightful readers.

Heartfelt thanks also go to my agent, Anne Williams at KHLA. You loved this book from your first encounter and gave me valuable input. We came very close with mainstream publishers, in fact achingly close, but you continued to believe in this project. I am very happy to be publishing this independently now. Thank you for your continued support.

To Alexi Francis, the superb artist who is responsible for my beautiful front cover. I'm so thankful for your work, and that we discovered each other via Twitter after writing on a mutual project: *Seasons*, for the Wildlife Trusts. I will be calling on you again.

Most grateful thanks too, to the East Kent Badger Group, who have trained me, used me, and given me opportunities I could only have dreamt of. I'm so glad I found you.

To my community who feature (mostly unwittingly) in this book – you are much appreciated!

And to the badgers, for showing up. I owe you.

ABOUT THE AUTHOR

Caroline Greville teaches Creative Writing at Christ Church University, Canterbury, and for Kent Adult Education. She is married with four children, and lives in a village with one shop, one pub, and many, many badgers.

Printed in Great Britain
by Amazon